Human
Sexual Behaviour

Human Sexual Behaviour

Philip Feldman
Psychology Department, University of Birmingham

and

Malcolm MacCulloch
Park Lane Special Hospital, Liverpool

JOHN WILEY & SONS

Chichester · New York · Brisbane · Toronto

British Library Cataloguing in Publication Data:

Feldman, Maurice Philip
  Human sexual behaviour.
  1. Sex
  1. Title II. MacCulloch, Malcolm John
  155.3   HQ21   79–41220
  ISBN 0 471 27676 6

Photoset by Thomson Press (India) Limited, New Delhi,
and printed in The United States of America

Contents

Preface... vii

Chapter 1 Sex and Society 1

Chapter 2 The Biological Bases of Sexual Behaviour.............. 24

Chapter 3 Social Learning and Sexual Behaviour................. 58

Chapter 4 Individual Differences in Sexual Activity 89

Chapter 5 Problems of Sexual Response........................ 122

Chapter 6 The Homosexual Preference......................... 149

Chapter 7 Other Sexual Behaviours 177

References 203

Author Index 218

Subject Index.. 224

Preface

Since we began working on this book our careers have passed through a number of changes, both of location and of professional emphasis, but we have remained constant to the central theme of the book: human behaviour, in most areas, is the result of an intimate and complex interaction of biological predispositions and continuing influences, social settings and rules, and the details of individual learning experiences. The importance of such an interactionist approach is particularly clear for human sexual behaviour and we have tried to follow it in this book. We have also included considerable material on minority sexual practices and sexual activities and preferences, and on the major methods of helping with the problems and difficulties sometimes associated with sexual encounters.

Chapter 1 deals with the social context of sexual behaviour. It begins with an historical overview of religious and medical assertions before reviewing current social attitudes towards heterosexual and homosexual behaviour and sexual materials. We then consider sex education, prostitution, and pornography, concluding with a brief reference to the wide range of cultural variations in sexual behaviour. The next chapter gives a fairly detailed account of the biological bases of sexual behaviour, covering general embryology, the structures of adult genitalia, the acquisition of sexually dimorphic behaviour, cerebral sexual mechanisms, sexual arousal, and the physiology of human sexual responses. Chapter 3 concentrates on the social learning of sexual activities, from acquisition, through performance, to maintenance by reinforcing consequences and includes material on attitude change, and observational and direct learning, as well as a wide range of situational and cognitive determinants. We then review the fast-growing research area concerned with mate-selection, attraction, and love. Chapter 4 reviews a sample of quantitative data on the remarkable range of individual differences and the frequency and variety of sexual behaviours and examines trends from Kinsey to the present. It looks also at some data which relate sexual attitudes to individual differences in personality.

Considerable advances have been made in our knowledge of problems of sexual response and in how to cope with them, but many uncertainties remain.

This area of research in clinical practice which owes so much to the work of Masters and Johnson is discussed in Chapter 5.

The final two chapters are concerned with minority sexual practices, Chapter 6 with homosexual behaviour and the last chapter with a range of behaviours, some legal, others classified as sex offences. In both chapters we include both biological and social learning explanations, as well as material on methods of various forms of help, ranging from changes in the behaviour to methods of producing for the subject a greater ease with his preferred practice.

We hope that this book will be of interest to undergraduate and postgraduate students of psychology and the social sciences, and to medical students, as well as to practitioners ranging from physicians to marital and sex therapists.

It is a pleasure to acknowledge the work of several secretaries over the years of preparation of this book, including Barbara Hudson, Sue Garvey, Sian Lunt, and Christine Bennel. We are most grateful to Carolyn MacCulloch for her patient proof reading and indexing.

Philip Feldman and
Malcolm MacCulloch, 1979

CHAPTER 1

Sex and Society

INTRODUCTION

All societies have formal or informal conventions to regulate sexual activities, including those considered deviant in some societies and 'normal' in others. A number, particularly the non-Western ones studied by anthropologists, are relatively clear-cut in their system of sexual rules, others such as those of the developed nations are marked by considerable disagreement, even concerning the desirability of 'society' attempting to make general rules enforceable by law, let alone the content of those rules. Speaking of Britain in particular, and of the Western world in general, Lord Justice Devlin has asserted: 'Society cannot ignore the morality of the individual any more than it can its loyalty; it flourishes on both and without either it dies' (Devlin, 1959). The alternative view was put by the Wolfenden Committee Report (1957) which led to the reform of the British law on homosexual behaviour. 'It is not in our view the function of the law to interfere in the private lives of citizens, or to seek to enforce any particular pattern of behaviour.' The report continued: 'Unless a deliberate attempt is to be made by society, acting through the agency of the law, to equate the sphere of crime with that of sin, there must remain a realm of private morality and immorality which is, in brief and crude terms, not the law's business.'

Many areas of sexual behaviour have been, and are still, considered 'the law's business', even though the law is often enforced very intermittently. In many states of the USA heterosexual oral–genital contact is illegal under statute, as in some states is premarital intercourse. In others all positions for sexual intercourse other than the 'missionary' position (male superior) are technically illegal. Throughout the West there is a legally enforceable 'age of consent'. While many countries have now legalized homosexual behaviour in private between consenting adults many still have a much higher age of consent than for heterosexual behaviour. The law is similarly involved in attempts to regulate exposure to materials—pictures or words—which are potentially sexually arousing. In 1967 the US Congress appointed a Commission on Obscenity and Pornography which produced a massive report three years later (Lockhart, 1970). A self-appointed group, led by Lord Longford (Longford Report, 1972), attempted a similar

1

exercise in Britain, though in this case the 'report' was largely lacking in factual evidence. Most countries have attempted a censorship of films, plays and books with constant and costly legal battles over particular productions. The battle ground shifts from time to time. Whereas the law now seems largely to ignore female strip shows, in contrast to earlier attempts at control, the recent phenomenon of male strippers has led to legal responses in both Britain and the USA.

AN HISTORICAL OVERVIEW

The Christian Church

The majority traditional view of the Christian Church has been that all forms of sexual behaviour are by nature suspect, and that only those that make up a bare minimum, necessary for the purposes of reproduction, are permissible. But it is fair to say that there has also been a contrasting minority element. Christian teaching comprises both liberal ideas and the deep seated anti-sexuality of a long tradition of virgins and celibates. In the hey-day of Christendom, in the Middle Ages, the contrast in terms of sexual licence and behaviour was even more marked. Two diverging currents could be distinguished: extreme indecency showing itself freely in social customs and in literature, contrasted with an excessive formalism bordering on prudery (Huizinga, 1955).

A comparison between a recently published Quaker pamphlet *Towards a Quaker View of Sex (Guardian,* 1966) and a fourteenth-century manual of female instruction suggests that we are rather restrained today. The medieval author of the latter used stories of a near obscene nature to demonstrate the necessity for virtue (Henriques, 1968). A nineteenth-century authority on the medieval period states, 'the conception of morality does not seem to have been very developed and great licentiousness and immodesty appear to have been general in every class of society' (Nyrop, 1888).

Henriques sums up the view that there has always been a clear contrast between what is prescribed by the guardians of social behaviour and what actually occurs: 'It is perhaps not extravagant to suggest that the conception of modern sexuality as departing widely from Christian standards of the past is very largely a myth. It is the myth of the Golden Age—that things were always better in the old days. The difference between the Middle Ages and ourselves is to be seen in terms of self-consciousness. Today there is an agonizing search to find an acceptable standard of behaviour, to find the satisfactory compromise between Freud and Pauline Christianity' (Henriques, 1968, p. 325). Henriques also points out that nowhere in the Old or New Testaments is there any explicit condemnation of premarital sexual intercourse, the foundation of the attitude being found in St. Paul, whose famous dictum: 'It is better to marry than to burn' was followed by successive Holy Fathers.

There are marked differences between the view of different contemporary camps within Christianity. That of the Quakers is well exemplified by the pamphlet (1966) referred to earlier: 'Without the fear of pregnancy (which modern contraceptives are steadily reducing), without the special guilt-feeling which her upbringing has often laid on the girl, man and maid are in this position on equal terms. Either can be frightened, hurt, and damaged by what is for them the wrong kind of sexual experience. It must, however, be accepted as fact that light hearted and loving casual contacts can occur without profound damage or moral degeneracy being the result for either partner.' By contrast, a contemporary Anglican has restated the traditional Christian view about chastity, his main contention being that sexual intercourse belongs to marriage alone—it can never be justified in the wrong context: 'Casual indulgence in venereal adventures yields at most a sensual pleasure or physical relief which is far removed qualitatively from the complete personal satisfaction attained when cohesion is the natural expression of true love.' (Bailey, 1962; cited by Henriques, 1968, p. 329.)

Medical Assertions

Bullough (1974) has given a lively account of the writings on sex of the eighteenth- and nineteenth-century doctors. (We cannot know, of course, in any factual sense the degree of acceptance of such views as followed by those living at the time. As in the case of the Church's attempts to limit sexual conduct, medical writings may have had less effect on everyday behaviours than their authors hoped.) Many doctors, such as the major eighteenth-century medical figure Herman Boerhave (1728) argued against non-procreative sex (sexual behaviour not intended to lead to pregnancy, such as masturbation and sexual intercourse involving the use of some contraceptive). He stated that 'rash expenditure of semen brings on a lassitude, a feebleness, a weakening of motion, fits, wasting, dryness, fevers, aching of the cerebral membranes, a decay of spinal cord, fatuity, and other like evils' (Bullough, 1974, p. 100). As Bullough points out Boerhave's views fitted in with traditional Christian prejudice as well as into much medical theory. Nineteenth-century doctors also asserted such ideas. For example, Graham (1848) believed that the loss of an ounce of semen was equivalent to the loss of several ounces of blood. He urged his many readers (his book went through 10 editions in 10 years) to take a diet of rye meal and other ingredients said to cut down sexual desire, and to limit sexual outlets to one per month. Kellog (1882) noted many suspicious signs of the masturbator including love of solitude, unnatural baldness, fondness for salt, pepper, spices and vinegar, the use of tobacco, and obscene words and phrases. In a sense, he was right: masturbation (see Chapter 4) is universal among males and widely found in females. The full list of 'signs' of the masturbator would include almost all members of the population as displaying at least one of them! A nice touch was that Kellog considered habitual masturbation to be revealed differently in boys and girls: the clue in the former was an aversion to girls, in the latter a strong liking for boys, fitting in very well with the prevailing notions concerning what was 'normal' for the two sexes—a strong heterosexual interest in the case of boys, none in the case of girls. Towards the end of the nineteenth century several medical writers looked on non-procreative sex as a contagious disease. Oral sex was said to cause cancer (Bergeret, 1898). Scott (1889) extended the dangerous consequences of 'perverseness' to the offspring of the person concerned, who would be born with 'perverted instincts'. For many years the book *Psychopathia Sexualis* by Kraft-Ebbing (1894) was regarded as the scientific last word in the field of sexology. He preached strongly the dangers of excessive sexuality, including frequent masturbation, which he saw as a causal factor for a wide range of unpleasant consequences, arguing that human progress depended on a constant struggle with sensuality. In general it can be said that until the scientifically based sex research of this century was carried out the prevailing medical and scientific view was that non-procreative sex had pathological elements.

Homosexual behaviour has had a varied historical treatment by medical writers. On the one hand, this form of sexual expression is clearly non-procreative (and hence undesirable), but because the condition was held to be inborn it was not more dangerous to those carrying it out than procreative sex to married people (Ulrichs, 1868). On the other hand, *because* it was non-procreative it was inevitably deviant and was seen by many as indicating sickness. Tardieu (1857) went further, regarding all those with homosexual 'appetites' as criminal or vicious. Until very recently homosexual behaviour figured in the standard classification of psychiatric problems, but in 1974 the American Psychiatric Association removed it from its *Diagnostic and Statistical Manual of Mental Disorders*. This does not mean that people whose preference is homosexual suddenly ceased either to suffer distress or to seek help; both remain true for some, but their sexual preference is no longer labelled as an illness. Whether it is a problem or a pleasure is a matter for the individual concerned.

Sex Research

While some of the nineteenth-century writings on sex were based on interviews with people, as opposed to *ex cathedra* assertions, they were confined to patients rather than the general population and used none of the controls basic to scientifically acceptable research. The key contribution of Freud and Havelock Ellis was to free human sexuality from the earlier notion that it was something for man to suppress or to use solely for procreative ends. Instead they sought to persuade a sceptical world that sexuality was a key feature of normal human life and development. Inevitably their work had severe shortcomings; it was influenced by the current notions of the central importance of biological, rather than social, control of behaviour. Thus it grossly underestimates the possibilities both of wide individual differences due to differing social training, and the related possibility of planned methods of changing individual sexual behaviour. Moreover, the work of Freud and Ellis was clinical, using the case histories of neurotic clients. They did not carry out controlled, descriptive and explanatory studies using properly constructed samples of the general population.

The first stage of the scientific enterprise proper began with studies in the 1920s which simply asked ordinary men and women about their sexual behaviour. This descriptive phase based on self-report culminated in the massive studies of Kinsey and associates in the 1940s and 1950s. These studies, and others since, provide the essential decriptive foundations for attempts to explain variations in sexual behaviour—between the sexes, cultures, and different time periods. They also help to chart the changing patterns of social behaviour and it is this dimension of social change and of the related widespread social awareness of matters sexual which are key features of contemporary cultural life. Research findings both reflect current social beliefs and help to influence them.

The biological tradition of sexual research has continued to be active in the important anatomical and physiological studies of Masters and Johnson in the 1960s, concerning the typical features of sexual intercourse. They used methods of direct observation inconceivable in the social climate of even 20 years earlier. Masters and Johnson have also pioneered methods of assisting sexual problems, but these involve social learning, rather than biological, methods. In general it is the social learning and cognitive approach which is increasingly making the running in sex research, due to the mounting evidence of the wide variability of human sexual behaviour in response to variations in previous experiences and current settings. However, despite this swing of fashion biological influences inevitably remain of great importance and they are discussed in Chapter 2.

From humble beginnings on the very margins of scientific respectability sex research is now active on a major and international scale. Beasley (1975) reported that the current files of the Kinsey founded Institute for Sex Research contained 1800 references to workers in human sexuality from 47 countries. Many of them refer to practitioners such as clinicians and educators, rather than researchers as such, but scientific enquiry into human sexual behaviour is clearly well established and growing.

CURRENT SOCIAL ATTITUDES

Introduction

The study of attitudes has been a major part of social psychology for the past half century. Many attempts at definition of the term attitude have been made, the most widely accepted emphasizing *evaluation*. Thus, attitudes are favourable or unfavourable beliefs about an act, event, object, or person. They represent both potential responses and the evaluation of previously made responses. Examples are: 'President X is strong', and 'Y's breakfast cereal is tasty'. But does an attitude predict actual behaviour—does the person vote for President X, or eat Y's cereal? Sometimes attitudes do predict behaviours rather accurately, at other times the two are well out of line, often because of social barriers against translating attitude into action. These barriers include the rules governing behaviour in a particular situation, and the penalties for not observing those rules, as well as the opportunity for carrying out the behaviour. Sexual behaviour requires an able and willing partner—for example, it is one thing for a boy or girl to favour sex before marriage (attitude); actually doing something about it (translating attitude into behaviour) requires a partner who both shares the attitude and finds the person concerned attractive enough to have intercourse with. Moreover, the couple still require opportunity; if the two live with their parents the behaviour is less likely to follow the attitude than if either one owns an apartment. It follows that studies of social attitudes to sexual behaviour tell us what people believe and what they would like to do about their beliefs, not necessarily what they do or have done. Nevertheless, such studies are of considerable interest; they explore beliefs concerning majority and minority practices, indicate the effect of current social influences such as films and television, and provide information which might predict forthcoming changes in actual sexual behaviour. Ideally, it is desirable to study actual behaviour but such studies are both immensely time consuming and they are not always practicable because of the nature of the subject.

How helpful attitude surveys are depends on the care with which they are designed and carried out: for example, questions have to be extensively pre-tested so that the researchers and the public both understand the same thing by them, and the sample questioned should be representative of the population under investigation. It is no use asking questions of young dockworkers in language used by professors (and vice versa). Nor is it good practice to question a group of college students and regard their answers as representative of all college-age people. If the 18–22 age group in general is your target then you must also question people not in college. A large number of attitude surveys are simply unreliable due either to the way questions are framed or to unsatisfactory sampling. Even the way questions are asked, and by whom, affects the answers which are received: attitude surveys sent out through the post yield only a small return out of the total possible—and that return may be a very biased fraction of the sample; in a face-to-face interview the questioner's behaviour has a major effect on the answers given, particularly in an area like sex in which there are powerful rules and expectations. Interviewers must therefore be carefully selected and trained.

Heterosexual Behaviour

The Kinsey researchers (Kinsey *et al.*, 1948, 1953) concentrated their main attention on American sexual behaviour (see Chapter 4) but they also asked questions about sexual attitudes.

One question concerned the reason why some single people avoided sexual intercourse. Females mentioned, in decreasing order of importance, that it was wrong, lack of desire, fear of pregnancy, fear of discovery, lack of opportunity and fear of venereal disease. The factors mentioned by males were lack of opportunity, lack of desire, fear of venereal disease, fear of pregnancy and fear of discovery. Whereas less than a quarter of the unmarried females wanted their husbands to be a virgin, nearly half the unmarried males sought virginity in a future bride.

The Kinsey data were collected before 1950. A very good study of British teenagers, by Schofield (1965a), was carried out in the early 1960s. Nevertheless it found some results which were not very different from Kinsey's, for example, the reasons for avoiding premarital intercourse and attitudes to virginity. 'It is clear that all teenagers expect girls to be much more circumspect than boys. Girls are much more likely to realize that there is a double standard for men and women and the majority accept the view that girls who have sex before marriage get a bad reputation ... From this section there emerges the impression that there is a group of boys who are keen to lose their own virginity but are critical of girls who provide them with this opportunity. If they wish to marry at all they are intent on marrying girls who are virgins and thus preclude marriage from their premarital sexual relationships. Girls, aware of the dangers, play a defensive role. They wish to protect their own virginity but expect boys to gain sexual experience, and find it acceptable that boys should be able to do what they rule out for themselves' (Schofield, 1965a, p. 112).

We are supposed to be living in a period which is characterized by an increase in sexual permissiveness; how true is this and when did the change, if it has occurred, take place? So far as attitudes are concerned there has indeed been a distinct shift and its onset can be located in the 1960s. In 1958, Rettig and Pasamanick (1959) readministered an attitude questionnaire which had been previously used in 1929. In both instances the subjects were college students. No change was found for either men or women in their evaluation of pre- or extramarital sex. Another readministration study of sexual attitudes by Coombs (1967) repeated in 1966 a survey carried out in 1927. This time there was a marked change, both 'adultery' and 'seduction' were found to be more acceptable to the 1966 group than to the 1927 group. British evidence suggests that the change occurred in the middle 1960s. In 1970 Wright and Cox repeated a study they had first carried out in 1963 on 17–18 year old school students. In 1963, 81 per cent of the girls considered premarital intercourse 'always' or 'usually' wrong, only 2.5 per cent considered it never wrong. In 1970 the figures had altered considerably, to 34 and 18 per cent respectively. The same change was true for the boys. A report from Germany by Schmidt and Sigusch (1972) helps us to pin down the shift in terms of an overall approach to what is desirable for the two sexes. They classified a range of attitudes to premarital sexual behaviour under four heads. The *orthodox double standard* means that men are allowed premarital intercourse under any circumstances, while women are not allowed it under any circumstances. It follows that the males' partners must be women other than their future wives (e.g. prostitutes, women of a lower social class, or a different ethnic group, etc.). The *transitional double standard* means that while both sexes are permitted premarital intercourse, males need not feel affection for their partners, whereas women must do so. *Permissiveness with affection* refers to the acceptability of premarital intercourse, for both sexes, but *only* in the context of a love relationship. As a sub-classification, there may be a single such relationship, culminating in marriage, or there may be a succession of relationships, each characterized by mutual affection. The final attitude, *permissiveness without affection*, means that premarital sex is acceptable for men and women equally, even when a love relationship does not exist. Generally speaking the rules are now more similar for men and women than in the past. 'Double standards' are strongly opposed by both sexes; the most popular category is now permissiveness with affection, with however an increasing emphasis on one sub-category—'even if there is no likelihood of marriage'— rather than another—'if there is a chance of marriage'.

Nevertheless, Schmidt and Sigusch (1972) considered the basic philosophy still to be a romantic one, *ultimately* aimed at marriage and family, the change being from 'premarital monogamy' to 'successive premarital monogamy'—meaning that being faithful to the person one eventually marries has been replaced by being faithful to one person at a time. Although the attitudes of males and females have become closer than in the past and have continued to move closer together, some sex differences still exist. We do not know what the final position will be; we are still in the middle of the major social revolution called Women's Liberation. Nor are we clear to what the shift in sexual attitudes is due: the appearance of the contraceptive 'pill' in the early 1960s or the general sexual liberalization of that period which both influenced the mass media and was influenced by them. What will happen in the 1980s is difficult to predict. Those who lament the development of permissive attitudes and behaviours predict that now the floodgates are open there will be further shift from a relatively greater incidence of 'permissiveness with affection' to an increase in 'permissiveness without affection'. On the other hand, the changes in sexual behaviour and attitudes which occurred during the 1920s were succeeded by over thirty years of stability in sexual attitudes. It would be reasonable to guess that if further changes do occur they will be connected with the continuing progress of female emancipation in other areas of life (for example, economics and politics) in which it is hardly likely that we have reached stability.

The effects of such future changes, both on the sexual relationships of males and females and parent–child relationships, can only be conjectured. It may be that female emancipation in the work area will speed the rate of change in the female role in the sexual area and vice versa. The general picture will probably be one of *female* change and the male *adaptation* to that change.

Homosexual Behaviour

The attitude of the Christian Church to homosexual behaviour, adapted from the Old Testament sex codes, has been strongly condemnatory. The ecclesiastical courts had the right to punish homosexual offences and did so by torture and death until the French Revolution of 1789 , the effect of which was a limitation of the penal code to more obvious harmful acts, such as sex with children. This more liberal approach gradually spread throughout Europe and North America and the control of sexual behaviour, both heterosexual and homosexual, now rests with the civil rather than the ecclesiastical courts.

It is undeniable that the homosexual members of the community have suffered, and do suffer, gross disadvantages in many areas of life. Levitt and Klassen (1974) reported a section of a 1970 American survey on attitudes to homosexuality, carried out by the Institute for Sex Research, which involved a rigorously constructed national sample of 30,000 American adults. These results may be generalized to the whole American adult population. Homosexual behaviour was perceived as 'always wrong', even when the participants 'were in love', by 70 per cent of the sample and as 'almost always wrong' by another 8 per cent. (It can be assumed that the homosexual section of the sample can be numbered among the remaining 22 per cent.) Adultery was regarded almost as unfavourably, but adolescent heterosexual intercourse was considerably less disapproved of. Another question concerned in which of the professions homosexual men should be allowed to work. The results fell into three groups: a quarter supported homosexuals being judges, teachers and ministers of religion, and a third supported their being doctors and government officials; by contrast over three-quarters agreed that homosexuals should be allowed to be beauticians, artists and florists. Nearly half the sample 'strongly agreed' that it was dangerous to allow homosexuals to be teachers or youth leaders and that they are high security risks; over a third were equally firm that homosexuals seek out children for sexual purposes and a quarter that they seek to corrupt their co-workers. Other (and equally incorrect) stereotypes were even more strongly held. Nearly three-quarters strongly agreed that homosexuals act like the opposite sex and two-thirds that they have an unusually strong sex drive (a nice contradiction; other survey evidence indicates a popular belief that women have a weaker sex drive than men). While half or more were strongly opposed to homosexuals dancing together in public and to the existence of 'gay' bars, only a small minority favoured excluding them from Church membership—this finding suggests that it is 'public display' which causes objections.

Average American attitudes may have changed in the years since the survey and British attitudes may be less hostile to homosexuality, but the probability is that a British survey would reveal evidence of inaccurate stereotypes and hostile perceptions. Various organizations such as the Gay Liberation Front, some more militant in style than others, are pressing hard for changes in both the law and in social attitudes. Essentially they would like equality in both areas with heterosexuals. For example, in 1967 the British Parliament passed the Sexual Offences (No 2) Bill which made sexual behaviour between consenting males no longer an offence in England and Wales so long as it was conducted in private and both participants were over 21. The next target for British homosexuals and their sympathizers is a reduction of the age of consent to 16, the same as that for heterosexuals.

Sexual Materials (Pornography)

Social attitudes to pornography vary from the view that exposure to explicit sexual materials at virtually any age is almost inevitably beneficial to the one that such exposure is inevitably harmful. In the latter connection some members of the President's Commission cited the views of prominent policemen. For example J. Edgar Hoover, Director of the Federal Bureau of Investigation, writing in *This Week* magazine stated 'I believe pornography is a major cause of sex violence. If we can eliminate the distribution of such items among impressionable school-age children we shall greatly reduce our frightening sex crime rate' (Lockhart, 1970, p. 637). The views of the American public, sampled by a variety of polls, are diverse and perhaps even inconsistent. 'Between 40 and 60 per cent believe that sexual materials provide information about sex, provide entertainment, lead to moral breakdown, improve the sexual relationships of married couples, lead people to commit rape, produce boredom with sexual materials, encourage innovation in marital sexual techniques and lead people to lose respect for women' (Lockhart, 1970, p. 27). The British public's view is likely to be equally varied. The diversity of opinion is reflected in the recommendations of the President's Commission and of the dissenting minorities who disagreed in whole or in part. In general the Commission recommended: 'Legislation should not seek to interfere with the rights of adults who wish to do so to read, obtain, or view explicit sexual material'. They exempted 'live' sex shows which were not studied by the Commission. On the other hand they recommend 'regulations upon the sale of sexual materials to young persons who do not have the consent of their parents' (p. 57). In short, allow adults access to most materials; allow young persons access only with the consent of their parents. The latter view is more permissive than legislation in other contentious areas such as the use of alcohol and of actual sexual experience, in both of which there is a legally defined minimum age and parental consent is irrelevant. One minority group opposed the recommendation concerning adults, argued for strict legal control over sexual materials, and asserted 'that it is impossible, and totally unnecessary to attempt to prove or disprove a cause–effect relationship between pornography and criminal behaviour' (p. 458). In contrast another minority group recommended the 'repeal of all existing statutes concerned with obscenity or pornography' (i.e. both for adults and children). In the event, the Nixon Administration did not accept the report of the Commission and its recommendation for the removal of legislative control over the use of pornography by adults has not been put into effect. Legal attempts to control exposure to sexual materials continue in both Britain and the USA.

What is the current state of the evidence on the social effects of pornographic material? The Oxford English Dictionary defines pornography as 'the expression or suggestion of obscene or unchaste objects in literature or art'. 'Obscene' means 'offensive to modesty or decency, expressing or suggesting lewd thoughts'. 'Lewd' means 'lustful' which in turn means 'desire for indulgence of sex'. Some (but rarely all) specific erotic stimuli (pictures, writing, etc.) are labelled as pornographic by some people, some of the time. The range of stimuli covered by the label varies according to time, place and the person applying it. Thus, when we apply the label 'pornographic' to a picture or a piece of writing, we are asserting: 'the effect of exposure to this will be that the person so exposed will wish to engage in the sexual activity portrayed in the picture or described in the writing'. At this point the law becomes involved because some of the activities concerned are thought undesirable. The law attempts to separate what is allowed from what is banned, the latter being represented by a phrase such as 'the tendency to deprave or corrupt'. The exact terminology varies between countries and across time, but 'depravity and corruption' sum up usefully the general language of the law in its frequent attempts to control or limit exposure. We can express this in psychological language as follows:

1. People have the opportunity to observe sexual materials, both verbal and pictorial.
2. They often attempt to copy what they observe and so acquire new behaviours.
3. Some of the behaviours that are acquired are undesirable; some for all members of society, some for certain members.
4. Therefore society must lay down rules as to which materials are to be made available and to whom, and should use the machinery of the law to enforce those restrictions.

The assumption is that all members of the 'society' would agree as to what is undesirable (i.e. what would tend to deprave and corrupt). D. H. Lawrence put the opposite view succinctly: 'What is pornography to one man is the laughter of genius to another'. Eysenck (1977) showed the range of views by an empirical study. He asked what activities, carried out by an adult male towards a number of categories of females, ranging from a 15 year old virgin to a married woman (the male being her husband) are either depraved or corrupt, or both (i.e. are socially undesirable). The sample of activities listed ranged from a kiss on the mouth, through taking a person to blue films, to using force to have intercourse; the questionnaires were administered to several hundred students. Opinion ranged widely, both according to the nature of the activity and the category of person concerned. There was a clear implication that most people believed that sexual development should occur in a gradual step-wise manner, proceeding from total innocence to considerable experience with increasing age. While the in-experienced middle-aged male, shocked by the mildly erotic (by current standards), is a figure of indulgent fun, the teenage girl experienced 'ahead of her years' is seen as equally unusual but much more disturbing. Indeed, both legal definitions and judges' instructions to juries in obscenity cases try to include this sense of what is likely to be disturbing to the average member of society *at the moment*. Unfortunately, it is not only the average person who is exposed to sexual material but a range of individuals even wider than that covered in Eysenck's study described above. How does society ensure free access for the groups considered not to be 'at risk', but also protect from exposure those thought likely to be affected adversely? Films are graded in terms of the audience allowed to see them, but box-office assistants clearly cannot discriminate with complete accuracy between teenagers old enough to see an X film, and those still too young to be allowed legal access to the show. In the case of sexual material displayed in shops and news-stands, discriminating between those 'legally' allowed to view and those who are not is, of course, quite impossible.

What is the extent of damage, if any, and what kind of 'damage' do we mean?

As Court (1977) points out, it is not possible to measure moral damage objectively, and in practice the main measure of damage has been the occurrence of sex crimes. Some years ago Denmark removed controls from the free dissemination of pornographic material. Several reports indicate that the result, over the past 10 years, has been a sharp and continued reduction in the number of heterosexual crimes reported to the Danish police. At first sight this supports the view that, at the least, pornography is unrelated to sex crimes, and indeed might even be a positive social benefit. However, there are many problems with police statistics in general, which are even more marked with those for sexual crimes; these problems caution against an uncritical acceptance of the Danish sex crime figures and against accepting the existence of a relationship between them and the availability of pornography.

First, many more sex crimes occur than are reported to the police. This effect may have become more marked recently than in previous years (so that perhaps even more sex crimes occurred, but fewer were reported). There is some evidence (Court, 1977) that this factor accounts for part of the apparent decline of sex crimes in Denmark. Second, the broad category of sex crimes ranges from the relatively mild, such as exposure of the male genitals, to the relatively serious, such as rape. The decline in sex crime figures could have been contributed to much more by the former than by the latter; there is evidence that this is partially true. Court analysed data from a number of countries of reports to the police of the serious sex crimes of rape and attempted rape for the past 15 years. The general pattern was of a steady increase (USA, Britain, Australia and New Zealand) but with some variations, notably Copenhagen—increasing up to 1972 (the law on pornography was eased in 1967) and then a decline—and Singapore, which changed little up to 1973 and then showed a marked increase in 1974. The Singapore Government has maintained a strict control of pornography in contrast to the other named countries. We have to conclude that such surveys show no clear evidence of a relationship between pornography and rape, in either direction.

A more direct approach was attempted as part of the research work for the President's Commission by Goldstein *et al.* (1971). They carried out a series of interviews designed to assess experience with erotic material (photographs, films and books) during adolescence and adulthood. The interviews were administered to a number of groups including convicted male rapists, homosexual and heterosexual paedophiles, and a sample of current users of erotic material (books, movies, etc.). The comparison groups were black males living in a Los Angeles ghetto, a group of middle-class black males, and a group of white males, all matched with the sex offender sample by age and educational level. The major findings were as follows: adolescent exposure to erotica was significantly *less* for all deviant and offender groups than for the control groups. During adulthood the sex offenders continued to report less exposure to erotic stimuli than the controls. However, the homosexuals and users both reported greater exposure during adulthood than adolescence. As adults, the controls and the rapists showed a sharp decrease in arousal to masturbation by erotic materials while the users' rate remained high and that of the homosexuals increased. Less than a quarter of respondents in any group imitated sexual behaviour as depicted in erotic material immediately, or shortly after, viewing it. It appeared that exposure during adolescence to erotic materials was not positively associated with later sexual deviation and offending. In fact, the evidence of this study was that the control groups had significantly *more* exposure to erotic material during adolescence than had the convicted sex offenders or the heavy adult users of pornography. However, the possibility of wide individual variation within the group of convicted male rapists remains. Some rapists may be called 'sub-cultural'—that is, the culture in which they have grown up is one in which rape occurs fairly frequently, and rape is committed in groups (see Chapter 7). For others, rape is extremely deviant within their own culture and they commit their rapes on their own. Goldstein *et al.* (1971) made no attempt to compare these two, possibly very different, subgroups within the overall group of rapists.

Current social beliefs about the harmful effects of pornography have been studied by Merritt *et al.* (1975). They divided by age a national sample of nearly 2,500 American adults aged 20–80. Regardless of education, sex and differing previous exposure to sexual materials, attitudes were more unfavourable with increasing age. The youngest group attributed desirable or neutral effects to sexual materials, the oldest one solely undesirable ones. This finding ties in with a study by Colson (1974) who found that if material was experienced as sexually arousing, it was more likely to be labelled 'clean' than if its effects were not arousing, when the label 'obscene' was more likely to be attached. Thus it may be that successive exposure to material, initially liked and so labelled 'clean', which was gradually shifted to more obscene material, might result in the latter material eventually being rated more favourably than would be achieved by initial and sudden exposure to it. This is precisely the argument of the anti-porn lobby, and the extensive experimental findings on the desensitization of initially aversive stimuli by gradual exposure provide strong support for this view, as does a brief comparison between the current content of the media and that of 20 years ago. Of course, whether the favourable evaluation of the initially unconventional is actually harmful, either to the person concerned or to others with whom he comes into contact, is a separate and more difficult and complex question, as we have already seen.

We can now attempt to sum up the controversy concerning the relationship between pornography and its social effects. If the link between pornography and sexual crimes is a positive one the implication would be that society should exert a much stricter control over all aspects of the pornography industry. But even if the evidence suggested this would be desirable, how practicable would it be—and at what cost (including the corruption of the police, see below). The alternative link (a negative correlation), if strongly suggested by the evidence, is highly attractive—not only could law enforcement agents simply switch from a near impossible task to other forms of crime, there would be the real social benefit of fewer serious sex offences such as rape. Unfortunately, the evidence does not clearly support either view. Perhaps the answer lies somewhere between the two views—as follows: allow sexual materials representative of non-violent sexual activities and in which both partners are adults; control as strictly as possible those materials depicting violence between partners of any age, as well as those involving children as sexual partners, whether or not the activity is violent. Finally, it is as well to keep a sense of perspective. Even if it is both desirable and possible completely to ban all exposure to pornographic material, as currently defined, sex crimes will continue to occur. Verbal and visual materials are but one source of information and sexual arousal.

Concluding Comment

The study of social attitudes to sexual behaviours, particularly the more unusual ones, is at an early stage and there are many gaps, but there seems to be a general trend towards a greater permissiveness, which was rather rapid in the middle 1960s, and particularly so towards majority type activities. Minority activities may still attract much opposition, the more so in respect of those which are the most infrequent. We know little of how attitudes change over time, both as a result of particular personal experiences and of increasing age in general—long-term individual studies are indicated.

SOCIAL PLANNING: SEX EDUCATION FOR THE YOUNG

Schools

A survey by Ford and Beach (1952) makes it clear that some primitive societies go about the sexual education of their young in a much more planned and thorough way than does the advanced West, where before this century sex education barely existed. With the general increase in objective approaches to sexual behaviour formal programmes of sex education have now begun; they are often given in the middle or late 'teens. Despite these attempts all the studies agree that the primary source of sex education is the peer group. Children learn from other children, often inaccurately, particularly concerning contraception and sexual intercourse. Mothers talk to their daughters more than fathers to sons, but by the time they do so, or teachers make an attempt, children have had some information from their fellows. All the surveys, British and American, between 1915 and the present are in agreement on this basic finding. Increasingly children, particularly girls, are taught about sex in school and at an earlier age than in the past, but the majority of a group surveyed as young adults found their school sex education to be unhelpful (Schofield, 1973). Nor did school-based information affect in any direction the sexual behaviour of the boys and girls in Schofield's careful British survey. Those who received some sex education neither began sexual behaviour earlier nor were more sexually active before marriage. However, as young adults they did regret the lack of accurate information during their school years and the great majority said they intended to help their own children learn about sex.

School sex education pays more attention to describing the anatomy and physiology of reproduction and sexual intercourse than its psychology. It is, indeed, formal education, rather than skill-training. Nor is there usually an attempt to teach a set of rules, except in a purely negative sense. Instead, Schofield (1973) has argued, teachers, in addition to factual presentations, should adopt a clear positive stance on general issues. For example: partners should always be willing partners; contraceptives should be used if either of the partners does not want a child; and, the sexual behaviour of men and women should be judged by the same standards.

The Experts

Hill and Lloyd-Jones (1970) studied 42 sex education books put out by educational publishers and found that nearly all were inaccurate, misleading and moralizing. Among the inaccuracies noted were: masturbation is physically harmful; semen is colourless and odourless; those who have intercourse without intending marriage are mentally ill; premarital intercourse is illegal.

Schofield (1973) asked young adults in his sample where they would go for advice on contraception; a great majority said they would go to a doctor or to a family planning clinic. This suggests that contraception is a medical problem, the doctor the expert, and user a patient, all possibly inappropriate to what is essentially a form of social behaviour. Leaving this aside, how well prepared are doctors for their role as advisers? The Royal Commission on Medical Education in the UK (Todd, 1968) found that British medical schools offered little or no instruction about sexual behaviour and sexual problems. Another study (Ward, 1969) found that although only one-third of the doctors surveyed had received instruction in contraceptive techniques, more than 90 per cent offered contraceptive advice to their patients.

Concluding Comment

It is not known whether earlier, more accurate and more relevant sex education would prevent problems and promote happier sexual lives, but the attempt to find out seems very desirable. It is also possible that better education and an easier social climate concerning heterosexual behaviour may combine to reduce the demand for commercial pornography more effectively than do legal controls.

SEX AS A COMMODITY

Sexual pleasure is sold and bought every day in most, if not all, countries of the world which have a cash economy (the current regime in China claims to have eliminated prostitution). Such transactions are as old as recorded history, so far as prostitution is concerned. Pornography—in the sense of materials designed to arouse sexually—is certainly very old, as witness Greek and Roman artefacts; its commercial aspect may be more recent.

Prostitution

According to Clinard (1968) about 300,000 United States women live solely by prostitution. In view of Kinsey's figures, this is not surprising—although the majority of his male subjects had only limited experiences with prostitutes, nearly a fifth used this outlet more than a few times a year. The sums of money involved are obviously very considerable indeed, and the economic gains are more widespread than to the prostitute alone. According to Lemert (1951) 'Real estate owners and managers are able to earn far more on their investments and properties by renting to prostitutes or vice-resort operators than to other tenants. Better class hotels, along with the cheaper ones, owe part of their revenue to the prostitute, as well as taxi cab companies, laundries, amusement parks, vacation resorts and contraceptive manufacturers and distributors.' (Lemert, 1951; cited by Clinard, 1968, pp. 263–4.)

Prostitutes have a job hierarchy like any other occupational group, ranging from those who walk the streets to the call-girl. According to Henriques (1968) 'The aristocrat of prostitution is the call girl. Throughout the Western world, if she is personable and has the necessary capital to furnish her flat attractively, if not luxuriously, she can hope to earn a very high income. In Britain since the passing of the *Street Offences Act* in 1959, a whole hierarchy of call girls has developed. This varies from girls operating in sleazy back rooms in Soho to the undetectable inmate of the Mayfair penthouse' (pp. 313–14). Henriques quotes from a speech by a former British politician Anthony Greenwood, to the International Abolitionist Federation Congress in Cambridge (*Guardian*, 1960): 'There has been a tremendous growth in the call girl system, the girls adopting such methods of advertising as the use of touts at railway stations to invite travellers to their "parties"; the use of advertising for "models" or "dancing partners" in shop windows; and the insertion of advertisements in various publications. Earnings from customers collected in this way can be as much as £600 per week.'

Evidence of long-standing official leniency towards prostitution surfaces from time to time. Henriques (1968) described the trial of the well-known brothel keeper Mrs Jeffries in April 1885: 'The lady arrived at court in a brougham given her by an Earl, surrounded by guards officers and said to reporters: "Nothing can be done with me, my clients and patrons are of the highest social order."' She possessed a chain of brothels throughout London which catered for every conceivable whim of clients. Henriques states that matters were so arranged at the trial that she pleaded guilty and was fined £200, being also bound over for two years in the security of £200. She is reported to have said on an occasion prior to the trial: 'Business is very bad, I have been slack since the Guards went to Egypt' (pp. 283–4).

A similar kind of leniency towards prostitution was revealed in 1960, the date of the notorious case concerning the so-called Ballet Rose. A number of extremely prominent people in Paris were involved in a prosecution which alleged that the accused had organized sexual orgies on a magnificent scale with the forced co-operation of young girls including one of 12 years of age (Henriques, 1968).

Like other occupations, that of the prostitute requires training. Bryan (1965) interviewed 33 prostitutes, all currently or previously working as call-girls in the Los Angeles area, and ranging in age from 18 to 32. Immediately prior to entry into the occupation all but one girl had had personal contact with someone professionally involved in call-girl activities (pimps or other call-girls). The novice received her training either from a pimp or from another more experienced call-girl, more often the latter. She worked an initial two to eight months under the supervision of the trainer, often in the trainer's apartment, the latter assuming responsibility for arranging contacts and negotiating the type and place of sexual encounter. The major function of the training period was an induction into the general mode of thinking about being a call-girl. This involved exploiting the 'customers', by whatever means necessary, and defining the colleagues of the call-girl as being intelligent, self-interested and basically honest individuals. She also learned certain skills such as how to carry on the initial conversation, particularly by telephone, personal hygiene and how to satisfy the specific sexual preferences of customers. Bryan noted that lists of names and telephone numbers of customers were available for purchase from other call-girls or pimps. He pointed out also the importance of early success and financial reward as providing the necessary reinforcement for continuing the occupation, a social learning view demonstrated anecdotally by Young (1964), who carried out a series of interviews with London prostitutes and provided a vivid description of entry into prostitution. A girl who has a great deal of sexual contact at school may take work as a waitress or chamber maid at a provincial hotel. Next: 'she sleeps with the odd travelling salesman, and one day one of them gives her a pair of nylons. The next one gives her a pound to buy her own, and the penny drops. She has been paid for it. Next stop London and the big money' (Young, 1964, p. 113).

To some extent the system of homosexual prostitution parallels the hetero-sexual system. There are two homosexual sub-cultures, the overt and the secret (see Chapter 6). Reiss (1960) provides a detailed description of an American juvenile group which serves the sexual needs of homosexuals in the secret sub-culture. He terms the juveniles 'delinquent peers' and the homosexuals 'adult queers' (using this term because he writes from the perspective of the juvenile group). The transaction is one form of homosexual prostitution, between a passive young male and an active adult male. It is limited to sexual contact and is one in which the boy develops no self-conception as a homosexual person or sexual deviant of any kind, although he does perceive male adult clients as deviants, 'queers' or 'gay boys'. Reiss describes the street hustler as being one of three well-defined types of male homosexual prostitute, the other two being the 'bar hustler' who usually visits bars on a steady basis in search of homosexual clients, and the 'call-boy' who does not solicit in public. The street hustler has the lowest prestige among hustlers, partly because his is the most hazardous and least profitable form of activity.

Reiss provides a description of the induction into the peer–queer transaction which parallels the training of call-girls described earlier. Many boys from the lowest socio-economic level in large cities are prepared for such contact through membership in a delinquent group which has a knowledge of how to make a contact with homosexuals and relate to them. Within the group boys hear reports of experiences, how to make contacts, how to get money if the homosexual resists, how much one should expect to get, and so on. Boys may know all this before they have any contact with a homosexual. There are a number of norms which govern the transaction. The first is that a boy must undertake the relation solely as a way of making money; sexual satisfaction cannot be sought actively as the goal in the relationship. Second, the sexual transaction must be limited to mouth–genital contact (client active, boy passive). No other sexual acts are generally tolerated. Third, both participants should remain emotionally neutral during the transaction. Fourth, violence must not be used so long as the relationship conforms to the shared set of expectations. Provided that the boy conforms to all these norms his fellows in the peer group will not define him as homosexual, nor will he so define himself. When they get older, the boys enter adult groups in which working in a normal job becomes one of the acceptable ways of behaving. At this age they risk loss of status if they continue to solicit.

It will be apparent that there is some similarity between the descriptions of juvenile male prostitution for older homosexual males and female prostitution, both juvenile and adult, for older heterosexual males. The central element of both is that the transaction is entirely economic, no emotional commitment being sought or accepted by either side.

Many, such as Henriques, have argued that society should accept the inevitability of a hard core demand for prostitution. West Germany has accepted such an argument and has a long tradition of the state control of prostitution. For example, the authorities in Dusseldorf have built a prostitute hostel which is described as follows: 'It is an opulent new block with many floors, and the windows only a few feet away from the trains, are screened by little awnings of lemon coloured frosted glass . . . there are rooms in it much in demand for 180 girls. They work there, inspected by the sanitary authorities and registered by the city police, fed from a large communal kitchen, and charged eight shillings a day in rent (about $1 at that time) plus laundry, meals, drinks and the rest, visited by a steady stream of men, and earning on average, perhaps £50 ($125) per night. (Henriques, 1968, p. 317; cited from the *Observer*, 11 July 1965.)

The argument will continue, as will the practice of prostitution, so long as there are people willing and able to pay for sexual pleasure—it can be assumed that the demand will generate a supply.

Sexually Explicit Material

The American Commission on Obscenity and Pornography (Lockhart, 1970) estimated that the total market for sexually explicit material of all of those kinds which it was intended by Congress to investigate, amounted in the late 1960s to over $500 million. The great majority (about 80 per cent) of the 'explicit' market was represented by motion pictures—the R and X categories. ('R' means restricted to those over 17 unless accompanied by an adult and 'X' to those over 17 whether accompanied or not. In the UK the appropriate equivalents are AA and X, and the age restriction is 18 and over.) The Commission also included another unrated category of films known as exploitation films, or 'skin flicks', and often shown at private 'clubs' rather than in general cinemas. A further group, known in the trade as 'sixteen mm' films, often for home viewing or 'stag' nights, has developed recently and contains particularly explicit material. Sexually explicit films—the R and X, etc., categories—represented about half the total market in films. The report details the film section of the pornography industry, indicating its rapid growth, relaxing standards and economic success. Hard current evidence is less available but casual observation of the entertainment columns of any big city newspaper, particularly during the past five years, indicates an increasing proportion of cinemas given over largely or entirely to sexually explicit films of relatively low artistic merit, as well as a smaller number of films which are both erotic and of high artistic quality. Clearly the economic returns must justify the concentration on sex films. So far as the great range of films is concerned, again even the casual observer of the cinemas over the past 25 years will have noticed the difference between the content of films previously restricted and those now unrestricted or in the less restricted categories.

The Report also detailed the market in sexually explicit books and periodicals. Publishers concentrating on the 'adults only' (often termed 'secondary') markets had sought to expand into the mass market in the same way as has occurred in the film world. In the late 1960s, the secondary publication market was worth about $70 million in retail sales, including both books and magazines, no more than about 5 per cent of the entire book and periodical market, indicating the economic importance of success in relaxing the mass market's standards of sexual content. Other outlets for sexually explicit material—the mail order market and the 'under the counter' market, dealing in materials at the margin of or outside the law as then defined—were less important in total economic return and the Commission also doubted their profitability. However, there are grounds for scepticism on this last point, although of a somewhat indirect kind. In both Britain and the USA it has been well worth the while of those engaged in the production and sale of sexually explicit materials to offer bribes to police officers concerned with this area—usually termed the Vice Squad. The most recent and most spectacular British example was revealed in the summer of 1977 when a series of trials resulted in a significant number of London policemen, some of very senior rank indeed, being sentenced to lengthy terms of imprisonment (Cox et al., 1977). The sums of money involved in the bribes suggested either a very lucrative trade or an unusual anxiety on the part of the pornographers to help the previously underpaid police—the former seems more likely. On an anecdotal level, it is the view of senior policemen we have talked to that those involved in the currently illegal end of the sexual materials business are far from keen to have their activities legitimized—the result they fear is a very considerable reduction in the prices they could charge and hence in the profitability of their businesses.

A persistent feature of the market in sexual materials has been that, as public opinion has become more liberal, so allowing open access to materials depicting widely occurring adult heterosexual activities, so new and initially more deviant material has been introduced. Whereas 10 years ago, the Report of the Commission could state the use of pre-pubescent children in stag films to be almost non-existent, the late 1970s have seen this previous taboo widely breached, with a very hostile public reaction to certain widely publicized examples.

It seems, overall, that the commercial aspect of sex is more important for actual sexual behaviour, represented by prostitution, than for visual or written sexual materials, with the former again more important than the latter. A speculation would be that prostitution would survive full legislation, with the economic returns then depending on the usual laws of supply and demand (the most desirable commanding the highest price) while the sexual materials market might be much harder hit.

CULTURAL VARIATIONS

Sexual behaviour varies widely within the developed countries. When we look at the world in general, the variations are even more striking. Ford and Beach (1952) surveyed anthropological evidence from nearly 200 different peoples, usually pre-literate, but often with highly evolved cultures. The results are striking, both for sexual behaviour itself and for what is thought desirable in the appearance of a partner.

The current view among Western sexologists is that extended foreplay before intercourse is highly desirable. In the societies surveyed practices varied widely from virtual absence to several hours of foreplay before intercourse. In many societies, including our own, stimulation of the female breasts is a common precursor of intercourse; in a few it is completely lacking. Kissing, in some form, accompanies intercourse in most societies, but variations are considerable and include some societies in which saliva flows from one mouth to the other. In others kissing is unknown and members of those societies found very strange the sight of Europeans doing so. Most societies practise some form of mutual stimulation of the genitals but variations are again considerable. For many people in the West and in some pre-literate societies it has been regarded as something to be avoided. Conversely, it is regarded as an essential part of sexual behaviour by others, although with wide variations. In our own society, some people associate intense sexual arousal with painful stimulation—by scratching or biting. In some pre-literate societies, for most, if not all, members painful stimulation is a common feature of sexual behaviour. For example, among the Sirioni, kissing is unknown but mutual biting and scratching are frequent. The women of the Choroti spit in their lover's face during intercourse, while those of the Apinaye may bite the partner's eyebrows. All three peoples live in South America. Every society has social rules with which to regulate sexual intercourse:

there is a widespread insistence on privacy and a much greater occurrence at night. Most societies require a period of abstention by the immediate survivor of the deceased partner, some societies demand abstention by other close relations, and a few by all members of the community between death and burial. Many societies associate temporary sexual abstinence with the beginning of key events such as hunting, fishing or farming (in the West it is commonplace for athletes, particularly boxers, to refrain before a major contest—the physiological basis for the practice is far from clear). A few societies believe very frequent sexual intercourse to have lasting ill effects (as did our own in the recent past). Among the Seniang of the South Pacific advice on the desirability of spacing is given by the old men of the village—who also maintain that it is entirely permissible for a man with white hair to copulate every night.

Societies differ widely in what is considered 'sexually attractive', most attention being focused on the physical attributes of the female, those of the male being seen as less important than this skills and prowess. In Western society also, studies concerning attractive physical attributes have concentrated on the male view of the female, a situation which is changing with the advance of Women's Liberation. The variations between pre-literate societies are considerable. More emphasize plump than medium or slim body build, some specify small ankles, others fleshy calves, some societies prefer pendulous breasts, others emphasize upright breasts. In our society the contrast is obvious between the 'flat-chested' look admired in the 1920s, and the very different look of the 1950s, indicating a change in preferred appearance in the same culture over quite a short interval. The convention in the West is that the male initiates sexual advances, a view which is shared by most but not all pre-literate societies. However, practice does not always follow theory, any more than it does in the West. There are also some societies in which either sex is allowed to take the initiative, and a few in which it is customary for the woman to do so.

Before concluding this chapter, it is important to draw another lesson from the facts of cultural variation; our society's beliefs in what is desirable in the sexual area are inevitably temporary and relative to place and time. In an earlier section we outlined some early medical beliefs; few of today's doctors would share them. We have also pointed out the shifting boundaries of public taste in films and literature. The rapidly rising divorce rate is clear testimony to changing views concerning the sanctity of marriage. Yet some beliefs do seem reasonably permanent across time and place, pre-eminently the prohibitions against incest—sexual relations between close relatives—and intercourse with a menstruating woman. In contrast, there are wide variations in attitudes to homosexuality, the age at which sexual experience is allowed, and to extramarital relations. Ford and Beach (1952) found information on 76 pre-literate societies; homosexual behaviour by adults was absent, rare, or secret in about 35 per cent, but normal and socially acceptable for some individuals in the remaining societies. As we have seen, attitudes in our own society place us more in the former than in the latter group, although a slow change seems to be underway. Only a minority of pre-literate societies sharply restrict sexual behaviour by young children, some enforce rules rather laxly, others actually encourage pre-pubertal adolescent sexual behaviour, even to the extent of providing formal training. In the West, the central attitude is still one of strong restriction on pre-adolescents and a gradual lifting of restrictions in adolescence, though more rapidly for boys. More societies disapprove of extramarital liaisons than approve, but a few appear very permissive, even by current Western standards, which appear to be undergoing a period of change.

The massive evidence of cultural variations between place and time lends support to the social labelling view of social rules, which has been applied to a wide range of behaviours, including crime (Box, 1971) and psychological problems (Scheff, 1975). In the context of sexual behaviour the social labelling view states:

(1) no sexual act is intrinsically deviant;
(2) the act of labelling is a social act which tells us more about the person giving the label—doctor or judge (*and* by definition, sex expert)—than the act or person he is describing as deviant, or normal. The fact that all societies disapprove of a particular act does not necessarily invalidate the labelling view, it simply states that all societies have found it convenient—for social or economic reasons—to prohibit that act. In opposition to the social labelling view is that of religion, which holds that certain activities are ordained as wrong by God. The scientist (*as* a scientist, not as a mother/father, wife/husband, etc.) concerns himself or herself with the ascertainable facts of the situation: the biology of sexual behaviour, its social context and social learning and their various interactions.

We can conclude that despite some universals, or near universals, there are considerable differences between different societies, and over time within the same one, in sexual practices and the conventions of sexual attractiveness. Such variations can have only an environmental, rather than a biological, explanation. They are socially learned and are maintained by social reinforcement. In Chapter 3 we consider in detail the processes of social learning and performance applied to sexual behaviour and in Chapter 2 we describe the biological bases of sexual behaviour.

OVERVIEW

All societies have codes of sexual behaviour and try to transmit them to their members. In our own society the Church has played a major role in this process and to some extent still does, but there are now wide differences of opinion between different religious groups. The medical profession has also been a traditional source of exhortation. It is only recently, with the development of scientific sex research, that the views of medical and other socially designated experts have been based on accurate evidence as opposed to unfounded assertion.

An increasingly careful attempt is being made to chart social attitudes towards aspects of sexual behaviour as well as to collect self-reports of the behaviours themselves. The general trend is away from differing standards for men and women towards a common one for both sexes. A fairly marked shift towards greater permissiveness, for example the widespread acceptance of premarital intercourse in a relationship marked by affection, took place in the 1960s. Homosexual behaviour, traditionally opposed by both Church and medical authorities, still excites much social disapproval despite a relaxation of legal prohibitions.

There is a thriving market in pornography and much disagreement about its social effects and desirability. In general, the boundaries of what is permissible have shifted considerably in recent years; much current opinion would accept the depiction of heterosexual acts between adults but not materials involving violence or children. Another version of sex as a commodity—prostitution, both homosexual and heterosexual—continues to thrive economically, although the greater sexual freedom of women may be decreasing its importance as a source of sexual outlet for some males. Prostitution has some of the features of a career—particularly recruitment, training and in certain countries social regulation of the place of work.

Our society is increasingly concerned to provide formal sex education for its young: current attempts tend to follow informal and often inaccurate sex education from peers. Unfortunately, many so-called experts also fall short of a desirable standard of accuracy. Sex education tends still to be at the stage of anatomy and physiology, rather than extending into personal actions, feelings and experience.

Finally, there is very powerful evidence of widespread cultural variation, both in sexual behaviours and in the physical features which are considered to be attractive. Such evidence indicates that there is a major social learning component in sexual behaviour which interacts with a biological component.

CHAPTER 2

The Biological Bases of Sexual Behaviour

INTRODUCTION

The differential development of male and female sexual organs in separate individuals is called sexual dimorphism. The associated dimorphic sexual behaviour is part of the evolutionary process by which higher species are maintained and modified under the influence of environmental change.

This chapter begins by describing the embryonic differentiation of sexual organs, the anatomy of adult sex organs and the physiological basis of sexually dimorphic behaviour. It continues with a discussion of sexual arousal in men and women and a description of the major sexual acts. Overall, it provides a survey of the crucial biological bases which enable human sexual behaviours to be developed and performed.

GENERAL EMBRYOLOGY

The Developing Individual: The First Six Weeks after Conception

The development of the mammalian embryo, be it of a cat, dog, horse or man, is a process of immense physical, spatial and chemical complexity.

The fertilization of an egg from one individual by a sperm from another is the crucial mechanism by which higher species evolve. It is an event which has led to the development of highly elaborate systems to serve the production of eggs and sperms, copulation, fertilization, embryogenesis and the birth of the new individual. Immediately after fertilization the egg undergoes a rapid series of mitotic divisions to produce a number of smaller cells called blastomeres. At this time, the developing embryo is propelled down the fallopian tube and at the 12 to 15 cell stage, enters the uterine cavity at about five to eight days after ovulation. Between six and nine days after ovulation the young embryo becomes attached to the uterine wall and is called a blastocyst; at this point the embryo contains the potential to develop all the structures present in the adult of the species. When the cells of the blastocyst cease rapid division, they enter a phase of movement *relative to one another*, a process called gastrulation. In gastrulation, certain cells seem to play an organizing role which leads to the production of layers of cells. Newly contiguous cells interact to form structures appropriate to their new spatial position within the embryo; thus each cell acquires a 'developmental fate'. This process, which orders the spatial structure, is called pattern formation. Each cell's final development stage occurs when those cells express their final determined status and go on to develop into the appropriate cell type. This differentiation requires the production of specialized organelles and specific biochemical end-products which characterize the hundreds of different cell types of the adult organism.

The Formation of the Gonad

Embryonic sex is determined genetically at fertilization and depends on the presence or absence of the Y (male) chromosome in the fertilizing sperm (see below for a full discussion).

The primordial sex cells are first seen in the wall of the yolk sac which is later taken into the body of the embryo and forms the hind gut. These cells migrate at about the sixth week and come to lie beneath the coelomic epithelium on the medial side of the mesonephros (see Figure 2.1).

The cells of the coelomic epithelium multiply and form sex cords which

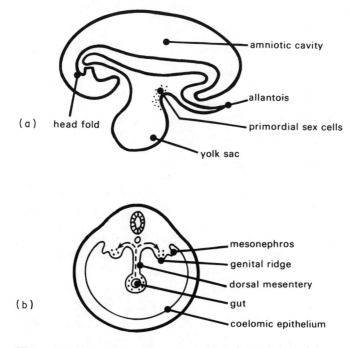

Figure 2.1 Formation of the gonad. (a) Left hand view of the embryo. (b) Cross-section showing sex cell migration to the genital ridge

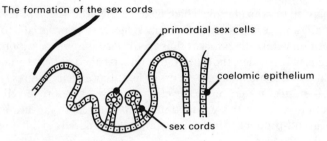

The formation of the sex cords

primordial sex cells

coelomic epithelium

sex cords

Figure 2.2 The migration of primordial sex cells and formation of the gonad

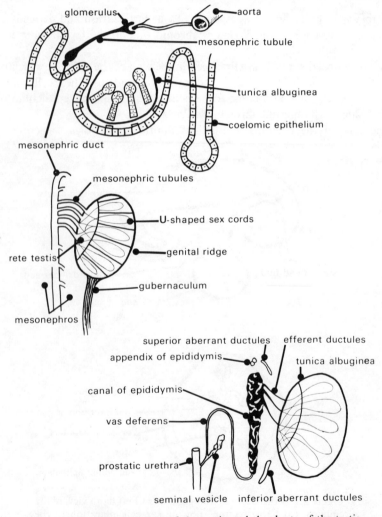

glomerulus

aorta

mesonephric tubule

tunica albuginea

coelomic epithelium

mesonephric duct

mesonephric tubules

U-shaped sex cords

rete testis

genital ridge

gubernaculum

mesonephros

superior aberrant ductules   efferent ductules

appendix of epididymis

tunica albuginea

canal of epididymis

vas deferens

prostatic urethra

seminal vesicle   inferior aberrant ductules

Figure 2.3 The formation of the testis and the ducts of the testis

increase in size to make a ridge on the medial side of the mesonephros, called the genital ridge. At this stage, when the embryo is examined, it is not possible to differentiate between the male and female gonads.

Differentiation of the Testis

The sex cords become separated from the coelomic epithelium at about the seventh week of development. In the fourth month the sex cords become U-shaped and form the seminiferous tubules. The primordial sex cells in the seminiferous tubules form the spermatogonia and the sex cells form the cells of sertoli.

The rete testis (see Figure 2.2) becomes canalized and the tubules extend into mesonephric tissue and join the remnants of mesonephric tubules. These tubules then become the efferent ductules of the testis. The duct of the epididymis, the vas deferens, the seminal vesicle and the ejaculatory duct are formed from the mesonephric duct (see Figure 2.3).

The Differentiation of the Ovary

The female gonad differentiates a little later than that of the male. The sex cords, with their primordial germ cells, break up into irregular clusters. The primordial germ cells eventually form primary oocytes which become surrounded by a single layer of cells derived from the sex cord, called the granulosa cells. The primordial follicle has now been formed (see Figure 2.4).

The Uterine Tube, Uterus, and Vagina

The paramesonephric duct (see Figure 2.5) appears on the posterior abdominal wall of the six-week-old embryo and starts as an invagination of coelomic epithelium into the underlying mesenchyme on the lateral side of the mesonephros (see Figure 2.5).

The paramesonephric ducts grow tailwards and inwards and fuse to form a solid bud (see Figure 2.5). The cranial part of the paramesonephric duct forms the upper portion of the uterine tube, the middle part forms the lower portion of the uterine tube and the caudal part, which fuses with its fellow on the other side, forms a common tube from which the uterus and part of the vagina develop. The origin of the formation of the vagina is not certain, but is it generally held that the fused lower ends of the paramesonephric ducts form the body and cervix, and the uterus and the vagina are formed from the wall of the urogenital sinus.

Paramesonephric Ducts in the Male

These degenerate in the third month, leaving behind small portions of the appendix, testis, and prostatic utricle.

28

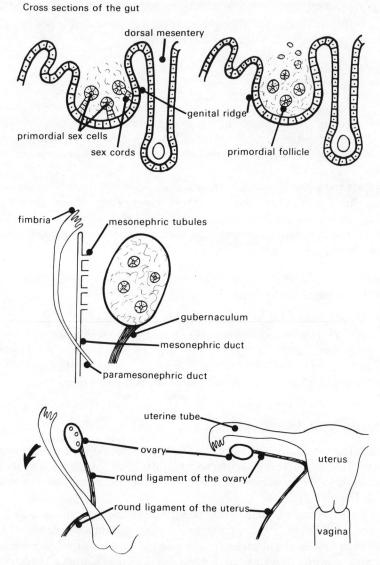

Cross sections of the gut

dorsal mesentery

genital ridge

primordial sex cells

sex cords

primordial follicle

fimbria

mesonephric tubules

gubernaculum

mesonephric duct

paramesonephric duct

uterine tube

ovary

round ligament of the ovary

round ligament of the uterus

uterus

vagina

Figure 2.4   The formation of the ovary and the developing uterine tube

Development of the External Genitalia

A swelling occurs between the cloacal membrane and the umbilical cord in the mid-line called the genital tubercle (see Figure 2.6). This is surrounded by the genital fold.

At the seventh week the tube elongates to form the phallus and develops and expands at the glans. The anterior part of the cloacal membrane ruptures so that

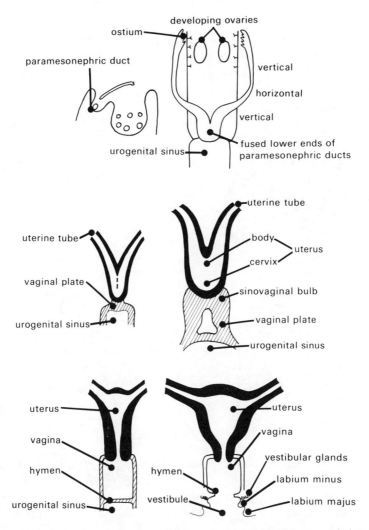

Figure 2.5   The formation of the uterine tubes, the uterus, and the vagina

the urogenital sinus opens on to the surface. A second pair of swellings appear laterally called the genital swellings. At this stage the genital areas of the two sexes are identical.

Differentiation into the Male Organs

The phallus elongates and causes the genital folds to form the urethral groove. The urogenital folds fuse to form the penile urethra. Incomplete fusion leads to hypospadias in the male.

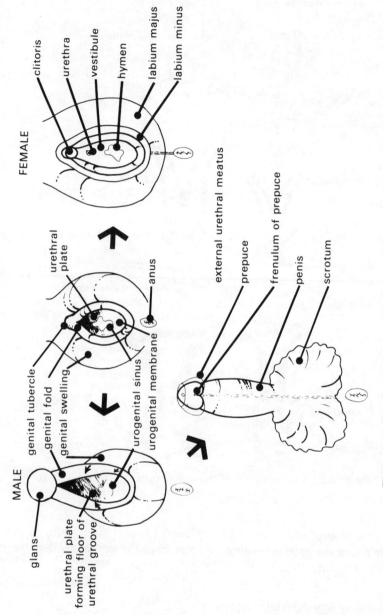

Figure 2.6   The development of the male and female external genitalia

Differentiation in the Female Organs

The changes in the female are less extensive. The phallus becomes bent and forms the clitoris. The genital folds do not fuse but form into the labia minora and the genital swellings enlarge to form the labia majora.

THE ADULT GENITALS

The Male

The male organs and ducts comprise: the testis, the epididymis, the ductus deferens, the seminal vesicle, the ejaculatory duct, the prostate gland, the bulbourethral glands, and the penis with its contained urethral passage. All the structures are paired (bilateral) except for the prostate gland, penis, and urethra (see Figures 2.7 and 2.8).

The *testis* is ovoid, the paired glands are supported outside the abdomen in the scrotal sac, the left testis being more dependent than the right. Each gland is covered by a peritoneal sac. The testicles are divided into lobules containing 600 highly tortuous seminiferous tubules of about 60 cm in length. The cell layer, or epithelium, which lines the thin muscular walls contains several cell layers which are the precursors of the sperm which, when mature, lie freely in the lumen of the tubes. The tubules converge into a network called the rete testis and from there, 15 to 20 efferent ductules go to the head of the epididymis where they form the duct of the epididymis. Clumps of interstitial cells are found in the connective tissue of the testis between seminiferous tubules and they represent the endocrine component of the gland. The ductus (the vas deferens) is a continuation of the duct of the epididymis and goes from the tail of the epididymis to form the

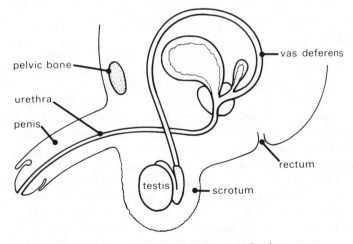

Figure 2.7   Left lateral view of male reproductive organs
(cross-section)

32

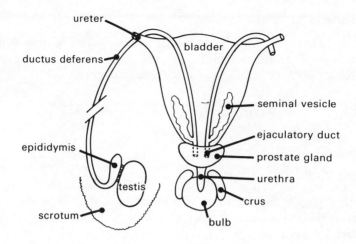

Figure 2.8   Male reproductive organs—rear view

ejaculatory duct. These tubes convey the sperms from the testes to the seminal vesicles which act as stores. The ducts ascend the scrotum to the groin and pass through the inguinal canal into the abdomen. In the abdomen they enter the pelvis and ascend retroperitoneally to the side of the bladder. They join the seminal vesicles immediately above the prostate gland to form the ejaculatory duct. The seminal vesicles are highly coiled tubes, 15 cm in length, which lie bilaterally against the base of the urinary bladder.

The *prostate* gland is chestnut-shaped, and lies with its base upwards against the neck of the bladder. It is 4 cm wide, 3 cm from base to apex and about 2 cm across. The prostatic urethra tunnels through the prostate gland and the ejaculatory ducts open through minute slits into the prostatic urethra (see Figure 2.8).

The *penis* consists of three cylindrical columns of spongy erectile tissue; on the upper or dorsal part the two corpora cavernosa lie side by side. The third small column, the corpus spongiosum, lies ventrally on the underpart and its anterior end is expanded to form the conical cap which fits over the anterior end of the corpora cavernosa and which is called the glans penis. The two proximal ends of the corpora cavernosa are attached to the pubic bones. The urethra runs up through the corpus spongiosum to the tip of the glans (see Figure 2.9).

The bulb and the crura of the corpora spongiosa have voluntary muscles attached to them. The erectile tissue of the corpora cavernosa and spongiosa contains sinus spaces which are fed by winding arterioles. These arterioles have special walls which normally are expanded to close the lumen of the artery. In this condition little blood is allowed to flow through the penile arteries. During sexual arousal the arterial lumen becomes dilated and the consequent increased blood flow leads to engorgement of the penis as part of the mechanism of erection.

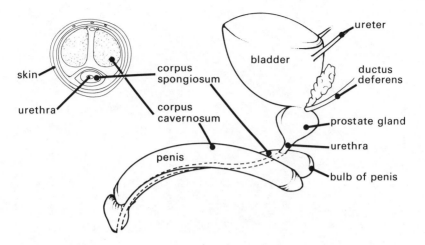

Figure 2.9   The bladder, prostate, and penis from the left side. Insert: cross-section of the penis

The Female

The female organs comprise:

(a) an internal group in the pelvis—the ovaries, uterine tubes, uterus, and vagina

(b) an external group situated inferior to the pubic arch, collectively referred to as the vulva.

The two *ovaries* are situated bilaterally on either side of the uterus next to the open end of the uterine tubes. They are almond-shaped about 3 cm in length, 2 cm in width and 1 cm in thickness.

The *uterine (fallopian) tubes* represent the unfused proximal ends of the paramesonephric ducts. They are 10 cm in length, attached to the side of the uterus in its upper end. The part running through the uterus is about 1 cm in length. The inner lining of the tubes is arranged in complex folds.

The *uterus* is pear-shaped, hollow, and highly muscular. It measures 7 to 8 cm in length, is 5 cm across at its upper part and is about 2.5 cm in thickness. Its neck or cervix is almost cylindrical and projects into the upper part of the vagina. Surrounding this area, the vagina has four recesses or fornices: one anteriorly, one posteriorly and two laterally. In the adult female who has not borne children the uterus is in front of the rectum but partly behind the bladder in a bent forward attitude (see Figure 2.10).

The *vagina* is about 7 to 10 centimetres long and extends downwards and forwards from the uterus to the external opening in the vestibule of the perineum. It is situated behind the bladder and urethra and in front of the rectum and anal canal.

The *external group* includes the mons pubis, the labia and the clitoris. The mons pubis is a mid-line fatty lump overlying the bony pelvis, formed by

34

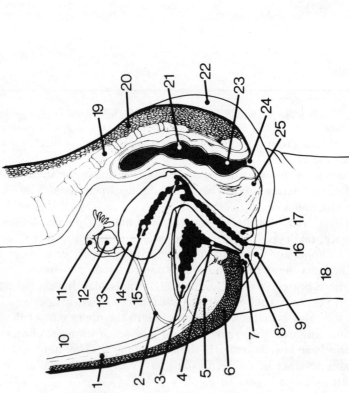

1 anterior abdominal wall
2 round ligament
3 bladder
4 urethra
5 joint of pelvic bones
6 mons pubis (symphysis pubis)
7 clitoris
8 labium minor
9 labium major
10 abdominal cavity
11 right fallopian tube
12 ovary
13 uterus
14 cavity of uterus
15 cervix of uterus
16 hymen
17 posterior vaginal wall
18 right leg
19 bones of spinal column
20 fat layer
21 colon
22 right buttock
23 rectum
24 anus
25 anal sphincter

Figure 2.10   Cross-section of the female pelvis viewed from the left

subcutaneous fat. The labia pudendi are two longitudinal skin folds on each side of the vulva; the lateral pair being larger are called the labia majora and the medial pair, being smaller, are called the labia minora. The former are analogous to the two halves of the male scrotum. The labia minora are split anteriorly to enclose the clitoris, uniting on its upper aspects to form the prepuce and frenulum of the clitoris. The clitoris is the analogue of the penis with a similar structure but does not contain the urethra. It contains the corpora cavernosa and the corpus spongiosum. In the vestibule of the vagina, which is a cleft between the labia minora, the urethra opens out, its opening being 2.5 cm behind the glans clitoridis and immediately in front of the vagina.

THE ACQUISITION OF SEXUALLY DIMORPHIC BEHAVIOUR

Introduction

Studies in the acquisition of sexual identity and sexual behaviours in humans are as complex as they are important. Even after many decades of research in disciplines as diverse as steroid chemistry and sociology, we must still draw heavily and by implication on studies in both lower and higher vertebrates in order to gain insight into the development of human sexual responsiveness. Both because the sexual organs of men and women are different and insemination normally requires co-operation it follows that the sequence of sexual behaviour has to be dimorphic—that is men and women perform specialized functions in order to achieve the result both seek.

In developmental biology the realization of a 'plan' (of an adult animal) is a highly useful notion, which can be seen as the sum of inherited genetic factors. The fruition of such a plan depends in part upon the genetic information which is contained in the genes coming into play in the correct order.

Sexual Differentiation

Genetic sex depends on the chromosome constitution which is established at conception; the fertilization of an ovum by an X-chromosome bearing sperm produces a genetic female and that by a Y-bearing sperm a genetic male. In the first eight weeks of intrauterine development in humans there are no differences other than the sex chromosome configuration XX and XY; however, from the eighth week onwards the primitive intra-abdominal gonad on the genital ridge of the embryo differentiates into a testis in the individual where a Y chromosome is present (male), and in the female (XX) foetus the ovary differentiates some two weeks later, at the end of the tenth week (see pp. 25–27).

Further sexual differentiations in the next month of the male foetal life depend on a testicular hormone as yet unidentified, which acts at a local tissue level to develop the epididymis, vas deferens, seminal vesicles and ejaculatory ducts from the mesonephric ducts, and causes degeneration in paramesonephric ducts (see Figures 2.1 and 2.2). If this testicular hormone is absent (i.e. in the XX chromosomal configuration), the male (mesonephric) ducts degenerate and the female (paramesonephric) ducts develop into the fallopian tubes, uterus, and vagina. It is thought that testicular androgens are responsible for the fusion of the urethral folds to form the penile corpus spongiosum, and the labio-scrotal folds to form the scrotum; in the absence of testicular androgen these primordial structures form the labia of the female (see Figure 2.6).

Sexual Dimorphism and Dimorphic Sexual Behaviour

The reproductive anatomy of the normal human (and other animals) is thus seen to be dimorphic. It logically follows that if a species is to reproduce, the species *behaviour* must also be sufficiently sexually dimorphic to permit copulation and conception to take place. We now show that the dimorphic nature of sexual behaviour is disrupted by genetic and hormonal abnormalities. Beach *et al.* (1969) have successfully analysed male and female sexual behaviour in the rat, on an empirical basis. Money and Ehrhardt (1971) have remarked that there is, as yet, no conventionally agreed differentiation of the components of human sexual performance. 'The lack no doubt reflects contemporary scientific reluctance to watch human beings copulate, as well as the relatively un-stereotyped nature of human sexual activity, as compared with that of other primates' (Money and Ehrhardt, 1971, p. 243).

The evidence from animal sexology is that sexually dimorphic behaviour is not solely male or female; it tends to be bisexual in *potential* but is mainly male or mainly female in manifestation (Beach, 1947; Whalen, 1968). Each sex at some time displays elements of sex behaviour appropriate to the other sex. The antecedents of such 'aberrant' behavioural elements are of interest; for example, crowding disrupts rat sex behaviour (Calhoun, 1962); isolation in the rhesus monkey has a similar effect (Harlow and Harlow, 1965); castration of adult rats followed by treatment with opposite sex hormone can release heterotypical (opposite) sex behaviour patterns (Beach, 1947); more recently the same findings for the male hamster have been reported (Swanson and Gossley, 1971). Money and Ehrhardt (1971) suggests that the dimorphic sex behaviour which is observed in animals will be a product of early hormonal manipulation (see later) and the animal's pubertal hormonal status at the time of observation.

Evidence from the animal literature suggests that the form of sexual behaviour exhibited by adult mammals is governed in two ways:
1. by 'cerebral sexual centres'
2. by the gonads, sexual apparatus and the nature of the circulating hormones.

There is complex relationship between 1 and 2 which depends on the development of the individual under genetic influences, the hormonal metabolic performance of the foeto/placental unit and the sensitivity of the various target organs to circulating hormones.

CEREBRAL SEXUAL MECHANISMS

Berthold (1849) found that castration of adult cocks resulted in genital atrophy and decrease of the male sex behaviour; re-implantation of testes prevented these changes. It was therefore supposed that a substance was produced by the testes which was responsible for the development and function of the sex organs, and also for the development and maintenance of sexual behaviour. Aschner (1912) observed gonadal atrophy in dogs after experimental damage to the pituitary gland. This gave the first hint that part of the brain had an influence over the gonads. Brain-produced hormones which affected the gonads, the so-called gonadotrophins, were simultaneously discovered in 1927 by Zondek and Ascheim and by Smith and Engle. Since 1929, various male and female gonadal hormones have been identified and some have been synthesized.

The pituitary gland is a small pedicle-like structure, apparently separate from the brain although connected to it via the pituitary stalk. It was Hohlweg and Junkmann (1932) who suggested that the brain might control the gonadotrophin production of the pituitary and so indirectly regulate both the gonadotrophin production and gonadal function. This crucial idea has been discussed by Dörner (1970) who has updated the original unit: CNS → hypophysis → gonads, to the following: hypothalamic sex and mating centres → hypophysis → gonads.

The present status of Hohlweg and Junkmann's 'cybernetic unit' is as follows:
1. Part of the basal central hypothalamus, called the hypophysiotrophic area (HPT), secretes follicle stimulating hormone (FSH) and luteinizing hormone (LH) *releasers*.
2. These chemical releasers are transported from the hypothalamus in the brain itself to the anterior pituitary gland, in blood vessels which run in the substance of the central nervous system, in the so-called hypothalamohypophysial portal vessels.
3. In the anterior pituitary they stimulate the secretion of the specific gonadotrophin, which in turn exerts a negative feedback (regulatory) function on the source of the hypothalamic releasers. In the female, an additional sex centre functions in the rostral (front) hypothalamus in cycles, and *over* produces LH releasers. The consequent over release of pituitary LH leads to ovulation (this function is under afferent control in the rabbit at least).
4. The pituitary gonadotrophins regulate both gonadal generative activity as well as the secretion of sex hormones.
5. The sex hormones regulate the physiological function of their target organs, for example the genitals.
6. The sex hormones (from the gonads) may inhibit (negative feedback) or stimulate (positive feedback) both the hypothalamic releasers and the pituitary gonadotrophins depending upon their combination.
7. Importantly, the gonadal hormones sensitize the hypothalamic mating centres to sensory excitation which reaches the diencephalon via the cortex. Androgens play a dual role here, because they can stimulate *both* the male and the female centres which have been shown to be located in the anterior hypothalamus (male centre), and the central hypothalamus (female centre). Dörner *et al.* (1968) distinguished these male and female mating centres in rats and showed that sexual behaviour could be *selectively stimulated or abolished*

either by intrahypothalamic sex hormone implantation or by hypothalamic electrolytic lesions in these areas.

8. The sensitivity of the centres to androgen depends on the degree of their differentiation, e.g. when the male centre is more highly differentiated it is prepotent in effect when the brain is later exposed to circulating androgen, and the resulting sexual behaviour is male. The reverse is true if the female centre is the more highly differentiated, although it should be noted that oestrogens mainly stimulate the female mating centre.

The Differentiation of Brain Sex Centres by the Influence of Sex Hormones

The evidence for the existence of cerebral sex centres is taken from the animal literature. The absence of testes during a *critical* phase of neonatal development in the rat resulted in *cyclic* hypophysial gonadotrophin secretion, while the presence of testes produced continuous (tonic) gonadotrophin secretion (Pfeiffer, 1936). If a male rat was castrated at birth and implanted with ovaries when it was adult, then ovarian cycles resulted; but if female rat neonates were exposed to androgen by neonatal testicular implants (ovaries intact) no ovulations resulted. Similarly, post-critical period male castrate rats failed to produce ovarian cycles when they were transplanted with ovaries in adulthood. The tentative conclusion was that the mammalian organism went through a critical phase of development during which the presence or absence of testes pre-ordained the adult capacity for ovarian cycling and, as cycling could be produced in the genetic male, it seemed likely that the biological substrate for cycling (a *female* pattern) was actually present in the male, but not normally manifested. In 1941 Wilson *et al.* added further weight to this model by showing that if *female* neonate rats were androgenized during their critical period, no ovarian cycling ensued in adulthood, and their ovaries failed to show corpora lutea. Barraclough and Gorsky (1961) established that the development of cyclic or acyclic (tonic) hypophysial gonadotrophin secretion is determined by an *androgen* dependent *hypothalamic* phase; that is, low critical phase androgen gave cyclical hypophysial secretion (female pattern) in contrast to high androgen which resulted in tonic secretion (male pattern). It is of interst that Dörner (1970) has shown that abnormally high levels of sex steroids in male and female rats during the hypothalamic differentiation phase result in hypogonadotrophic hypogonadism during the hypothalamic functional phase, and precisely the same result is obtained by administering abnormally high levels of male gonadotrophin. It therefore appears that the differentiating hypothalamus is not only critically sensitive to normal amounts of androgen and oestrogen, but may be critically affected by excess gonadotrophin in a way which leads to hyposexuality (i.e. reduced sexuality) in the functional (adult) period.

Phoenix *et al.* (1959) distinguished a *pre-natal differentiation period from a post*-pubertal activation period, based on pre-natally androgenized female guinea pigs who were caused to show male sexual behaviour under the influence of post-pubertal androgen. In the first phase, the differentiation of the hypothalamus is dependent on the androgen level, and in the second phase, the hypothalamus is activated either by androgens or oestrogens. Grady and Phoenix (1963) and Harris (1964) showed that neonatal orchidectomized (castrated ma[l]e) rats showed marked female sex behaviour when treated with exogenous oestrogen in adulthood.

In summary, these observations, also confirmed by Feder and Whalen (1965) and Neumann *et al.* (1967), strongly suggested the great significance of brain androgen level in the critical hypothalamic differentiation phase with regard to the *direction* of sex drive and behaviour in the post-pubertal mammal. The critical phase is perinatal in rats (Diess, 1969), but *pre*-natal in guinea pigs, monkeys and probably in humans (Dörner, 1970, p. 283).

Concluding Comment

New human beings result from the fertilization of a normal human egg by a normal human sperm. All the information that is necessary for that cell's development is contained as a code in the cellular DNA. Certain cells in the early embryo reorganize the structure (no doubt under the instructions of DNA codes), so that the primitive human takes shape. If we discount the complex mass of structure which goes to make up the rest of the organism we may focus on two areas primarily relevant to later sexual behaviour, the brain and the gonads.

The instructions for the development of sexed gonads, i.e. ovaries (XX) or testes (XY), are present because the fertilization contributes either a second X or a second Y chromosome. The gonad cell strings develop between the seventh and the fifteenth weeks. It is not clear at what time the primitive gonads produce sex steroids, but the presence of circulating sex steroids (particularly androgen) is vital to the development of the brain. It now seems certain that there are male and female sex centres in the human brain; the male centre becomes prepotent over the female centre if it is exposed and sensitive to androgen in the third month of embryonic life.

Androgens available to the foetus may be produced by the foeto-placental unit, the male foetus, and possibly by the mother. There are therefore several possible mechanisms which could account for the development of abnormal cerebral sexual dimorphism. If in a female foetus there is too much androgen circulating at the critical third month, the male centre may be sensitized, thus gaining prepotence over the female centre, leading to abnormalities in gender acquisition and post-pubertal behaviour. Similarly, in the male there may be an absence of androgen or a specific hypothalamic androgen insensitivity, which leads to a female brain showing cyclical activity and the female type of gender acquisition.

However, abnormal levels of sex steroids can affect the developing gonads without affecting the brain, because the critical periods of the genital and cerebral cells differ. Thus it is possible to observe a number of inter-sex states in which the cerebral sexual differentiation (and hence aspects of behaviour) differs from the body phenotype. Gender is not infrequently mis-assigned soon after birth

(Money and Ehrhardt, 1972). There are now several dozen well-documented cases of gender reassignment. A number of authors point out that gender role can apparently be reassigned and therefore, by implication, initially mis-assigned; however the bulk of the animal literature strongly suggests that brains have sex, and that cerebral sexual dimorphisms contribute significantly to the production of sexually dimorphic behaviour.

The acquisition of sexual identity and sexual behaviour in the human is thus a subject of wide scope; it has its roots almost at the base of life itself. We cannot attempt to understand sex fully without far reaching knowledge in cell physiology, hormones, genetics, and embryology as well as in social learning and social organization.

SEXUAL AROUSAL IN THE HUMAN

Sexual arousal is a periodic phenomenon; both humans and animals rarely maintain a constant level of arousal. There is a relationship between the level of arousal at any one time and the ease with which the organism can be elevated to orgasm at that time. Arousability is a concept which is analogous to 'trait versus state' theory in discussions on emotions (Cattell and Scheier, 1961; Spielberger, 1966; Zuckerman *et al.*, 1967). A subject's trait characteristic can be measured both as the average of the state, and the capacity for variation in measures of that trait. Specifically, in the sexual sphere, Whalen (1966) has distinguished between level of arousal and arousability, the latter being an 'individual's characteristic rate of approach to orgasm as a result of sexual stimulation' (Whalen, 1966, p. 52). Sexual arousability is, therefore, defined by the responses to a standard series of sexually arousing stimuli. Measures of sexual arousability have been achieved in the rat (Beach, 1958) but not yet in man. However, two general approaches to the problem of measuring sexual arousal are available to us in man: verbal report and behavioural/physiological observation.

The Mechanisms of Sexual Arousal

Sexual arousal is mediated by both the central and the autonomic nervous system. Money (1961) predicated three 'co-ordinates' of sexual function:
1. the local genital surfaces
2. the brain
3. the hormones.

Money stated that 'loss of any one of these three co-ordinates is an immense handicap to effective sexual functioning' (Money, 1961, p. 1396). There are both species and sex differences in the components of sexual arousal which are subserved by the neocortex and hormones, and Beach (1958) has noted the evolutionary trend which places the balance of importance on the neocortex.

Sexual Arousal and the CNS

MacLean (1965) has stressed the importance of teleceptors (sight and smell) in initial sexual stimulation in animals. Specific sex arousal centres have been found in the limbic system of the squirrel monkey and intracranial electric stimulation to hippocampal projections produced penile erections. The areas concerned are quite widespread in the septum, anterior thalamus, hypothalamus, mammillary bodies, anterior cingulate gyrus, medial orbital gyrus, and medial dorsal nucleus of the thalamus. In addition, there is quite a strong suggestion that hippocampal discharges (associated with throbbing erections and followed by calmness) are linked to orgasm and post-orgasmic decline in sexual arousability. The cerebral areas associated with seminal discharge are different from those listed above; these findings fit in with Beach's (1965) suggestion that there exists a sexual arousal mechanism (AM) and a consummation mechanism (CM) in the male. MacLean's evidence shows the neural structural difference of the two mechanisms in animals; in man it is possible to display ejaculation without erection and vice versa (Hohmann, 1966). Thus, clinical findings in man are in line with experimental findings in animals.

Sexual Arousal and Autonomic Nervous System

A series of rabbit and rat experiments have shown that destruction of a large area of cortex did not impair sexual behaviour provided that the hypothalamus was intact (Gellhorn and Loofburrow, 1963). These authors suggest that the sex act is accompanied by both sympathetic and parasympathetic neural discharge (it will be remembered that the hypothalamus may be regarded as containing the head ganglia of both the sympathetic and parasympathetic systems). The problem of emotional specificity (particularly of physiological dependent variables) has been discussed by Shachter and Singer (1962). However, it appears that sexual arousal is unique in its 'invariable increase' in surface temperatures, colour, tumescence, genital secretions, rhythmic muscular movements and orgasm. Masters and Johnson's (1966) description of human sexual responses fit Wengener et al.'s (1968) theory of early parasympathetic activity predominance, followed by sympathetically mediated phenomena in the later pre-orgasmic phases of arousal.

There seems to be a strong suggestion from drug reports that sympathetic depressants interfere with ejaculation (CM, see above; Blair and Simpson, 1966) and that MAO (monoamineoxidase) inhibitors (which have anti-parasympathetic effects) interfere with erection (AM, see above; Simpson et al., 1965). Thus, it seems reasonable to suppose that, in man, sympathetic tone dominance inhibits arousal and facilitates ejaculation, the *exact* situation which is seen in premature ejaculation.

Sexual Arousal and Hormones

Money (1961) has adduced considerable evidence in support of the idea that androgen relates to sexual arousability in *women* as well as in men. Zuckerman (1971) concludes that sex hormones probably operate to lower thresholds for sexual arousal, but that beyond a certain level additional hormone supplies do not make much difference.

Physiological Measures of Arousal in the Human

Zuckerman (1971) has provided an excellent review of the physiological concomitants of sexual arousal. Work on skin potential, heart rate and respiration are disappointing as single or joint measures of sexual arousal because of that lack of specificity which has been the bane of research into all aspects of arousal. However, measures of penile response, although unsatisfactory at the present time, appear to hold out the greatest promise in this field. Once a simple unobtrusive plethysmograph or strain-gauge has been developed it will be possible to investigate subjects' sexual arousability more fully. To date vaginal blood flow is the most satisfactory indicant of female sexual arousal. Fluctuations in vaginal blood flow during REM sleep phases have been found to be similar to those occurring in the big toe; it is tentatively concluded that fluctuations in the vaginal tube volume express general cardiovascular changes seen in the REM periods. This general unison of the autonomic system is further illustrated by Bardwick and Behrman (1967) who have shown that the uterus responds to both anxiety and sexual stimulation (reading *Playboy*!) with an increased mean amplitude and amplitude variance of its contractions. The technique involved is painful and, therefore, unlikely to be helpful for that reason alone. Similarly, pupillary response and cortical evoked responses failed to provide a reliable index of sexual arousal.

Biochemical Studies of Sexual Arousal

There do not appear to be any direct studies on hormones and sexual arousal in humans. Levi (1969) examined catecholamine excretion in males and females in response to erotic films. The results were interesting in that both groups showed increase in adrenalin production and sexual arousal but the females reported a significant degree of unpleasant emotion. A similar effect was found in response to non-sexual films of violence, sadism, and also to comedy. Urinary acid phosphatase (AP) seems to be correlated with sexual arousal in men (Clark and Treichler, 1950; Barclay, 1970). There are strong indications that AP measures will relate to sex-drive and arousal.

Concluding Comment

Although the field of enquiry is new there is now an extensive literature on sexual arousal and arousability. It seems clear that the hypothalamus is implicated as the immediate mediator of a push–pull, sympathetic/parasympathetic system which, in the male at least, has two separate functions: arousal and consummation. At the same time, erection and consummation may be influenced by higher centres, predominantly in the limbic system and it is this link with fight/flight and anxiety mechanisms that is probably at the root of many human sexual problems. We may now confidently assume that anxiety and its consequences are causally related to human sexual arousal and sexual arousability. We are thus still at a stage where the investigation of sexual problems is predominantly a clinical matter.

THE PHYSIOLOGY OF HUMAN SEXUAL RESPONSES

Introduction

Masters and Johnson (1966) conducted a long series of experiments on the physiological changes produced in men and women by genital stimulation. The experiments were undertaken 'because of the immense ignorance concerning human sexuality in lay and professionals alike'. They studied a number of distinct groups of people. All the individuals observed were specially chosen for their studies and therefore represent highly selected groups. The sex responses of 111 pregnant women were looked at separately and 61 aged women and 39 aged men were also investigated. In addition, Masters and Johnson have investigated 118 female and 27 male prostitutes, 8 and 3 of whom, respectively, were studied psychologically.

The major sample consisted of 382 women and 312 men mainly from an academic community. The age ranges were 18–78 for females and 21–89 for men. The cohort included 276 married couples, 106 single women, and 36 single men. All the subjects who were approached were given a detailed interview and the selected subjects ultimately provided data on 10,000 complete sex response cycles: 7,500 female and 2,500 male. Experimental stimulation was manual and mechanical genital stimulation, and both natural and artificial coitus, the latter in women being produced by a mechanical transparent artificial penis.

Masters and Johnson leave at least one important question unanswered and it is worth quoting their view of it. 'How does the sexuality of male and female study subjects differ from that of our general population, and are there significant differences? These biologic and behavioural questions are of major moment. Unfortunately, these are questions for which there are no answers, because there are no established norms for male and female sexuality in society . . . . Without established norms of human sexuality there is no scale with which to measure or evaluate the sexuality of the male and female study subject population . . . comparisons may be drawn selectively between the reported response patterns of this highly selected research population and the reader's personal experience or his concept of norms of human eroticism in today's society. From these prejudiced levels of comparison, there is no appeal at this time' (Masters and Johnson, 1960). Although aspects of their sample selection are capable of technical criticism none the less they have increased greatly our knowledge of human sexual physiology; this knowledge is undoubtedly worth while scientifically and is being used every day to help people who complain about their sexual performance and satisfaction.

The Sequence of Events

The total human sexual response in both the male and the female is divided into four phases as follows: the excitement phase, the plateau phase, the orgasmic phase, and the resolution phase. All the phases are in general analogous, with one exception; in the male there is no immediate post-orgasmic

44

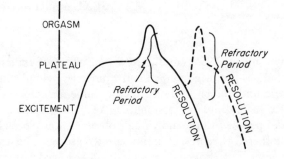

Figure 2.11   The male sexual response cycle

ability to return to a fresh orgasm. The successive phases of the sexual cycle are shown in Figures 2.11 and 2.12.

The excitement phase in both sexes may be initiated and develop in response to thoughts, mental imagery, general physical contact, and specific sexual contact involving the erogenous zones. The plateau phase is entered if sexual stimulation is maintained in an effective way. When the degree of sexual tension is very marked, it is shown by deep and superficial vasocongestion. If stimulation ceases in this phase, a long tension-laden resolution phase occurs. More often, sexual stimulation continues until the plateau phase proceeds to the orgasmic phase. Masters and Johnson (1966) state that, in the orgasmic phase 50 per cent of females have the capacity to return immediately to full orgasm. This pattern is most infrequent in the male. Another important physiological difference is that the female's orgasm can be terminated at any point by an unexpected extraneous distraction such as noise or change in lighting. However, the male's ejaculatory process cannot be stopped once it has started. In the resolution phase, the male

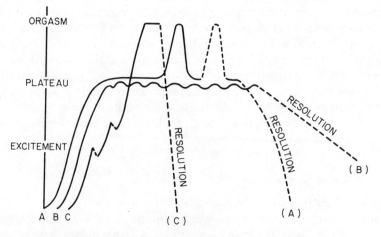

Figure 2.12   The female sexual response cycle

has an acute refractory period in which further full erection is virtually impossible. The general body reactions associated with the four phases of the sexual responses are shown in Tables 2.1 and 2.2. The specific sexual responses are shown in Table 2.3, and the sexual response cycles for humans are described for each sex separately (pp. 45–53).

HUMAN SEX RESPONSE CYCLES

The Female

The physiological reactions in the female to sexual stimulation are multiple and occur in all the body systems. The vasocongestive reactions can occur in any phase of the sexual cycle but the muscle tension changes usually become obvious during the plateau phase of sexual excitation, and continue into the orgasmic phase.

The breasts. Nipple reaction, which consists of an enlargement and increased protuberance of the nipple, is usually the first evidence of the breast's response to sexual tension increase. During the excitement phase, there is often increased engorgement of the veins on the breast and there is an increase in the size of the breasts. During the plateau phase, there is areolar engorgement and the breasts increase in size by one-fifth to one-fourth over their unstimulated size. The breast develops a mottled appearance described as a maculo-papular rash.

During the resolution phase, the sex flush (rash) disappears and the breasts detumesce.

The sexual flush. It is thought by Masters and Johnson (1966) that the intensity and severity of the flush reaction is directly related to the degree of the sexual tension experienced by the women. The rash first appears over the upper abdomen (epigastrium) in the late excitement or early plateau phase. It then spreads over the breasts. As orgasm approaches, the rash can spread over the lateral walls of the thighs, over the buttocks and back, and there is a flushing of the face just prior to orgasm. Approximately three-quarters of all women flush as they approach orgasm.

Muscle tension. Muscle tension becomes obvious late in the excitement phase and during the plateau phase and is both generalized and specific. A foot and hand clutching spasm is noted. It is thought that the degree of muscle tension increase is related to the level of sexual tension. As tension increases during the excitement phase, the female shows general restless body movements which increase in their speed with time. In the plateau phase, the individual may frown, scowl or grimace. The neck muscles contract involuntarily and the respiration rate increases; the abdominal musculature tightens as orgasm is imminent and clutching and grasping is a clear behaviour pattern. Late in the plateau phase, prior to orgasm, pelvic thrusting in either sex is said to be involuntary in

Table 2.1. Sexual Response Cycle of the Human Female—Extragenital Reactions

	I. Excitement phase	II. Plateau phase	III. Orgasmic phase	IV. Resolution phase
Breasts	Nipple erection; increased venous patterning; increase in breast size; tumescence	Turgidity of nipples; further increase in breast size; marked areolar engorgement	No observed changes	Rapid detumescence of areolas and involution of nipple erection; slower decrease in breast volume and return to normal venous patterning
Sex flush	Appearance of maculopapular rash late in phase, first over epigastrium, spreading rapidly over breasts	Well developed flush; may have widespread body distribution late in phase	Degree of flush parallels intensity of orgasmic experience	Rapid disappearance of flush in reverse order of its appearance
Myotonia	Voluntary muscle tension; vaginal wall expansion, tensing of abdominal and intercostal musculature	Further increase in voluntary and involuntary tensions; semi-spastic contractions of facial, abdominal, and intercostal musculature	Loss of voluntary control; involuntary contractions and spasm of muscles	Myotonia resolves in 5 min into phase but not lost as rapidly as many evidences of vasocongestion
Rectum	No observed reaction	Voluntary contraction of rectal sphincter as stimulative technique	Involuntary contractions of rectal sphincter occurring simultaneously with contractions of orgasmic platform	No observed changes
Hyperventilation	No observed reaction	Appears late in phase	Respiratory rates as high as 40/min; intensity and duration indicative of degree of sexual tension	Resolve early in phase

Tachycardia	Heart rate increases in direct parallel to rising tension regardless of technique of stimulation	Recorded rates average from 110 to 175 beats per min	Recorded rates range from 110 to 180+ beats per min; higher heart rates reflect more variation in orgasmic intensity for female than for male	Return to normal
Blood pressure	Elevation occurs in direct parallel to rising tension regardless of technique	Elevations in systolic pressure of 20–60 mm Hg, diastolic 10–20 mm Hg	Elevations in systolic pressure of 30–80 mm Hg, diastolic 20–40 mm Hg	Return to normal
Perspiratory reaction	No observed reaction	No observed reaction	No observed reaction	Appearance of widespread film of perspiration, not related to degree of physical activity

Table 2.2. Sexual Response Cycle of the Human Male—Extragenital Reactions

	I. Excitement phase	II. Plateau phase	III. Orgasmic phase	IV. Resolution phase
Breasts	Nipple erection (inconsistent and may be delayed until plateau phase)	Nipple erection and turgidity (inconsistent)	No observed changes	Involution of nipple erection (may be prolonged)
Sex flush	No observed reaction	Appearance of maculo-papular rash late in phase (inconsistent); originates over epigastrium and spreads to anterior chest wall, neck face, forehead and occasionally to shoulders and forearms	Well developed flush; degree parallels intensity of orgasm (est. 25% incidence)	Rapid disappearance of flush in reverse order of its appearance
Myotonia	Voluntary muscle tension; some evidence of involuntary activity (partial testicular elevation, tensing of abdominal and intercostal musculature)	Further increase in voluntary and involuntary tension; semi-spastic contractions of facial, abdominal and intercostal musculature	Loss of voluntary control; involuntary contractions and spasm of muscle groups	Myotonia resolves in 5 min into phase
Rectum	No observed reaction	Voluntary contraction of rectal sphincter as stimulative technique (inconsistent)	Involuntary contractions of rectal sphincter at 0.8 s intervals	No observed changes
Hyperventilation	No observed reaction	Appearance of reaction occurs late in phase	Respiratory rates as high as 40/min; intensity and duration indicative of degree of sexual tension	Resolves during refractory period

Tachycardia	Heart rate increases in direct parallel to rising tension regardless of technique of stimulation	Recorded rates average from 100 to 175 beats per min	Recorded rates range from 110 to 180 beats per min	Return to normal
Blood pressure	Elevation occurs in direct parallel to rising tension regardless of technique of stimulation	Elevations in systolic pressure of 20–80 mm Hg, diastolic 10–40 mm Hg	Elevations in systolic pressure of 40–100 mm Hg, diastolic 20–50 mm Hg	Return to normal
Perspiratory reaction	No observed reaction	No observed reaction	No observed reaction	Involuntary sweating reaction (inconsistent), usually confined to soles of feet and palms of hands

Table 2.3. Human Sexual Response Cycle: Genital Reactions

Male	Female
Excitement phase	
Penile erection (3 to 8 seconds) as phase is prolonged	Vaginal lubrication (5 to 15 seconds) as phase is prolonged
Thickening, flattening and elevation of the scrotum	Thickening of vaginal walls, flattening and elevation of labia majora as phase is prolonged
Moderate testicular elevation and size increase	Expansion of inner 2/3 vaginal barrel and elevation of cervix and body of the uterus
Plateau phase	
Increase in penile coronal circumference and testicular tumescence ($\frac{1}{2}$ to 1 × enlarged)	Orgasmic platform in outer 1/3 of vagina
Full testicular elevation and rotation (30 to 35 degrees)	Full inner 2/3 vaginal expansion, uterine, and cervical elevation
Purple cast to corona of penis (inconsistent, even if orgasm is to ensue)	'Sex-skin' discoloration of labia minora (constant, if orgasm is to ensue)
Mucoid-like emission from Cowper's gland	Mucoid-like emission from Bartholin's gland
Orgasmic phase	
Ejaculation	Pelvic response

1. Contraction of accessory organs of reproduction
  a. Vas deferens
  b. Seminal vesicles
  c. Ejaculatory duct
  Prostate
	1. Contractions of uterus from fundus toward lower uterine segment

2. Relaxation of external bladder sphincter	2. Minimal relaxation of external cervical os
3. Contractions of penile urethra at 0.8 s intervals for 2 to 3 contractions (slowing thereafter for 2 to 4 more contractions)	3. Contraction of vagina orgasmic platform at 0.8 s intervals for 4 to 8 contractions (slowing thereafter for 2 to 4 more contractions)
4. External rectal sphincter contractions (2 to 4 contractions at 0.8 s intervals)	4. External rectal sphincter contractions (2 to 4 contractions at 0.8 s intervals) External urethral sphincter contractions (2 to 3 contractions at irregular intervals)
Resolution phase	
1. Refractory period with rapid loss of pelvic vasocongestion	1. Ready return to orgasm with retarded loss of pelvic vasocongestion
2. Loss of penile erection in primary (rapid) and secondary (slow) stages	2. Loss of 'sex-skin' colour and orgasmic platform in primary (rapid) stage Remainder of pelvic vasocongestion as secondary (slow) stage

character. In orgasm, most of the myotonia is involuntary. There is involuntary contraction of the external rectal sphincter, together with contraction of the glutei muscles during the excitement and plateau phases. Hyperventilation develops late in the plateau phase and respiratory rates go up to 40 a minute. Similarly, there is tachycardia (increase in heart rate), with rates up to 180 beats per minute. These changes are mirrored in increases of blood pressure (systolic) of between 30 and 80 mm of mercury.

Perspiration. The female may perspire over the back, thighs and anterior chest wall at the immediate post-orgasmic stage. About one-third of women display the perspiration reaction.

The external genitalia. There is a marked expansion in the labia minora during sexual stimulation, so that in the plateau phase they increase in volume between two and three times, to protrude beyond the edges of the labia majora, and change in colour from pink to bright red. Masters and Johnson state that no pre-menopausal woman has been observed to reach the plateau phase of sexual tension, develop sex skin colour changes (labia minora engorgement) and not experience an orgasm. Within 10–15 seconds of orgasm the labia minora change from deep, bright red to light pink as part of the resolution phase changes.

The clitoris. When sexual tension develops, the clitoral glans increases in size, the clitoris as a whole engorges, and increases its shaft length. In the plateau phase, the body of the clitoris retracts from the normal pudendal overhang position. In the resolution phase, the clitoris returns to the normal pudendal overhang position within 5–10 seconds of orgasmic platform.

The vagina: excitement phase. The first physiological evidence of the female's response to sexual stimulation is the production of vaginal lubrication, a material which appears on the walls of the vagina within 10 to 30 seconds after the onset of effective sexual stimulation. The origin of the secretion is in doubt, but it appears to be a vaginal wall transudate. During the lengthening and extension of the inner two-thirds of the vaginal barrel, its walls expand involuntarily and relax in an irregular fashion. The cervix and the body of the uterus are pulled back and upwards into the false pelvis and during the excitement phase, the vaginal walls change colour from purplish red to a darker purple red.

The vagina: plateau phase. There is a change in the outer two-thirds of the vagina which becomes grossly distended with venous blood, so as to reduce the lumen of the outer one-third of the vaginal barrel by a factor of one-third. At orgasm, the major changes are confined to the orgasmic platform and are confined to the outer one-third of the vagina and vulva. The vulvar musculature contracts strongly in a regular fashion at a rate of 0.8 second intervals.

The vagina: resolution phase. The changes seen during increase of sexual tension are reversed.

The subjective experience of orgasm. Masters and Johnson have described the subjective experience of orgasm as follows: 'There is, lasting only a small time, a sensation accompanied by an intense sensual awareness orientated from the clitoris . . . edging up into the pelvis. There is a simultaneous loss of auditory acuity. A number of subjects have expressed a feeling of receptive opening (presumably in the vagina). Some women describe giving birth as an experience very similar to that of orgasm. In the second stage of orgasm subjects report a feeling of warmth which suffuses the body starting from the pelvic area' (Masters and Johnson, 1960). In stage three there is usually a feeling of involuntary contraction of the vagina and rectum, with a sensation of pelvic throbbing. Pregnancy has been reported to sharpen the sense of sexual awareness during orgasm.

The Male

As with the female, there is some physical evidence of the development of sexual tension throughout the entire body in the same basic pattern. Widespread areas of superficial and deep congestion develop, followed by an increasing muscle tension which is itself both generalized and specific.

The breasts. Nipple erection is seen in the male in the plateau phase of sexual stimulation, but there are no other specific breast changes. The male develops the same maculo-papular sex flush as that described in the human female, which, as in the female, arises primarily from the epigastrium and spreads over the anterior chest wall.

Muscle tension. Increased muscle tension becomes obvious late in the excitement phase and during the plateau levels of sexual excitement. Foot and hand spasm and clutching has been noted as well as the involuntary trunk muscle movements which occur late in the pre-orgasmic plateau phase. During ejaculation the anal sphincter contracts involuntarily as does the bulbospongiosus muscle. There is hyperventilation, tachycardia, hypertension as well as sweating reactions which parallel those of the female.

The penis. When the penile arterioles are dilated, the flow of blood into the penis is increased and the spongy tissue sinuses fill with blood. It is thought that the veins of the penis possess valves that can slow down the venous return from the penis. The dilatation of the penile arteries, leading to the penile erection, is thought to be the result of stimulation in the splanchnic nerves. The first male response in the excitement phase is penile erection. In the plateau phase, the penis undergoes a minor vasocongestive increase in size as orgasm approaches. This additional swelling is confined mainly to the corona glandis and is accompanied by deepening of the mottled reddish-purplish colour of the glans. In the orgasmic phase, ejaculation occurs and develops from regular contractions of the urethral sphincter and the bulbospogiosus muscle. Seminal fluid is expelled down the full length of the penile urethra and high pressure is created by these muscles, sufficient to project semen several feet. In the resolution phase, the penis detumesces in two phases. Initially, it shrinks rapidly down to a 50 per cent erection, then more slowly to its pre-stimulated size. The rate of the second stage detumescence depends on the post-orgasmic behaviour; partial erection is prolonged by continued physical (sexual) contact.

The scrotum. As sexual tension increases, there is a tensing and thickening of the scrotal skin covering caused, in part, by the contraction of the smooth muscle of the dartos layer. These changes are reversed in the resolution phase. In the testes during the excitement phase, there is elevation of both testes towards the perineum. The superior pole of the testis rotates anteriorly so that the posterior testicular wall comes into direct contact with the male perineum at the peak of excitation. If the testes do not undergo at least partial elevation, the human male does not experience a full ejaculatory sequence. There is, in addition, an increase in testicular size which occurs in the late excitement or early plateau phase. Masters and Johnson state that the testes increase in size by 50 per cent. There is no specific change in the testicles at orgasm. During the resolution phase they detumesce and descend once more.

Testicular and ovarian pain has been reported in both males and females who have not achieved orgasm, notably during prolonged petting where orgasm has not been possible. (A female junior medical officer reported sick, complaining of abdominal pain which, on subsequent questioning by a consultant surgeon, turned out to have followed a long period of sexual excitement without orgasm.) A similar kind of pain, but specifically related to the testicle, is described in the male and is presumably due to vascular congestion and its effect on the relatively inelastic testicular integument.

HUMAN SEXUAL ACTS

Human sexual acts are defined as behaviours which initiate and increase sexual arousal. We include fantasy under this heading because we believe it to be a very important element in the development and maintenance of both sexual attitudes and overt sexual behaviours.

There is some difficulty in the analysis of human sexual acts because they may be active or passive. For example one person may accidentally see another person and experience a degree of sexual arousal which in turn leads to active behaviour (such as conversation) which promotes the arousal. Alternatively a person may initiate sexual fantasy or sexual approach behaviour in a more planned way, both of which may produce sexual arousal.

It is generally held that visual, auditory and olfactory stimuli are responsible for the early stages of sexual arousal in man and there are convincing animal analogues for this (Schein and Hale, 1965). Both sexes tend to perform approach behaviour when they see a sexually interesting person. The next stage in this behavioural chain is usually a verbal exchange which is designed to gain the partner's attention or interest and to allow a gradually increasing physical proximity. The content of the conversation may include intimate or sexual themes or it may simply contain comments of general interst. Conversation continues with an increasing level of eye contact to the point where physical contacts such as hand touching develop; kissing and/or frank body caressing develops when it seems clear from the nature and frequency of the 'casual' body contact that a firm rejection is unlikely. Sexual arousal increases with kissing and body contact. Subsequent encounters between the same partners follow a similar but compressed pattern.

Different pairs of partners and different members of pairs are aroused in different ways which seem to depend on prior experience. Beliefs and attitudes play an important part in the mode of arousability; for example, males differ in the different emphasis which they attach to the arousing properties of the female anatomy. Different men are aroused by special features of face, hair, eyes, breasts, legs, voice, mannerisms, and so on. Similarly, different women are aroused by differences in men's faces, muscle-structure, height, hair, voice, by their manner and their position on a power hierarchy. Thus the way that physical attributes are perceived is an important early component in the production of sexual arousal within a pair. The intermediate state of sexual approach behaviour which involves the use of socio-sexual approach skills to increase sexual interest is one which causes many people great difficulty. We discuss the social stimuli to arousal in more detail in Chapter 3.

Assuming that the pair have reached the stage of tacit or explicit consent to proceed to orgasm for one or both of them, the methods of increasing arousal still further vary widely.

Genital/Genital Stimulation

Genital/genital stimulation contains an important element of sex *dissymmetry* in that it only requires sexual arousal in the male. The erect penis is inserted into the vagina and either or both partners make pelvic thrusts to move the penis in the vagina. The variations in 'sexual positions' are considerable and include the following:

Face to face, horizontal, man on top.
Face to face, horizontal, woman on top.
Face to face, lying on right side.
Face to face, lying on left side.
Face to face, both sitting.
Face to face, standing.
Face to face, woman lying, man sitting up.
Face to face, man lying, woman sitting up.
Face to back, man lying, woman sitting up.
Face to back, both sitting.
Face to back, both standing.
Face to back, both lying on right side.

The above sequence represents a desirable and frequently attainable ideal pattern of human sexual behaviour. In Chapter 5 we describe the many problems which prevent full sexual satisfaction by partners and the methods which are now being develped to overcome these problems. The information provided in this chapter on the biological bases of human sexual behaviour is essential both to a complete explanation of sexual problems and the development of effective methods of help.

OVERVIEW

Embryonic sex is determined by the presence or absence of the Y chromosome. Primordial sex cells first appear at about the sixth week after fertilization and, following migration from the wall of the yolk sac to the underside of the coelomic epithelium, they differentiate between the sexes to form the testis and male sex organs in the male embryo and the ovary and the female sex organs in the female embryo. The anatomy of the male and female sex organs is dimorphic and it is described in detail. Because the human species has a dimorphic reproductive anatomy the species behaviour must also be dimorphic to permit copulation and fertilization to take place.

The animal literature suggests that the form of sexual behaviour which is shown by adult mammals is governed on the one hand by cerebral sex centres which are differentiated into male and female during embryogenesis under the influence of hormones and on the other hand by the adult gonads, sexual apparatus, and the hormones which circulate after puberty.

The concepts of level of sexual arousal and arousability have been defined and the parts played in sexual arousal by the central nervous system, the autonomic system, hormones and other biochemical substances discussed. The detailed physiology of the human sexual response has been described and the important relative gradients of arousal rate between male and female noted.

Human sexual acts are described in terms of genital/genital stimulation, genital/non-genital stimulation and non-genital stimulation. Human sexual behaviour tends to fall into the following sequence: pair formation, the pre-copulation phase, the copulation phase and the post-copulation phase. Each of these phases has characteristic behaviours which in general need to be present for the couple to progress successfully through stages of increasing sexual arousal to mutual orgasm. The post-copulation phase is particularly important in the context of affectional bonding and love.

CHAPTER 3

Social Learning and Sexual Behaviour

INTRODUCTION

The previous chapter provided a biological framework for sexual behaviour—its anatomy, physiology, and biochemistry. The sexual lives of all human beings have certain broad features in common irrespective of the biological differences between males and females. However, within this broad framework there is room for much variation in what human beings actually do concerning sexual activities, and in their selection of partners. The details of individual variation in sexual behaviour, including frequency of activity and age of first experience, are given in Chapter 4. In this present chapter we concentrate on how people learn their own particular pattern of sexual activities. We apply to sexual behaviour the psychology of learning and performance, detailing the processes of acquisition, the situational cues which elicit sexual responding and the consequences which either maintain it or cause it to reduce. By sexual responses we mean the physiological and physical concomitants of arousal, the physical actions which maintain or increase sexual arousal, and the verbal and non-verbal behaviour which occurs between people in socio-sexual encounters. Finally, we consider attraction and love, an area of research which psychologists have only recently begun to explore.

SOCIAL LEARNING: ACQUISITION

Social Setting

Whereas each pre-literate society tends to have only one preferred set of practices and partner attributes, Western societies provide a number of sub-sets of practices and attributes. However, *within* each social group there will also be variations, due both to biological differences between individual members, for example in the ease of sexual arousal, and to the details of individual learning experiences.

Western society provides a range of social settings within which sexual behaviours are learned; additionally, social settings change over time. We noted in Chapter 1 that the sexual attitudes and behaviours of university students changed during the 1960s in the direction of greater permissiveness. The annual entry of new university students of the 1970s was exposed to a different socio-sexual setting than the entry of the 1950s. Bauman and Wilson (1976) compared the unmarried students of 'two generations'—1968 and 1972—of the University of North Carolina. The 1972 group had more permissive attitudes to premarital sexual behaviour, and less adherence to the 'double standard'. Finger (1975) reported that actual premarital sexual behaviour also increased for college students in the years 1974–75. In Chapter 4 we shall note further evidence of change between the generations, particularly that collected by Kinsey *et al.* (1948, 1953) whose study is unique in containing data reported by Americans born in the later years of the nineteenth century, as well as those born in the 1920s. As might be expected, the latter reported, for example, an earlier age of first sexual intercourse and a greater frequency of female orgasm. However, it would be wrong to conclude that the direction of change of the socio-sexual setting is one way—towards greater and greater permissiveness and an increasing emphasis on pleasure for the female as well as for the male. A scholarly review by Stone (1977) sets out the evidence available from pre-sex research days. It suggests that eighteenth-century women were expected to experience orgasm, and that conception was thought difficult without it.

Persuasive Communications

Even before the opportunity for actual sexual behaviour is available, people are exposed to all kinds of information concerning sexual behaviour, both factual ('this is how to do it') and persuasive ('X does it and enjoys it, why don't you?' or 'its wrong to do it because you'll be punished/catch a disease'). Such statements, which are available from a wide range of sources, including other people, books, films and the television, may change the probability of a particular behaviour actually occurring. Once the behaviour has been carried out and enjoyed (positively reinforced) it is likely to be repeated. If the behaviour is disliked, repetition is less likely, at least until after a longer interval than that which occurs following an enjoyable experience.

McGuire (1969) has reviewed in detail the variables which determine the probability of change of an attitude due to a persuasive communication. He divides the communication into five components: source, message, channel, receiver, and destination.

Source. A persuasive communication in favour of increased sexual activity will be more effective when the source of the message is physically attractive, socially admired, has the ability and willingness to deliver valued rewards (such as attention and approval) and is in frequent contact with the 'receiver' of the message.

Message factors. When the message is very discrepant from the receiver's present position the credibility of the source is very important. If this is initially low, then the greater the discrepancy, the less the change from the original attitude. However, if credibility is very high, attitude change may be very great.

Channel factors. Essentially, hearing something is more persuasive than reading it, similarly a face to face message is more persuasive than one seen on TV.

Receiver factors. These are concerned with differences between the persons to whom the message is addressed. People with a poor general opinion of themselves tend to be more persuasible, as do those who have just failed in something specific they have attempted.

Destination factors. These concern the impact of a message; the usual finding from laboratory research on the impact of messages is that they fade over the course of time. However, this very much depends both on the message and on the receiver. Laboratory messages are usually designed to be trivial; real-life ones may be of crucial importance. People are also likely to differ in their general tendency to rehearse (that is to repeat to themselves) what they have heard. It follows that a person in receipt of a message with sexual connotations of great personal relevance from a close and very attractive friend is likely to rehearse it much more frequently than if the message was fairly trivial and received from a neutrally viewed stranger. The former is likely to be much more influential on actual behaviour than the latter, because of the nature of the message, its source, and the greater cognitive rehearsal to which the combination will have led.

Immunization against persuasion. This term is used when someone likely to be exposed to a persuasive communication is 'immunized' against it by being given a weak form of the communication together with a strong counter-argument. In the sexual area an example would be a mild statement of the joys of intercourse in the context of material on the dangers of sexually transmitted diseases.

Persuasive communications are an example of a *social influence* procedure and we have concentrated on the situation in which one person is exposed to a communication from one other person. There are also group influences on behaviour. Membership of social groups provides ready possibilities for learning both by observation and through one's own direct experience.

Social Models

People who add to the cohesiveness of a group by conforming to its approved practices will be rewarded, those who do not will be punished in a variety of ways, for example by exclusion from the group. The group both rewards, punishes, and provides a clear message of what is desirable behaviour. In addition, it gives examples of the approved behaviours and provides opportunities to carry them out. Spanier and Cole (1975) found that 'informal sex education' by other young people had a much more powerful effect on premarital sexual behaviour than formal sex education programmes.

Behaviour Changes Which Follow Attitudinal Changes

A change in attitude may result in a change in behaviour, but whether or not it does so depends largely on the features of the particular situation, including the opportunity available, the perceived rewards and the perceived risks. In the sexual context this means that an inexperienced person newly persuaded of the desirability of premarital sex will be more likely to have intercourse if an attractive interested partner who is already known and liked is available and the physical surroundings are suitable.

Behaviour Changes Which Precede Attitudinal Changes

Conversely, an initial change in behaviour can lead to an attitude change by a process known as cognitive dissonance reduction. A vast amount of research, beginning with Festinger (1957), has been carried out on cognitive dissonance, generally based on the assumption that discrepancy is psychologically uncomfortable, so that people will act in order to remove a discrepancy between attitude and behaviour by changing their attitude, their behaviour or their perception of what is happening in the situation. The more important the behaviour is in the life of the person, the greater the pressure to deal with the dissonance which is experienced at two points: the first occurs immediately a decision is taken to carry out a new behaviour, the next after the behaviour has been completed. At both points dissonance is dealt with by a common mechanism. The new behaviour is perceived as more attractive than the old one and failure to carry it out is perceived as less attractive than carrying it out. The change in perception is assisted by attending to information which supports the decision to change or the actual change in behaviour, and by ignoring or reducing the perceived weight of contrary information. The process of dissonance reduction seems to be easier still after the behaviour has been carried out. This is likely to be particularly true when the behaviour concerned is a first experience of sexual intercourse because virginity cannot be restored. It may be the reason why such a large proportion of those disappointed with their first sexual experience nevertheless try again after an interval because their behaviour has committed them to a change of status from virgin to non-virgin.

Essentially, behaviours are learned both by direct personal experience and by observation. Direct and observational learning both involves forms of learning conventionally termed 'classical' (or 'Pavlovian') and 'instrumental'. Recent research (Miller, 1969) has thrown some doubt on the absoluteness of the distinction, but for our purposes it is useful to regard them as separate types of learning.

By 'learning' we mean a change of behaviour as the result of experience and 'experience' simply refers to a sequence of environmental events. It may include, and for human beings does include, the subjective awareness and evaluation of those events. Learning is distinguished from maturation—developmental changes due to heredity (assuming a normal physical environment).

Classical Conditioning

In classical conditioning a previously neutral event, such as a light or a tone called the conditioned stimulus (CS), is paired with a stimulus that automatically elicits a particular response termed the unconditional stimulus (UCS). After a number of pairings the previously neutral event alone comes to elicit the response. Experiences during the early years of life appear to be of importance in providing the basis for the later classical conditioning of emotional responses to the stimuli provided by other animals or people.

As a part of a larger programme on the effects of early infantile experiences on later behaviour, Harlow (1965) reared monkeys apart from their mothers. Monkeys reared totally apart found great difficulty in carrying out normal sexual behaviour, even when paired with normally raised and sexually experienced monkeys. Those who were reared apart from their own mothers, but were allowed to play with other monkeys in infancy, were able to engage both in sexual behaviour and to provide maternal care for their young.

It is widely held that normal heterosexual and emotional development requires considerable contact with others of the same age, and of both sexes. The effect of the deprivation of such opportunities has been found to extend, in monkeys, to poverty of response to facially conveyed expressions of distress (Miller *et al.*, 1967), and in humans there may be a similar lack of emotional discrimination and responsiveness in those deprived of emotional contacts during their early years. For emotional responsiveness to occur in the adult, it seems a basic requirement that a variety of emotional responses be consistently and reliably provoked in childhood, in the presence of distinct, clearly discriminable, cues. Such experiences provide the basis for the classical conditioning of feelings and other states appropriate to social situations. The occurrence of emotional learning experiences is thus necessary for the adequate development of affection. Sexual behaviours between individuals occur more easily against a background of a capacity for sexual affection.

The mechanisms of classical conditioning provide an excellent explanation for the very wide variety of stimuli which evoke sexual arousal, including both those observed by anthropologists and described in Chapter 1, and some of the apparently bizarre sexual behaviours found in the West, for example, sexual arousal to such previously neutral objects as rubber articles and boots.

Instrumental Conditioning

Classical conditioning is concerned with contiguity—the association between two stimuli. Instrumental conditioning emphasizes the consequences of a single response or a response sequence. In the sexual context we often find that people habitually approach or avoid particular cues which signal the sexual intention of the other person in the situation. The case of sexual avoidance is discussed in detail in Chapter 5. So far as actually carrying out sexual behaviour is concerned, there is a gradual 'shaping' as a result of which the practice and execution of a variety of instrumental social responses, directed at first towards peers of both sexes, is later directed towards members of the opposite sex. (With the exception, of course, of those whose sexual preference is homosexual: we discuss this in Chapter 6.) This range of instrumental responses includes not only the initial contact with another person but also responses involved in the subsequent sexual interaction. A large variety of acts which later in life are brought together to form the complex sequence of human sexual behaviour are practised earlier in life in many non-sexual situations. Such acts includes both verbal and non-verbal behaviours, examples of the latter being eye contact and touching.

What consequences are likely to lead to repetition of the sexual behaviour concerned, that is which reinforcers are positive? Increased sexual arousal is a positive reinforcer, as is orgasm. There are also other positive reinforcers which have an application in all types of social situation such as attention and approval. Negative consequences include premature loss of erection, physical discomfort and pain (although pain may also be associated with sexual arousal and hence experienced as pleasant, depending on the prescription of the particular culture and the exact circumstances of previous sexual experiences). Reinforcement is not only external, as described above; people also reinforce themselves, both positively and negatively, for attaining, or failing to attain, some target or standard. Self-reinforcement may be either material or verbal.

Fully mature sexual behaviour consists of a gradually developed complex set of instrumental responses which takes the form of a sequence. Social contact is followed by dating, then by kissing, petting, and so on. There is a rather gradual progression along the sequence of instrumental acts. At each stage the consequences, positive or negative, of the previous behaviour, together with the opportunity to proceed, determine the nature of the behaviour which follows.

Observational Learning

People may acquire responses by observing the experiences of others (observational learning). Observational learning is concerned with responses which are acquired without any direct reinforcement to the learner; instead he observes the experience of another person, termed a model. The observer is exposed to the full sequence of events involving the model, from stimulus, through response, to reinforcement.

Bandura (1973) points out a number of reasons for the major importance of observational learning, including avoiding costly mistakes and speeding up the rate of learning. The effects of observational learning include the acquisition of new patterns of behaviour, the strengthening or weakening of previously learned inhibitions, and the facilitation (in performance) of previously learned responses. In addition, observational learning can facilitate the suppression of existing behaviours.

Observational learning is governed by a number of sub-systems. The *attentional* process requires exposure to a model, the selection of relevant behaviours and their accurate perception. A key factor here is the individual's existing associational preference. When there is a range of available models, the observer will pay attention to those models who are successful, attractive, and have a high status. In general, selective attention is given to those features of the model's behaviour which are the most positively reinforced by his environment and hence will be perceived as most potentially reinforcing for the observer. In the sexual context, the observer will copy the model of highest social status, greatest physical attraction, and most evident sexual competence and success. Observational learning is not confined to any one period of time, for example childhood, but is a continual process throughout the whole of a person's life.

Next the products of observational learning need to be *retained*. Effective retention requires that the memory of modelled behaviour be transformed into verbal and visual symbols. These may be rehearsed by the individual away from the presence of the model. Indeed, the apparent speed of observational learning makes it almost inevitable that rehearsal occurs. With increasing practice, both observation and copying become more accurate. The accuracy of copying is assisted both by practice and by external positive reinforcement of correct, and negative reinforcement of incorrect, imitation. However modelled responses may or may not be *reproduced* by the observer. To do so he must possess the requisite skills and physical capabilities as well as opportunity.

Finally what is termed *participant modelling* is likely to be particularly important in the sexual context. Participant modelling means that the more experienced partner carries out the sexual response, which is then copied by the less experienced one, or the former tells the latter what to do. In both cases, when the response has been copied, it can be corrected by the partner immediately and positively reinforced by approval when correct.

There is a great deal of evidence from anthropological literature (Ford and Beach, 1952) of the direct modelling of children by adults. For example, in several pre-literate societies, children are free to watch adults, including their own parents, having intercourse. In Western societies modelling by parents has often taken the form of instruction in which behaviours are to be inhibited. For example, Bandura and Walters (1963) found that parents who were anxious about sex had sons who were similarly anxious. The present generation of young parents may provide less inhibitory models for their children.

The First Sexual Experience

Once it has occurred, an experience is available for reinforcement, positive or negative, externally or self-administered. Moreover, such consequences are not necessarily short-lived. The human capacity to recall and rehearse an experience means that it may be kept alive for a long time after it actually occurred, possibly with important effects on subsequent opportunities for the same behaviour. This is true of the entire sequence of sexual activity from the initial social encounter to the various forms of sexual intercourse. Because of the great emotional weight our society places on the first experience of sexual intercourse, its outcome—whether it met expectations or fell short—seems to be of particular importance.

Unfortunately there has been little research, and certainly none of a prospective kind, into the consequences of the first sexual experience, and the nature of the first partner, on the future choice of partners, preferred activities and situations. All existing data are retrospective in nature. Schofield (1965a) carried out a careful survey of the sexual life of British teenagers. He found that the first experience of sexual intercourse did not always result in sexual gratification. Less than half the boys (48 per cent) and less than a third of the girls (30 per cent) said they 'liked it' when they were asked for their reaction to the first experience of sexual intercourse. In fact some said that they had actively 'disliked it' (7 per cent of both boys and girls), while others said that they were 'disappointed' (14 per cent and 7 per cent of the sexes respectively).

Schmidt and Sigusch (1972) cite studies in Denmark and the USA which suggest that the conditions and the subjective experience of the first intercourse may vary with the permissiveness of the given social group: the more permissive, the more intercourse tends to be enjoyed, and to occur without the use of alcohol or the application of force. Hence, they predicted that the more permissive climate of the late 1960s would be associated with a greater enjoyment of the first experience than the less permissive atmosphere of the early 1960s. Their own results, obtained from a sample of German young people, supported their prediction. The differences between the 'generations' were particularly clear for the girls, the later generation being more likely to experience the first intercourse with their steady boyfriend, to have had a greater sexual motivation for it and to have enjoyed it. They were less likely to have been under the influence of alcohol, to be disappointed about it or to have found it unpleasant or disgusting. The same trends were true for the boys, though less markedly so, so that there was a greater similarity between the sexes in their response to the first intercourse in the later, than in the earlier, born groups.

A French enquiry into premarital sexual activity (le Moal, 1964) studied 149 married males who were practising Catholics. Sixty per cent admitted premarital activity. Of these, 8 per cent had their first sexual experience with the girl they later married, 44 per cent with another girlfriend, 47 per cent with a prostitute. By contrast, Schofield's findings (1965a) support the view that present-day British adolescents have little contact with prostitutes. The Kinsey (1948) findings suggest a considerable decline over the course of this century in the proportions of males who are sexually initiated by prostitutes.

THE PERFORMANCE OF SEXUAL BEHAVIOURS: SITUATIONAL DETERMINANTS

Once a particular response has been acquired, whether by direct or by observational learning, it may be performed. It then comes under the control of the stimuli associated with its occurrence. Such stimuli may be external—such as the general appearance of another person, some significant detail of that appearance, or an action on his or her part—or internal, such as the recollection of an earlier experience or scene. In either case, a sexual stimulus is much more likely to evoke its associated sexual response from someone who has already acquired the response than from someone who has not yet done so. This is particularly the case when the response is well established—that is, it has been performed so many times that it can reasonably be described as habitual.

Sexual behaviour is a complex sequence of actions which begins with a rather simple verbal or visual response, which may or may not be followed by physical contact culminating in intercourse. We are concerned in this section with those events (stimuli) which evoke a response indicating sexual arousal.

Physical Appearance

In a study concerned with body shape alone, Lavrakas (1975) found the most popular male shape with a group of Chicago women aged 18–30, to be the 'V' look—thin legs, slim lower trunk and a broader upper trunk. Least popular was the pear-shaped look. There was some individual variation also, with overweight women, for example, opting for relatively broader shapes. This might be an instance of a tendency to realism in sexual performance. If we think in terms of a 'pecking order' for both males and females, composed of a number of attributes such as physical appearance, social status, wealth, 'personality', and so on, those high on all attributes would be at the top, and vice versa. It is obviously not sensible for those low in the order to find attractive only those in the higher positions; and, in practice, there seems to be a clear tendency for pairing between people in similar positions—although the positions may be achieved by different combinations of attributes. For example, a pairing of a high status, wealthy but fairly plain male and a lower status but very attractive female (and vice versa as women begin to gain the higher status positions in our society).

The above findings for body shape are of course very limited and also reflect the learned conventions of a small sample of American women. So far as facial appearance is concerned, we do not have even this amount of information. Anthropological observations suggest that there is a wide range of what is considered attractive, indicating that the perceived attractiveness of particular physical attributes may be a learned response, with few or no universals. All we can conclude is that male physical appearance in general is an important cue to female sexual arousal; the precise elements can vary widely.

The same generalizations seem true of male response to female physical appearance. Matthews and Bancroft (1971) studying British men found a tendency for manual workers to prefer women of more conventionally well-dressed appearance, whereas psychologists were a little more likely to prefer those who were unconventional or 'trendy'. Wiggins et al. (1968) reported findings which indicate that males who were outgoing sportsmen preferred large-breasted women, and those who preferred small breasts tended to drink very little and to be religious. But these were only trends, and there was much overlap. It would certainly not be possible to predict with confidence the preferred female partner of an extraverted athlete or an introverted booklover.

Indeed, it is most probable that for both males and females we can conclude only that *some* aspects of appearance are important cues to sexual arousal. The response of any particular individual will depend on the prevailing standards in the particular society, individual learning experiences, and the range of physical appearances of available partners (the pecking order idea mentioned above). Later in this chapter we describe work on attractiveness, particularly as it relates to liking and loving.

Display of Interest by the Other Person

It is the convention in our society that it is the male who initiates the sexual encounter. In line with this, Kolaszynska-Carr (1970) reported that a sample of British heterosexual women had experienced a display of interest by the opposite sex more frequently than had a sample of British heterosexual males. On the other hand it may be that female advances are more subtle and hence less easily detected, or that males are simply less good at perceiving interest. A display of interest may be either welcomed or not, depending on the recipient's attitude to a new sexual encounter and on the general appraisal of the other person's sexual acceptability. If A (male) is aroused by B (female), displays interest, and that interest is returned (presuming the signal has been read accurately) the return signal is likely to heighten arousal. Similarly, A's interest, if welcomed by B, will in turn heighten her arousal, and so on. Conversely, if A's signal is unwelcome, B, far from experiencing increased sexual arousal, may feel very differently. Kolaszynska-Carr (1970) noted a variety of such adverse reactions, including 'embarrassment' and a 'desire to get away'.

Aggression

Leading personality theorists since Freud have asserted that sex and aggression are closely related, but very little human research has been carried out into this relationship. Jaffe *et al.* (1974) found that people sexually aroused by erotic literature delivered more intense 'electric shocks' (using an impressive but fake machine) than did those who had read neutral material, suggesting that sexual arousal facilitates aggression. However, a number of studies such as that by Donnerstein *et al.* (1975) suggest that mildly erotic stimuli can have the opposite effect, that of inhibiting aggression. It is only highly erotic material which increases aggression in a subsequent aggression-arousing situation.

The more important question is whether the opposite effect occurs: does the prior arousal of aggression increase sexual arousal in response to erotic stimuli? The question is of obvious everyday importance: is a sexually frustrated and angry man more likely to assault a sexually arousing female than one who is equally frustrated but not angry? There appears to be no available evidence to answer the question but the notion that all sources of physiological arousal combine to increase the tendency to perform a well-established response would suggest that the answer is yes.

The above discussion is concerned with relations between anger arousal and sex arousal in the same person. Is a display of aggression by A likely to increase the sexual arousal of B? There can be no general answer. The outcome will depend on such factors as B's sexual experience in relation to displayed aggression by a partner. For example, has it frequently been followed by sexual pleasure? If so, aggression by a prospective partner might be a more powerful instigator of sexual arousal than a neutral display. Clinically, this form of behaviour is termed masochism. Conversely, if aggression has been associated with sexual failure and distress, its display will be very unlikely to evoke a sexual response.

Alcohol

The use of alcohol in the Western world is so widespread that its use is significantly associated with social and sexual behaviour. Recent experiments (e.g. Farkas and Rosen, 1976) suggest that a very small dose of alcohol may increase sexual arousal—indicated by penile diameter increase—to erotic films. However, as the dose is increased penile response decreases steadily. In the same way, a very small amount of alcohol improves performance on a wide range of tasks, particularly by rather anxious people; a higher dose worsens performance. It seems likely that the well-known sexual facilitating effect of alcohol is due to its effect on mood and its powerful disinhibitory effect.

The Presence of Models

It is the general finding of research on observational learning that the presence of a model already carrying out a particular behaviour increases the likelihood of an observer carrying out the same behaviour. Conversely, if the model fails to respond to a particular situation, observers will also tend to refrain from doing so. In both cases modelling effects are greatest when the model is physically in close proximity, is of high status and is strongly and visibly reinforced for his own behaviour. Applying this general rule to the sexual area, it would be expected that when an individual is exposed to a potentially arousing stimulus, a sexual response is more likely when there are, close at hand, models of high status, responding sexually and being positively reinforced for doing so.

Lack of Prior Sexual Outlet

The lack of opportunity for sexual outlet prior to a situation where the opportunity exists is thought to increase the likelihood of sexual activity taking place. Regular separation of couples for short periods such as a working week may enhance their weekend sexual activity to produce for them an optimum sexual way of living. Zimbardo (1969) has given an anecdotal account of scientists and others based at the South Pole, who in the early weeks of their stay reported an increase in heterosexual arousal, followed later by a sharp decrease. Zimbardo considers that because the behaviour was not possible, eventually sexual arousal diminished and became then a minor part of life.

Specific Erotic Stimuli

In Chapter 1 we discussed some of the social dimensions of the controversy over pornography. In this section we concentrate on laboratory studies of response to erotic stimuli. Such studies have used both self-report data and physiological measures of arousal. We have already noted the potentially distorting effects of the laboratory situation. Not surprisingly the usual finding is that erotic material is often arousing, with visual presentation more effective than auditory and moving pictures more arousing than stills. However, there are complications according to the time intervals between repeated presentation, the sex of the observer and his or her previous experience.

There are increases in both masturbatory activity and sexual intercourse in the 24 hours after a single presentation of erotic material. But what are the effects of repeated presentation? Mann et al. (1974) were interested in the effects on married couples of repeated exposure to explicitly sexual material, earlier work by Mann and others having suggested that satiation is likely to occur. Their experimental group consisted of 46 married couples, mainly well educated, all of whom rated their marriages as happy and their sexual lives as satisfactory. When they were told the exact nature of the study, only one-fifth declined to participate. The median age of the group was in the forties, and the median length of marriage 17 years, the minimum being 10 years. They were shown two films. The first, labelled 'conventional', depicted heterosexual intercourse and female self-masturbation. The 'unconventional' film showed male and female homosexual intercourse, group oral–genital sex and flagellation. A third, termed 'non-erotic' consisted of a day in the life of a teenage expectant mother. The films were shown at the rate of one a week for three weeks in all, in counter-balanced order, and the major measures taken were the participants' reports of their sexual activity during the three week viewing period. More activity was reported on the 'movie night' than on other nights for both sexual films, but not for the control film. The difference between movie and non-movie nights declined after week 1, suggesting a 'satiation' effect, which was somewhat *less* marked for the unconventional film. The group which saw the conventional film first reported more unpleasant feelings after their viewing than the group which saw the non-erotic film first. No such differences were found for the groups which saw the unconventional film first—perhaps because the behaviours depicted were so removed from their own experience as not to provoke a comparison. Mann and colleagues draw two major conclusions from their studies. First, filmed sexual stimuli elicit a relatively transient sexual reaction. Second, repeated exposure produces satiation. However, it should be noted that they cite other studies which indicate that a recovery period of at least a month rather than a week combats satiation. Moreover, a variety of stimuli, rather than repetition of the same, reduces even short-term satiation. Erotic stimuli carefully spaced out can increase the frequency of whatever sexual activity is already well established—intercourse in the case of couples, masturbation by the solitary, and perhaps even sex assaults by particularly disturbed individuals. It does not appear from the Mann *et al.* study that viewing unconventional sex films initiates those novel activities. At least this was true so far as adults with well-established conventional practices were concerned. It may be that more deviant activities would be initiated in those without well-established socially acceptable sexual behaviours. However, even in the case of normal adults a combination of exposure to deviant stimuli and a total absence of opportunity to carry out the previously preferred practices is likely to increase the probability of deviant activities. Our speculative answer to the question of the relationship between pornography and sex crime raised in Chapter 1 is thus a very complex one: men with well-established habits of sex with consenting partners and ready and continuing access to such partners who are exposed to 'porno-violence' movies will merely show transient increases in their previously preferred sexual activities; those with poorly established conventional sex habits, no access to consenting partners, and a solitary social life in general, who are exposed to a continued diet of film-depicted rape will both show heightened arousal to such films and will be more likely to commit rape, particularly if they have a strong tendency to rehearse 'in their head' what they have experienced. It may be desirable to ease the access of such males to normal sexual opportunities and stimuli, by a wider access to sex counselling, the provision of registered brothels, and the removal of censorship from films which show normal loving and caring heterosexual behaviour.

Individual differences: males and females. The popular belief has been that men are more 'sexy' than women—that is exposed to the same erotic material, men will both report more arousal and also show more physical and physiological sexual changes. A second social belief is that women respond more to romantically toned material than do men. Are these beliefs true, and if so, for all men, or for men on average? If they are true, whether for all men or for men on average, what is the explanation: different social learning experiences, or some basic biological difference between the sexes which will persist irrespective of equal learning opportunity? Schmidt *et al.* (1973) tried to answer the first question. They asked 240 young Germans, half of them male and half female, to read one of two stories describing the sexual experiences of young couples. The stories differed in the degree to which affection was expressed between the partners. The great majority of both sexes reported some physical sexual arousal while reading the stories; sex differences were trivial. During the following 24 hours many members of both groups showed an increase in sexual activity compared with the previous 24 hours, the increase being somewhat greater for the females. No difference was found between the two types of story—both sexes responded equally to the presence and the absence of affection. Schmidt *et al.* cite other recent studies which show a similar picture—in contrast to the marked sex differences in self-reported arousability to sexual materials noted by Kinsey and his colleagues (1948 and 1953), a generation earlier. The clear suggestion is that in sexual arousability, as in other areas of life, women are catching up. Biology remains the same; it is social learning opportunities which have changed. (NB. We are not talking about sex differences in the time taken to become fully aroused, in which there do appear to be biologically based sex differences—see Chapter 2—but to the fact of arousal to specific erotic stimuli.) Another study (Griffitt, 1975) indicated that female arousal to sexual stimuli depends on previous sexual experience. He showed slides of heterosexual behaviour to male and female college students and asked them to rate how arousing they found the slides. The results indicated that 'across all seven categories of sexual experience high-experienced females were more sexually responsive than low-experienced females' (Griffitt, 1975, p. 536).

Before leaving the topic of specific erotic stimuli, we should note as an important implication from all the studies that sexual materials vary enormously. The materials used vary from naked females to violent sexual assaults on children. We should avoid the blanket term 'pornography'. Nor do the terms 'soft' and 'hard' 'porn' help—their meanings constantly shift. Instead, the material concerned should be described in as precise a way as possible.

Specific Situations

The performance of a well learned behaviour is elicited reliably by a particular situation, or aspects of situations, previously associated with the particular behaviour. For example, in the field of crime, thefts are more likely in ill-lit places, such as subways or the public areas of apartment blocks, and in a crowded store during a sale than in the same store when there are few customers about and the staff have time to look out for potential shoplifters. Similarly, the performance of sexual behaviours is elicited by particular situations and inhibited by others.

Cognitive Cues

The human capacity to record and later recall experiences is particularly important. These mechanisms turn previous experiences and their consequences into stimuli for the performance of future overt behaviours. Cues to behaviour may thus become 'internal' as well as being 'external'.

External cues vary in their power to guide behaviour depending on previous learning (e.g. person A may have learned to associate a particular physical feature with sexual arousal, person B has never had the opportunity to do so). Internal cues may also vary in strength between two people, even when both have had the same actual experience associated with the original external cues. For example, both persons A and B have been sexually aroused by female C. But whereas A tends not to recall such experiences more than occasionally, B constantly relives the experience 'in his head' perhaps accompanied by masturbation. The behaviour concerned is often termed cognitive rehearsal. It is important, and we consider it again shortly.

Sexual Behaviour Viewed as a Skilled Performance

Sexual behaviour can be seen as a sequence of behaviours performed at a certain level of skill by both partners. There are extensive researches and theoretical analyses of skilled performance in the learning of motor tasks, and these extend to the field of social behaviour. Analyses are made of the patterning of speech, laughter, gesture, the physical distances apart adopted by the participants, the percentage of eye contacts, gaze aversion, and the nature of body-part contact.

Analysing sexual performance as a skill (both the social preliminaries and the actual sequence of physical acts) is an appropriate extension of such work. In the advanced Western countries many skills relevent to daily life are systematically trained, but the acquisition of social and sexual skills is left largely to chance. By way of contrast, anthropological evidence suggests that many pre-literate societies take care that the inexperienced adolescent is sexually initiated by an experienced older person with the intention that both skill and self-confidence are acquired by the initiate.

Incentives and Sexual Behaviour

The experimental literature on incentives shows that, within limits, learning is faster the greater the incentive provided. Similarly, the greater the incentive the more probable is the performance of well-learned response. Incentives can take the form either of deprivation or additional stimulation. In animal studies deprivation is achieved by withholding a particular reinforcer, such as food or sex, for some hours. For example, a rat deprived of access to a female for a sufficient period of time will cross an electrically charged floor in order to copulate with a sexually receptive female. The longer the period of sexual deprivation to which he has been subjected, the greater the intensity of shock he is willing to tolerate. The same applies to humans; events and situations which increase sexual responsiveness, either through deprivation or extra stimulation, can enhance the extent to which stimuli are perceived as sexually relevant and as potential sources of sexual gratification.

Learning and Performance

Finally, it is important to distinguish between the acquisition and the performance of a response. An individual may have a response in his repertoire but may not perform it, either because of lack of incentive, lack of reinforcement, or lack of opportunity. Inferences which are drawn from the absence of a given sexual response are quite inappropriate until the response fails to be displayed under optimum conditions.

Overview

Given that an individual is biologically capable of acquiring sexual behaviours and that he has already performed them on a number of occasions, the following are the situational determinants for the performance of a sexual response: the physical features of the prospective partner; his or her display of interest, specific erotic stimuli; opportunity factors, the level of sexual deprivation of the individual concerned, and the strength of the associated internal cues for all of these factors.

MAINTENANCE OF SEXUAL BEHAVIOUR

In the last section we concentrated on the events which initiate the performance of sexual behaviour; we now concentrate on the importance of the outcome of previous sexual experiences in maintaining, or diminishing, sexual behaviour over an extended period of time. We shall particularly emphasize the importance of reinforcement, both external, physiological, and self-administered, and of cognitive rehearsal. As a general rule of behaviour, outcomes subjectively judged pleasurable maintain behaviour; those judged unpleasant inhibit future repetitions.

External Reinforcement

Reinforcements under the control of other people include the responses displayed by the actual sexual partner, both verbal and non-verbal. Another sort of social response is administered by third parties.

The total pattern of previous outcomes of sexual behaviour, known as the *schedule of reinforcement*, is important. Schedules may be very complex, but for our purpose it is enough to contrast consistent outcomes with intermittent ones. We set out below three examples to illustrate the power of different schedules of reinforcement. In the first case, the previous 50 attempts at sexual intercourse were all mutually satisfactory. In the second, only 10 per cent of the 50 fell in this category, with no pattern to enable prediction as to whether the next one would be satisfying. The third case concerns an individual who has a 100 per cent record of sexual failure. All three have available to them a willing and attractive sexual partner, in a favourable situation. The first two people are very much more likely to respond to the opportunity for sexual behaviour than is the third. The behaviour of the first (approach) and the third (avoidance) is what commonsense would lead us to expect, but the second is an example of the general finding that reinforcement received on an intermittent and varying schedule is highly resistant to extinction. In this case the behaviour will be performed again and again despite only receiving occasional positive reinforcement. The phenomenon of partial reinforcement is the explanation of the persistence of people who play gambling machines. An occasional and *unpredictable* success keeps them responding through many hours of net financial loss.

Physiological Reinforcement

Sexual behaviour has a clear physiological basis. Overt sexual actions are preceded and accompanied by sexual arousal often, but not always, leading to the physiological changes associated with orgasm. Physiological consequences thus can be thought of as reinforcers for overt sexual actions. The physical responses described in Chapter 2 are available immediately as reinforcers of sexual behaviour and these responses may also be recalled at some later time to serve as cues for solitary sexual arousal and masturbation. This behaviour is in turn associated with physiological arousal and orgasm. The elements of sexual arousal and sexual response are cyclical in that arousal responses become stimuli for further responses.

Self-Reinforcement

As well as being externally and physiologically reinforced, sexual behaviour may also be maintained by self-reinforcement. People learn to set standards for their own performance in a variety of areas of behaviour, including sexual behaviour. Having performed the behaviour the individual can then compare his performance with his previously held standard. If this is reached, or even exceeded, he may reinforce himself, perhaps with a simple self-administered 'pat on the back', or in some more concrete way as in 'I deserve a good meal/holiday on the strength of that'.

Cognitive Rehearsal

A study by Bandura and Jeffery (1973) indicates that effective rehearsal improves the recall of well-learned responses. Several clinical researchers have used planned cognitive rehearsal to enhance the effectiveness of a training programme (e.g. Meichenbaum and Goodman, 1971; McFall et al., 1971). In general it is our view that learning continues to take place well after the actual overt behaviour and often well away from the place in which it occurred. Individuals may differ markedly both in their general tendency to rehearse a wide range of areas of behaviour and to rehearse particular areas. For example, A may rehearse most things, from sex to football, or he may be a high rehearser only for one area—sex or football, etc. Alternatively, he may be a high rehearser for certain types of material—pleasant rather than unpleasant, or vice versa. There is indeed evidence (Merbaum and Kazaoka, 1967) that some people do tend to be systematically more attentive to certain types of information, for example pleasant information, and systematically less attentive to unpleasant information. The converse is also true. Individual differences in rehearsal might be due to the particular experience—an intense and repeated experience is likely to be rehearsed more frequently than a relatively trivial experience—with a consequent difference in later behaviour. But over and above differences in rehearsal due to differences in the nature and frequency of the actual overt experience, we would also expect differences in rehearsal habits between individuals who have had the same experiences. We expect the effect of rehearsal on subsequent behaviour to be most powerful under the following conditions: when the experience is intense and repeated; when the individual is an habitual high rehearser for the particular material; and when the range of alternative materials is limited.

We can now apply this model to three examples of sexual behaviour by males. All three individuals are habitually high rehearsers. Person A has had a series of girlfriends. He has had mutually satisfactory sex with most of them, but he views the most recent as someone special—she is a person with whom he feels sufficiently in love to contemplate marriage, or at least a serious attempt at living together. As he repeatedly rehearses this very pleasant prospect, his conviction that marriage is the right course of action strengthens, as does the associated probability that he will actually carry out the necessary overt behaviour of asking her to marry him. The second example, B, is that of a shy young man. He is fairly interested in women sexually, and is under very strong social pressure to succeed with them, but lacks both the necessary social skills to read accurately the available signals and the sexual skills to bring about a mutually satisfactory sexual experience. The result is a series of failures which he rehearses, finally avoiding even appropriate opportunities for heterosexual encounters. At the same time he has had the not uncommon experience of a pleasurable homosexual encounter. Many young men do experience as teenagers homosexually induced orgasms without any change in their overall heterosexual responsiveness. But in the case of B there is an association of relative heterosexual failure and relative homosexual success plus a high tendency to rehearse experiences of failure. The result is a gradual shift of attitude from being relatively favourable to the heterosexual preference to being relatively favourable to the homosexual preference. The shift will be assisted by the continued avoidance of heterosexual attempts and the continuing occurrence of (pleasurable) homosexual encounters, as well as by further rehearsal of these events. The change will be further assisted by the cognitive mechanisms outlined earlier in the chapter, including distortion of perception and selective attention. This then is one possible mechanism for the development of the homosexual preference. Our last example is an individual exposed to highly deviant sexual material, with little exposure to more conventional material. The result of rehearsing deviant material may be an increased tendency to perform a potentially deviant sexual act. Once the act has been carried out it may be maintained by subsequent frequent rehearsal and intermittent performance. Paradoxically, it may be that the cognitive rehearsal of deviant material is particularly likely by patients housed in institutions for diagnosed psychopaths—which typically provide little or no opportunity for the normal social experiences which might provide alternative non-deviant material for rehearsal.

Concluding Comment

Thus far, in outlining the acquisition, performance, and maintenance of sexual behaviour we have drawn on principles of social learning theory which have been applied with success to a wide range of other human behaviours. We return now to a set of phenomena which many believe to be quite special and different from all other phenomena of behaviour, namely attraction and love. As we shall see, while it is essential to deal with attraction and love in any attempt to cover human sexual behaviour, they are not 'special' in the sense of requiring additional or novel explanatory principles.

ATTRACTION AND LOVE

Introduction

Until very recently there was no formal psychological research into romantic attraction and love. The field had been left completely to novelists and poets. There have been many definitions of love, but as may be expected none has been universally accepted. 'Love is such a tissue of paradoxes, and exists in such an endless variety of forms and shades that you may say almost anything about it that you please, and it is likely to be correct' (Finck, 1891, p. 244). In 1958 Harlow said, 'So far as love is concerned, psychologists have failed in their mission. The little we know about love does not transcend simple observation, and the little we write about it has been better written by poets and novelists.' A number of psychologists have responded to this challenge.

The difficulties involved in the study of attraction and love include the social taboo against the invasion of the privacy of the emotions, and the problems of measuring the phenomena involved.

There are problems in the measurement of interpersonal behaviour of all kinds, but they are even more severe in this most 'private' of human behaviours. It is very difficult to produce measures and ways of interpreting them which are free from implicit value-judgements. For example, marital satisfaction is often measured by scales on which high agreement on social and other attitudes and minimal overt conflict are interpreted as indicating high satisfaction. Yet there are undoubtedly marriages and partnerships judged satisfactory by the participants which are marked by frequent arguments. Conversely, lack of conflict could be associated with mutual boredom and dissatisfaction. Byrne and Griffitt (1973) have reviewed the measures used in studies of attraction, both verbal—a variety of scales and questionnaires—and non-verbal, including eye contact, distance apart, and the angle of body lean. The frequency and length of eye contact and body proximity are proportional to the degree of mutual attraction. Both partners can influence non-verbal situations—by altering eye contact, by altering inter-body distance and body orientation. All such non-verbal cues can be observed, recorded, and analysed.

We shall concentrate on a number of selected topics: the broad social rules for mate selection, the specific attributes which determine attraction between partners, the 'special' behaviour called love, and the complex patterns of mutual rewards which characterize established intimate relationships. The data on which we draw have been collected on heterosexual partnerships, but the same general features ought to apply, in principle, to homosexual partnerships, with the exception of the social rules for partner choice—which appear to be much more clearly defined and applied to the heterosexual situation.

Social Rules for Mate Selection

We are concerned both with prospective marital partners and the surrounding social context. The key idea has been 'the field of eligible spouse-candidates' (Winch, 1958); that is, those people who are viewed as possible marital partners. Kerckhoff (1974) has shown that spouses often have similar social characteristics. Husbands and wives tend to be similar in age, religion, ethnic groups, and social class. This homogamy (similarity of partner) has been stable in Western society through the twentieth century. The norms of what is an appropriate partner are learned by instruction, observation, and direct experience— conformity is rewarded and deviance is punished. The evidence for homogamy comes paradoxically from the minority of deviant instances. For example, those who marry outside their religious group tend to have either weak religious backgrounds, strained relationships with their parents, or both. However, opportunity is of key importance as well as group membership itself: many people simply have little chance to meet members from other groups. This is shown by the fact that as people move from one town to another, they are more likely to marry outside their own social group. There is much evidence that partners are found in the area in which one lives—mate seekers do not seem to explore far, and if the immediate neighbourhood consists of one's ethnic, religious, and social class group, the field of available partners is similarly restricted. Examples are areas in which most people are white, middle class, and Anglican, or black, working class, and Baptist—or, of course, vice versa. As the neighbourhood becomes more varied, so actual partner choice becomes more varied. Departures from homogamy are also more likely to occur when homogamous partners are scarce. For example, the older the person who is unmarried, the more likely is he or she to marry outside his or her ethnic or religious group. Again, with increasing age, the general rule concerning age (the same or nearly the same) is relaxed. Deviations from the rules seem more frequent in the poorer sections and it also seems more possible for males to 'marry down' than for females to do so; a male professional marrying a female office worker evokes much less social comment than the reverse situation.

Mate selection is influenced also by the broad view taken of the 'normal' pattern of the marital relationship. Two patterns have been indentified: the 'interactional' and the 'parallel'. The former emphasizes mutual involvement and interaction, shared interests and activities, frequent expressions of affection and a serious effort to understand and meet each other's needs (Bernard, 1964). It is said to be more characteristic of middle class than working class couples, whose typical pattern is the parallel type, in which emphasis is placed on distinct and separate roles and attributes. The husband is expected to be sober, kind, and a good provider, and reasonable in his sexual demands on the wife, who in her turn is considered 'good' if she is a competent housekeeper and cook, a good mother, and a willing sex partner. While the husband lives largely in a male world, the wife lives in a female one. The advance of Women's Liberation is obviously favourable to the interactional pattern and seems likely to result in a decreased frequency of the parallel form of relationship. The relevance of the two patterns to the process of mate selection is that for those favouring the interactional pattern, personal compatibility and being 'in love' are additional criteria over and above those of race, religion, and social class compatibility. A further class difference, which is also related to mate selection is that the middle class tend to date early, move through a number of partners and marry later than the working class who, by contrast, tend to begin dating later but then pair off fairly rapidly with the person whom they will marry.

Rosenblatt (1974) has pointed out that most of the data on partner choice are concerned with American college age students. Such data omit the key role of economic factors in non-Western and non-urban communities, in which marriage is often closely associated with the ownership and transfer of money and property and may be arranged rather than left to the chance results of unchaperoned meetings. Rosenblatt and Cozby (1972) found that freedom in the choice of the partner went along with 'impractical' grounds for choice, such as sexual attraction and love, and a mutual display of affection before marriage. Conversely when there is little freedom of choice, sexual attraction is much less emphasized. This enables the economic and other interests served by an arranged marriage to play the dominant part. In order to reduce the importance of attraction children in such societies are trained to accept the system of arranged marriages, the sexes are segregated before marriage, premarital sex is punished severely and marriage takes place at an early age. In the 'free choice' societies, attraction between potential partners is assisted by a complex set of 'flirting behaviours' which seem fairly universal and include joking and teasing, as well as certain non-verbal behaviours involving a pattern of smiling, eyebrow-raising, and turning away (Eibl-Eibesfeldt, 1971). The distinction between freedom of choice of partner and an arranged marriage is important also for directing the selection of partners (if any) with whom sexual intercourse can occur before marriage. It is inevitably restricted, at the very least, when the family authorities have an interest in the selection of the 'correct' partner. Where marriage has little financial implication there are fewer controls over premarital sex partners. The reason for this difference is that while premarital sex may increase commitment, it also puts at risk the marital chances of those concerned, particularly the female, and hence spoils the financial plans of the family. Finally, even in societies which restrict freedom of choice, those who are difficult to marry off are much less subject to restrictions, for example those placed on premarital sex.

This section has emphasized that attraction and love are far from universal features of mate selection. There is an inverse relationship between economic emphases and the importance attributed to love. The competence of a prospective partner in a wide range of activities, including earning a living, also plays a part. The overriding importance of attraction and love are further limited by the current tendency in several countries of the West for couples to set up house together before marriage, as well as merely having sexual intercourse. Such 'trial marriage' may provide a more rational basis for a long-term relationship than love alone.

Attraction

Physical attractiveness is one of the components of attraction—and in the sexual context is of particular importance. When people are asked what they look for in a prospective partner they tend to mention such attributes as honesty, warmth, and sense of humour. But these features are essentially the prerequisites for some relatively enduring relationship. In the short term, and certainly at the first encounter, physical appearance is of primary importance. A number of studies, carried out on American college students, are in agreement on this point. One method which was used in this kind of study is to give students tickets for a dance on condition that they accept a 'blind date' for the evening. Later the students are asked how much they liked their partners. Using this method, Walster et al. (1966) rated students for attractiveness before they met their date. The more physically attractive the person the more he/she was liked; personality and intelligence were of much less importance. Silverman (1971) found a close relationship between the level of attractiveness of each member of the pair of dating couples (rated by independent observers); an interesting illustration of the 'pecking order' notion discussed earlier.

Does the importance of physical attractiveness decline as the couple meet repeatedly? Mathes (1975) contacted students by telephone and secured agreement that they would be introduced to a partner with whom they would meet weekly for five 40-minute encounters. Attraction was rated on each occasion by each partner. Independent judges rated physical attractiveness at the outset. Contrary to other studies, attractive partners were not liked more than unattractive ones at the first encounter. However, by the second encounter the prediction was supported—the partner who was judged more attractive was now liked more. The difference persisted for the remaining three encounters, suggesting some stability in the importance of physical attractiveness for liking.

Physical attractiveness is not of course the only factor in the stability of liking. Byrne et al. (1972), again using the 'blind date' method, found that a partner was most liked when he/she was both physically attractive (as rated by independent judges) and was known to have similar attitudes on a variety of issues important to the judging partner. Liking was least when the partner was both unattractive and dissimilar in attitude. To sum up: physical attractiveness is the first 'test' to be passed when young people meet. If it is met successfully other factors come into play, but the importance of physical attractiveness remains over a lengthy series of encounters.

When independent judges are used to rate physical attractiveness in studies of liking there is a positive correlation between these factors. When the partners do the rating themselves, the relationship with liking is even more powerful because people are realistic in the targets they set for themselves (the evidence for this statement is summarized by Curran and Lippold, 1975). In this way a person's perception of his own position on the attractiveness hierarchy can come into play. Individual A may be rated as rather unattractive by independent judges, but is given a higher attractiveness rating by B, because of the latter's low 'objective' rating as given by the independent judges.

Berscheid *et al.* (1971) found that people, especially females, were keen to meet those of a similar level of physical attractiveness to themselves. Variations from this general tendency to match are associated particularly with males who are high in self-esteem, due to a number of factors including high social status, wealth, and a previous record of success with partners more attractive than themselves. An obvious example is the physically unattractive but very wealthy and powerful businessman who pairs with a woman of exceptional beauty and charm.

So far physical attractiveness has been prepotent, even to the extent that people considered physically attractive are also thought likely to have desirable personality attributes. Dermer and Thiel (1975) tried to establish the conditions, if any, beyond which beauty may fail. They found that as compared to unattractive women, attractive women are expected by both male and female college students to be more sociable, heterosexually and professionally successful and personally happy. However, they are also expected to be more conceited and adulterous. There were no differences in the way in which men and women students made their ratings. We can see this result both as evidence that beauty does have its limits in this context and as indirect support for the 'pecking order' view. Presumably men will tend not to seek as partners women who are considered both attractive and successful unless they themselves can match up to this hierarchical position. If they can they may feel confident of holding their highly desirable mates in the face of continuing competition from alternative partners.

The Nature of Love

According to Berscheid and Walster (1974) love is associated with fantasy about the loved one and is aroused more by fantasy than by reality which, because it is so often less rewarding that what was anticipated, tends to erode love. Whereas liking is closely responsive to both positive and negative reinforcement, apparently love fits less neatly into the reinforcement paradigm, in that it may be associated with distress, even agony. However, as we have seen, sexual behaviour may become associated with physical pain through classical conditioning. In the same way love may become associated with 'psychological pain'; the reinforcement paradigm still applies. That love is often associated with distress is shown by a study by Tennov (1973) who asked 80 single young men and women to answer a questionnaire on romantic love. More than half reported having been severely depressed as a result of being in love, and over a quarter of those who reported depression had also thought of suicide. Many members of both sexes read romantic novels and poetry and daydreamed about their affairs. Rubin (1974) suggests that love is further distinguished from liking by a greater emphasis on both needing and giving, that is more emotional interaction is both provided and sought. Additionally, love is distinguished by the intimacy of the confidences which are exchanged.

Current ideas on the nature of love are much influenced by the romantic ideal which stems from the courtly love of the medieval European nobility. The key features of this ideal are that love is fatal, uncontrollable, strikes at first sight, is single-minded, knows no boundaries and is lifelong. However, whereas courtly love was extramarital, contemporary thinking often stresses the marriage bond. The romantic ideal is transmitted by television, films, and books, all of which provide a mass of possibilities for the observational learning of 'love-related' behaviours as they do for behaviour in general.

A Theory of Romantic Love

Berscheid and Walster (1974) have proposed a detailed theory of romantic love which is based on Schachter's (1964) general theory of emotion. According to this, emotional experience requires both physiological arousal and the labelling of that arousal in specific emotional terms. An experiment by Schachter and Singer (1962) demonstrates the theory and its explanatory power. Volunteers were injected with a substance labelled 'suppoxin' which was said to be a new vitamin. In fact half were injected with epinephrine, which is sympathomimetic, and half with saline solution. Each half was then divided into three subgroups: the first was given advance warning of the physiological effects of epinephrine; the second was given incorrect information as to these effects (numbness, itching, slight headaches); and the third was given no information. It was predicted that the two latter groups would attribute their aroused state to whatever was going on around them when the drug took effect 20 minutes later. The environment was experimentally controlled as follows. Half of the members of each subgroup were joined by a confederate of the experimenter who hula-hooped and danced in an attempt to induce 'euphoria'; the other half were asked to fill out a questionnaire and hand it to another confederate. The confederate then threw the questionnaire in the waste paper basket and shouted at them. The results were as predicted. Physiological arousal due to the epinephrine was attributed to the emotion associated with the situation (euphoria or anger). Thus, Schachter concluded, emotion is due to both physiological arousal, the precise form of which is relatively unimportant, and the cognitive label attached by the person experiencing the emotion; the source of the label is the situation in which the experience occurs.

According to Berscheid and Walster (1974) passionate love is experienced when a person is (a) intensely aroused physiologically, (b) situational cues indicate that 'passionate' love is an appropriate label. This approach explains why intensely positive *and* negative experiences are both conducive to love—because both produce intense physiological arousal. The second element, that of labelling, now becomes crucial. Provided that the label seems appropriate it will be applied. Love dies when either arousal in the presence of the loved one declines, or an alternative label appears more appropriate.

There is as yet no direct support for this theory of love, but Berscheid and Walster (1974) cite some indirect evidence. A number of studies are relevant to the theory's first stage—that of the generation of physiological arousal, the source of the arousal, whether objectively unpleasant or pleasant, being relatively unimportant. Brehm *et al.* (1970) demonstrated that previously induced fear increased sexual attraction. Similarly, Jacobs *et al.* (1971) gave two groups of men a questionnaire test of personality followed by feedback of the result. For one group this was arranged to be flattering, for the other insulting. Half the members of each group then met a 'warm' girl, the other half the same girl but this time behaving in a 'cool' manner. Their liking for the girl was then measured. The result of particular interest was that the 'insulted' group liked the 'warm' girl more than the 'flattered' group. This finding can be seen both as indirect support for the theory under discussion and as a nice demonstration of the everyday belief of 'falling for someone on the rebound'—a rejected person is particularly vulnerable to flattery.

Walster *et al.* (1973a) then attempted a more direct test of the notion that an unpleasant source of arousal (in this case *frustration*) is conducive to love. They noted the wide agreement that the girl who is 'hard to get' inspires more passion than the one who 'throws herself' at any man. However, their initial studies failed to support the expectation. It was only when they changed their hypothesis from being 'generally hard to get' to being 'selectively hard to get' that support was found. In this study males were recruited for a computer date matching programme. They were told that five girls had been selected by the computer and were given their biographies. It was also possible for each of the men to discover how some of the girls had rated both him and the four other men with whom the computer had 'matched' her. One girl (easy to get) made it clear she was eager to date all five men, one (generally hard to get) said she rejected all five and one (selectively hard to get) said she was eager to date only the person in receipt of the feedback. The other two girls served as controls, no information being given on their preferences. This time a clear finding emerged; the selectively hard to get girl was liked much more than the others. However it is not clear whether this really is an example of frustration (a negative emotion) increasing arousal and hence liking, or instead relates to an increase in self-esteem (a positive emotion) following selection in a competitive situation, the source of the increase then being evaluated more positively.

More relevant to the suggested link between frustration and love is the study by Driscoll *et al.* (1972) which attempted to look at real life 'Romeo and Juliet' situations. They studied a large number of couples, some married, some 'going steady', others living together, to whom they administered a number of questionnaires concerning parental interference, conjugal love (mutual support), and romantic love (conjugal love plus trust and romance). Parental interference was found to be related strongly to romantic love and rather less strongly to conjugal love in the case of the unmarried couples, but only minimally with either scale so far as the already married were concerned. This suggested that parental interference increases love, a suggestion supported by a follow-up some months later: the more the initial amount of interference the greater the increase in love and vice versa. However, other explanations are possible. First, if the disapproved-of relationship is weak, the attempted interference is likely to be successful—ending the relationship and thus removing the couple from the study. Second, the direction of the effect may be the opposite of that assumed—parents may interfere *because* the couple are already in love. Finally, there is ample evidence that an increased attempt to achieve a goal is only one consequence of an obstacle to its attainment. Others include seeking an alternative goal (partner in this context) and withdrawing from the situation completely. The alternative which is taken depends on the outcomes of previous responses to frustrating experiences, both in general and in the love context itself, and the specifics of the current situation.

Bercheid and Walster also mention some pleasant emotional experiences which heighten arousal and hence facilitate the emotion of love. Most obvious among these is sexual gratification. Sexual arousal is proportional to general physiological arousal. Liking and loving tend to be attributed to the person who is associated with the arousal. Several forms of non-sexual physical activity are dangerous, extremely arousing physiologically and are subjectively labelled exciting. Examples include parachuting and skiing. In a similar way some sexual relationships, particularly those which carry a risk of punishing consequences if detected, are more 'exciting' than others, because they evoke particularly high levels of general arousal. Hence, there is a possibility that extramarital or extrasocial group sexual relationships are both more arousing sexually and are labelled as more passionately romantic than marital relationships and those which are formed within the social grouping. Finally, as suggested above in the discussion on the Walster *et al.* (1973a) study on the effect of 'hard to get' girls on liking, if the potential loved one supplies a particularly valued reinforcer a strong emotional response will result and this is particularly the case if reinforcement follows a lengthy period of deprivation. For example, an employee with a lengthy history of both job failure and socio-sexual failure and a resulting low self-esteem all-round is given warm congratulations for a piece of work by an attractive boss. The result may be that he/she interprets his/her resulting emotion as 'liking', perhaps even as 'love'.

The second step in the Berscheid–Walster theory of passionate love is to attach the appropriate label—love—to the state of heightened arousal. They suggest that children are trained to label their feelings correctly by parental labelling of the external behaviour (e.g. a child is hurrying to get to a party: 'I feel funny' says the child; 'You mean you feel excited' says the mother). By adolescence most of us have learned what external stimuli are generally associated with what emotional label. However, some emotions are labelled less reliably than others, love being a particular case in point, so that a great deal of influence is exerted by 'appropriate' situations and people.

Berscheid and Walster follow Schachter in asserting that when a situation is ambiguous the most plausible label will be used. They have suggested two influences in deciding what is the most plausible label: first, the presence of stimuli previously associated with the label; and, second, the balance of rewards and costs of the competing emotional labels. We also label as love certain violent emotional behaviours, as when a man and a woman seem to argue constantly over trivia. Much cultural encouragement is given to attaching the label love to a range of emotions. Linton has made the rather harsh comment: 'the hero of the modern American novel is always a romantic lover, just as the hero of an old Arab epic is always an epileptic' (Linton, 1936, p. 175).

Several questions remain concerning the label 'romantic love'. First, how is this distinguished from the more derogatory label 'infatuation'? Berscheid and Walster suggest that 'romantic love' is the label used by the participants during the course of a passionate relationship and 'infatuation' the one assigned when it is definitely over.

A second question concerns possible sex differences in the importance attributed to romantic love. One study suggests that men are, if anything, more concerned with romance than are women. Kephart (1967) found that two-thirds of a group of college males would not marry a person otherwise eligible unless they were in love. This may reflect stereotypes concerning male and female roles more prevalent then than now: the male is the economic provider; hence his earning power can make up for lack of romantic attraction. Berscheid and Walster (1974) make a number of predictions as to how individual expectations concerning love will affect the labelling process. First, those who label themselves as 'romantic' will fall in love more often than those who do not—perhaps because the former court situations in which love may happen and vice versa. Second, low self-esteem will be strongly associated with the need for affection. Dion and Dion (1975) tested this prediction on 156 male and female students. They found that people low in self-esteem expressed attitudes of greater love and trust towards their partners than those high in self-esteem. However, the latter group experienced romantic love more often, both requited and unrequited. Being more self-secure they are more willing to take risks. Finally, those who have (socially learned) expectations that love will happen will experience it more frequently because they are more likely to label ambiguous emotions as love.

Berscheid and Walster's two-stage theory of romantic love is a very useful beginning in a difficult field. It omits a number of elements of the general approach to behaviour we have outlined earlier in this chapter which would fit in very easily. First, exposure to social models of 'lovers' and 'loving behaviour' provides people with powerful opportunities for the observational learning of appropriate behaviour. Second, the occurrence of positive reinforcement, even if intermittent, of being 'in love'. Third, the very powerful emotions associated with love, together with the socially approved label 'love', both rightly stressed by Berscheid and Walster, provide an excellent source of intense and frequent cognitive rehearsal of love related experiences, thus maintaining and strengthening the associated overt behaviours.

Intimate Relationships

Having reviewed the variables leading to the formation of a relationship, we can now look at the relationship itself. Rosenblatt (1974) notes that 90 per cent of the societies he studied (including those of the developed countries) emphasized rituals and ceremonies in building attachment to a relationship. Other members of the family are also committed. There is a change of residence and new economic responsibilities. Some societies make considerable prior preparation for the change, including a long period of 'engagement'. Children born to the pair reduce the probability of the relationship breaking up by increasing the community of interests of the partners.

An attempt to develop a general theory of social behaviour, termed Equity theory, has been made by a number of social psychologists, most notably Elaine Walster (Walster *et al.*, 1973b). Equity theory has been applied with some success to industrial relationships, exploiter/victim relationships, and philanthropist/recipient relationships, as well as to casual social encounters, and Walster *et al.* (1976) have now generalized it to include intimate personal relationships. Essentially the theory states that people try to maximize their outcomes from relationships, become distressed when the relationship is inequitable, and try to eliminate their distress by restoring equity. This can be achieved by restoring either *actual* or *psychological* equity. The former is concerned with real outcomes, for example pay or conditions of work, the latter with perceptions, such as an employer asserting that a poorly paid worker is lazy, or exaggerating his own efforts and importance.

Is it appropriate to apply this 'market' approach to human behaviour to romantic and marital relationships, or are they so special and different that general psychological principles are not applicable? Some psychologists have asserted that love transcends equity: 'The principles of the inter-personal market place are most likely to prevail in encounters between strangers and casual acquaintances and in the early stages of the development of relationships. As an inter-personal bond becomes more firmly established, however, it begins to go beyond exchange. In close relationships one becomes decreasingly concerned with what he can get *from* the other person, and increasingly concerned with what he can do *for* the other' (Rubin, 1973, pp. 86–87). Walster *et al.* (1976) quote an alternative view in support of equity theory: 'Marriage is an interlocking, self-contained system. The behaviour and the attitudes of one partner *always* stimulate some sort of reaction from the other . . . we call this system of behavioural responses the *quid pro quo* (or "something for something") . . . the *quid pro quo* process is an unconscious effort of both partners to assure themselves that they are equals, that they are peers. This is a technique enabling each to preserve his dignity and self-esteem. The equality may not be apparent to the world at large: it may be based upon values meaningless to anyone else, and yet serve to maintain the relationship because the people involved perceive their behavioural balance as fair and mutually satisfying' (Lederer and Jackson, 1968, pp. 177–179).

Walster *et al.* (1976) have made a series of bold assertions about intimate relationships and are now engaged in a programme of research designed to test them. First they offer as a definition of an intimate relationship: 'loving persons whose lives are deeply intertwined'. Such persons include best friends, parents and children, as well as our present concern—lovers and spouses. Intimate relationships are characterized by: an intensity of loving; a depth and breadth of information exchange (e.g. mutual confidences); a long time-span (at least in intention, as in 'until death do us part'); the high value of the resources (rewards and punishments) exchanged and the variety of those rewards and punishments, which range from love to goods and services; the substitutability of rewards and punishments (e.g. a special Sunday dinner in return for a publicly made declaration of love); the unit of analysis—which is the couple (us) rather than the individual (me) as in casual relationships. The above list is of considerable interest. It makes it clear that the sexual element is only one component of an intimate relationship between lovers or spouses.

As a general statement Walster and her colleagues assert that contentment in a relationship is closely linked to the equity of the relationship: the more inequitable the relationship the more distress. Inequities are particularly likely at four crisis periods: marriage; a first child; the children leaving home; and retirement. 'At such times of precipitous change a couple may find that their once equitable relationship is now woefully unbalanced' (Walster *et al.*, 1976, p. 23). Either couples find ways of restoring equity or their relationship will founder. Walster and colleagues expect equitable relationships to be sturdy ones; an inequitable relationship is when one partner is clearly 'superior' to the other—in all of the variety of attributes such as attractiveness, status and education, and so on, by which people may be compared. They predict that in this case *both* partners will be unhappy—because both suspect that the relationship will be unstable. A brief study supported their expectations. Berscheid *et al.* (1973) sent out a questionnaire to the readers of *Psychology Today* concerning their satisfaction in their dating/mating/marital relationship and their perception of the desirability of their partner (from 'much more than I' through to 'much less than I'). As predicted, readers who were matched with appropriate partners ('as desirable as I') were more satisfied with their relationships than those whose partners were 'far more' or 'far less' desirable than themselves. Of course this study has a major flaw: people *first* may become dissatisfied *then* perceive differences in desirability. Such a study will need to be carried out from the point at which couples 'go steady' and then continue for some time, so as to look at the predictive power of the original perception of partner desirability for later satisfaction.

How is equity to be restored by the participants in inequitable relationships? The first method is to restore actual equity—by bringing about real changes in the relationship, either by one partner contributing more, or the other less. Areas in which this could occur include physical appearance, day to day talk, financial security, expressions of love and affection, self-sacrifice and sexual behaviour. This is very reminiscent of the reciprocity approach to marital therapy (Azrin *et al.*, 1973) which spells out the pattern of reinforcement each seeks from the other. The second method is to restore psychological equity by changing perceptions. For example the neglected wife might try to convince herself that her husband working all hours is really evidence of his concern for her. The 'psychological' methods of restoring equity are more fragile than are the 'actual' methods of restoration.

Finally, Walster and her colleagues point to some existing evidence for what they term the matching hypothesis—like marries like. (NB this must apply much more to the interactional pattern of relationship, increasingly emphasized as the sexes become more equal, than to the parallel pattern in which wide differences might be tolerated because of the separation of roles and the different worlds in which the two live for most of their working lives. It might well be that the rapidly rising divorce rate is one of the prices society pays for the equality of the sexes. Alternatively, couples might learn skills whereby the equity of marriages, and hence their stability, might be more effectively maintained.) Walster *et al.* cite for their matching hypothesis the kind of evidence some of which we have already listed: dating and marital partners do tend to be similar in physical attractiveness, mental and physical health, and intelligence and education, as well as social status, ethnic membership and religious affiliation. Of course, it is the total 'slate' which counts. As Murstein *et al.* (1974) put it: 'A handsome man is seen with a woman of mediocre attractiveness. " I wonder what he sees in her?" may be the quizzical question of a bystander. Quite possibly, she possesses compensating qualities such as great intelligence, inter-personal competence, and wealth, of which the bystander knows nothing ...' 'Another case of compensatory exchange might be indicated if an aged statesman proposed marriage to a young beautiful woman. He would probably be trading his prestige and power for her physical attractiveness and youth.' (Murstein *et al.*, 1974, pp. 3–4; cited by Walster *et al.*, 1976, p. 43.)

The research into love and attraction by Walster and other psychologists is of both great scientific interest as well as considerable social importance in view of the increasing evidence of unhappy marriages and of heavy demands on marital counsellors.

OVERVIEW

The social learning component of human sexual behaviour may be divided into the social settings within which sexual behaviours might occur and the sequence of the acquisition, performance, and the maintenance of those behaviours. Social settings provide a range of models of both behaviours and attitudes. The process of acquisition involves both classical and instrumental conditioning components. Individuals learn from their observation of others as well as from their own direct experience. The considerable weight attached to sexual behaviour by our society makes the outcome of the first sexual experience of particular importance.

The situational determinants of the performance of sexual behaviours include the physical appearance of a prospective partner, the partner's display of sexual interest, the level of sexual deprivation, and the presence of previously conditioned specific erotic stimuli and situational factors such as opportunity. Aggressive arousal and alcohol have complex eliciting or inhibitory effects whose interrelationship with sexual behaviour is not yet fully understood.

Over a period of time sexual behaviours, like behaviours in general, are maintained, or diminished, by their consequences. Reinforcement takes three forms: external (attention and approval), physiological, and self-reinforcement. The schedule of reinforcement which is experienced is of particular importance; an intermittent schedule will maintain attempts at sexual responses to partners despite only occasional success. In addition the cognitive appraisal and rehearsal of sexual behaviour is of great importance in maintaining or diminishing, perhaps even transforming, those behaviours.

All societies have social rules for mate selection which may interact with the socially learned criteria for physical attractiveness. Some societies place little or no weight on love. In our own it plays a central part. A current psychological theory of romantic love suggests two stages: non-specific emotional experience and its labelling as love or romance. The evidence to date suggests the value of the theory, particularly when supplemented by social learning principles. A development in social psychology, Equity theory, has been applied to intimate relationships. It makes predictions about what people do when the return from such relationships falls below some expected or experienced level of return in relation to their own contribution. Equity theory seems relevant to the explanation of why some relationships continue to flourish over time while others break down.

CHAPTER 4

Individual Differences in Sexual Activity

INTRODUCTION

In the previous chapters we have established a framework for looking at human sexual behaviours. They occur in a social setting and are determined by social conventions, biological predispositions, continuing biological influences, individual opportunities, and social experiences. In this chapter we shall look at one of the most striking features of the field; the vast range of individual differences in such variables as the rate of acquisition of sexual activities and the range of their frequency. We shall outline some findings concerning the relationship between individual differences and such potential correlates of behaviour in general as group membership and features of personality assessed by formal tests.

The evidence which is reviewed in this chapter has been obtained from individuals talking to interviewers of varying degrees of expertise about their own present and past sexual activities. Asking people to talk about themselves is one of the three standard techniques used in psychological research. The second is the observation of naturally occurring behaviours, and the third is to set up an artificial situation, all aspects of which can be systematically manipulated (this third method is the classical controlled experiment). In practice observation has hardly been used at all in the field of human sexual behaviour and, for obvious reasons, people would very soon become resentful of being observed by an uninvited individual, no matter how pure were his scientific intentions. However, a variation (naturally occurring behaviour recorded in a systematic manner) has been extensively used by Masters and Johnson (1966) in their meticulous and well-known work on the anatomical and physiological characteristics of sexual behaviour, which we referred to in detail in Chapter 2.

Much the largest, most detailed, and most thorough self-report survey ever carried out is the work of Kinsey, and his associates, in the USA. Their work is summarized in two massive books, one concerned with the sexual behaviour of the human male (Kinsey *et al.*, 1948) and the other with the sexual behaviour of the human female (Kinsey *et al.*, 1953). A more recent study, which has used more satisfactory sampling techniques than those of the Kinsey group was carried out in England by Schofield (1965a). A recent American survey of a very large, but non-random, sample of its readership was reported in *Redbook Magazine* (1975).

The data cited in the first part of this chapter are largely concerned with the reports of these three surveys, together with a series of German surveys by Schmidt and Sigusch (1972). Most important of all, almost the entire published quantitative research on human sexual behaviour to date has been obtained from the advanced industrial countries of the West. It might be, as the same systematic techniques are used in other parts of the world, that we will have to considerably revise our descriptive knowledge of human sexual behaviour. In turn, this might affect theories set up to account for the descriptions we obtain.

In the field of sexual behaviour we are concerned with an area of life in which what people have *actually* done, what they would have *liked* to have been able to do, and what they feel they *should* have done, are intertwined in such a way as to add to the difficulties which people experience when they try to recall accurately past experiences of any kind. The social prescriptions and proscriptions of the group in which any individual finds himself will affect any self-report data which are collected from him. For example, if a respondent is a member of a sub-culture in which a high rate of sexual outlet is deemed to be desirable, there are obvious temptations to exaggerate the true own level of outlet if it is actually below a level which he/she imagines to be normal. Conversely, he might be an individual whose sub-culture proscribes anything but a low level of outlet and then only in certain special circumstances. In this case, he might be tempted to deny the full extent of his sexual activities. The major surveys of sexual practice have been well aware of these problems and have attempted to bring them under control. One problem which may be less important than is often feared is that of volunteer bias. (A basic tenet held by most psychologists is that people who volunteer for research are different from those who choose not to volunteer.) Barker and Perlman (1975) compared the personality test scores of the two-thirds of the college sample which returned questionnaires sent to them on sexual behaviour with the third which failed to do so. No significant differences were found on a very large number of personality scales. Moreover, the percentage answering the sex questionnaire was very similar to that returning a questionnaire on parent–child relationships selected for its non-threatening nature. It is important to note that this result was obtained for college undergraduates, one of the main populations used in sex surveys and may not hold for other, older, and possibly more conservative, populations.

THE SURVEYS: RESEARCH TECHNIQUES

Kinsey

For many years, Alfred C. Kinsey and his associates (the associates carried on Kinsey's pioneering work after his death) conducted individual interviews with many thousands of Americans. Direct and detailed questions were asked concerning the intimate details of the respondents' sexual behaviour. Of the many thousands of people interviewed, fewer than ten had refused to complete the history once they had started (Pomeroy, 1963). Initially 521 items were included as possible areas of exploration, but since people were questioned in detail only about those items they had specifically experienced, the actual number of items covered was close to 300.

Nine broad areas were surveyed:

1. social and economic data
2. marital history
3. sex education
4. physical and physiological data
5. nocturnal sex dreams
6. masturbation
7. heterosexual history
8. homosexual history
9. sex contacts with animals

Each interviewer was both a trustee of the Institute for Sex Research and a member of its Policy Making Board. Great care went into the selection of interviewers—in the 22 years up to 1963, only 9 of some 300 persons considered as possible interviewers had been selected. The selectors were looking for interviewers who were both happily married, yet able to travel extensively, who were highly trained scientists, but acceptable to all sections of society. Moreover, the interviewers should both be fully aware of their own culture and yet so unaffected by it that they did not pass moral judgements on the sexual behaviours of others.

The people who were interviewed were not recruited by the standard sampling techniques used by Schofield (1965a, see below) but were contacted in various ways. A large number of interviews were set up through personal introductions requiring much cultivation of the appropriate community contacts. Frequently, individuals who themselves had given histories became 'contact men' for introductions to their acquaintances or other members of their groups. 'Contacts' included such individuals as editors, clergymen, clerks, housewives, lawyers, gamblers, physicians, police court officials, prison inmates, public school teachers, and welfare workers. The majority were recruited from a social group of some sort—church, fraternity, parent–teacher association, and factory. In every instance, the co-operation of the entire group was solicited. Once a significant proportion of a given group had contributed histories, social pressures operated in such a manner that others felt obligated to do so, assisting the goal of 100 per cent co-operation.

Very strict procedures were carried out in order to ensure confidentiality. The major feature was a cryptic code, used to record as well as store all data, which was developed with the help of an experienced cryptographer. All histories were kept behind locked doors and in fire-proof files with locks used only for that particular project. At the time of the latest report (Pomeroy, 1963) only six individuals knew any part of the code and only four had knowledge of the entire code.

Every attempt was made to make the interviews appear as informal as possible. The first few items were of a non-sexual nature and the whole followed a sequence which took into account the topics that might be most difficult for the particular respondent to discuss. Particular care was taken to phrase questions in the everyday language of the subject. Sexual questions were phrased in a direct, rather than an evasive manner, so that the burden of denial was always placed on the subject. This technique was intended to reassure subjects that the interviewer was unlikely to be surprised by any experience they might had had, however unusual.

Elaborate procedures were carried out to assess the extent to which individuals were falsifying and many individuals were re-interviewed after an interval of time varying from 18 months to 7 years, in order to check on the extent to which he gave the same information on each occasion. A further check on the reliability of information was the comparison of responses given by married couples. Finally, there were procedures to check the possibility that bias was contributed by the interviewer himself. It was shown that, by and large, different interviewers did not elicit significantly different sexual histories from comparable individuals.

Many of the large number of articles which have appeared, following the Kinsey books, have criticized the sampling methods used (e.g. Himelhoch and Fava, 1953). For instance, 75 per cent of the females interviewed were college educated; the proportion in the general American population was then 13 per cent. Moreover, while Kinsey took considerable care to show that the standarized interview techniques which were used with his male correspondents (Kinsey *et al.*, 1948) did not produce significantly different results between the three male interviewers, he did not, unfortunately, repeat these tests in his study of females (Kinsey *et al.*, 1953). Schofield (1965a) found interviewing women about sexual behaviour to be more variable and uncertain than interviewing men; Kinsey made it even more so by using men to interview women, whereas Schofield found they responded much more readily to female interviewers.

However, despite the doubts and criticisms, at the time of writing, over 30 years after the publication of the major Kinsey surveys, it can be said that as a body of work they have stood the test of time as major achievements of twentieth-century science. At the very least, they serve as a massive and exhaustive set of data on the sexual practices of many Americans in the first half of the twentieth century.

The quantitative figures are less important than the more qualitative findings which came as a considerable shock to many, but have received support from later studies; they include the massive variations between individuals, and within individuals over the life span, and the wide range of sexual *outlets* used by any single individual. The quantitative figures, such as those for premarital intercourse, serve as a rough base line for more recent studies, which are outlined later, so that a picture of long-term trends can be built up. The data collected by Kinsey and reviewed in this chapter are based on approaching 5,000 persons of each sex.

Schofield

This survey (Schofield, 1965a) studied the sexual behaviour of teenagers in Britain during the early 1960s. The interviewers were specially trained for the work, and a series of properly constructed samples were used, so that the results can be regarded with a fair degree of confidence. The primary aim of the research was to determine the extent of sexual experience within the 15–19 year age group.

The sampling method used was as follows. A list of National Health Service patients, covering 97.5 per cent of the total population, aged 15 to 19, in an area designated London C, was consulted. Similar lists were obtained from six other areas of Britain. In these seven areas it was estimated that the total number of unmarried teenagers aged 15 to 19 was 24,093. One thousand, eight hundred and seventy-three interviews were completed, so that one in every thirteen teenagers was represented in the sample which consisted of almost equal numbers of boys and girls classified into two age groups, 15–17, and 17–19, designated as 'younger' and 'older' respectively. Particular care was taken to secure equal social class representation. As in the case of the Kinsey work it was decided that valid information about sexual behaviour could only be obtained during the course of a lengthy face-to-face interview. Ten young graduates were used as the interviewers in the research, five male and five female, all of whom underwent an extensive preliminary course of training. The prospective interviewees were contacted by an introductory letter and a follow-up visit. In all 328 refused to be interviewed. Interviewers were not allowed to give up before six call-backs had been made, and all those who refused were asked to fill in a form containing 16 questions about background and leisure interests—about half consented to do so. This information was then used in order to assess the representativeness of the 85% who did consent to be interviewed.

The most usual reason given for refusing to be interviewed was 'lack of interest'. Others said they had no time, and some implied that they were going to be asked about things they did not want to discuss. Schofield argues that both particularly experienced and particularly inexperienced adolescents might be equally likely to refuse to be interviewed, the former because they thought that the information might be passed to their parents, the latter because they were ashamed of their lack of experience. A comparison between those who refused and those who accepted showed no marked differences in occupation, number of jobs, in church going, or in the number of times they went out dancing, all of which items were shown to be associated with sexual experience (see later). The entire schedule consisted of 261 items. When all the questions concerning behaviour had been answered the respondents filled in a 50 item social attitude inventory. As in the Kinsey work the form of the questions assumed that the interviewee had engaged in the particular activity, the burden of denial being placed on him. The interviewers made every attempt both to avoid value judgements, and to use words which would be understood by the respondent.

Certain aspects of sexual life were largely ignored by Schofield, particularly masturbation and sexual fantasy, as well as homosexual behaviour. These omissions severely limit the value of the study which, from the point of view of survey design, is admirable. As Schofield claims: 'No other research on sexual behaviour has used a better sample' (Schofield, 1965a, p. 210). A combination of the virtues of the Kinsey and Schofield studies seems indicated in any future survey.

In September 1975 *Redbook Magazine* published the results of a survey of the sexual behaviours of 100,000 of its (female) readers. This is one of a number of reader surveys. Others have been carried out by such magazines as *Playboy* and *Forum.* In its report *Redbook Magazine* did not state what percentage of the total readership returned the questionnaire, but they do point out that those who did so were younger, better educated, and financially better off than the population as a whole. Nevertheless, the magazine asserts 'the women who answered *Redbook*'s questionnaire are in the mainstream of American life'. Self-administered questionnaires cannot be submitted to any of the checks for reliability so carefully carried out by Kinsey and Schofield. Nevertheless the results are of some interest, particularly as they seem the nearest we have to the situation in America 25 years after Kinsey, at least so far as women are concerned.

THE SURVEYS: RESULTS

The Kinsey Studies

The Kinsey data will now be reviewed. Before doing so it will be useful to define the statistical terms used throughout the Kinsey researches:

1. *Individual frequencies*: Average per week of outlets to orgasm. (Whenever the term outlet is used, it refers to *any* sort of sexual activity leading to orgasm.)
2. *Group averages*: These were calculated for each type of sexual outlet, and for each five-year period. In all instances averages were calculated only for groups which exceeded 50 in number.
3. *Mean*: The mid-point of a set of scores.
4. *Median*: The score obtained by the 'middle-most' subject when subjects are arranged in order from the highest scorer to the lowest scorer.
5. *Percentage of individual outlet and percentage of group outlet*: These are self-explanatory.
6. *Incidence*: The percentage of persons who have experienced a given activity.
7. Finally, 'coitus' is used interchangeably with 'sexual intercourse'. It may or may not lead to orgasm.

Before adolescence: boys. Kinsey defines orgasm as the abrupt release of the extreme sexual tension which precedes the event, followed by sudden return to a normal, or sub-normal, physiological state after the event. In the mature male this tends to be accompanied by ejaculation. But orgasm as defined above may also occur *without* the emission of semen. Kinsey's report includes direct observations on 169 pre-adolescent boys, which supplement the retrospective self-reports of the adult respondents who form the great majority of the Kinsey sample. Kinsey reports that orgasm has been observed in boys of every age from five months to adolescence. In all cases it was a striking duplicate of orgasm in an older adult with the exception of ejaculation. Erection was much quicker in pre-adolescent boys than in adults, although the speed with which they reached climax varied considerably in different boys, just as in adults. The most remarkable aspect of the pre-adolescent population was its capacity to achieve repeated orgasm in limited periods of time. This capacity much exceeded the ability of teenage boys who, in turn, were much more capable of multiple orgasm than any older males. More than half of the pre-adolescent boys on whom there were adequate data readily reached a second climax within a short period of time and nearly a third were able to achieve five or more climaxes in quite rapid succession.

Pre-adolescent heterosexual activities were reported by 40 per cent of the male sample. They began their activities at an average age of nearly nine years. Such activity started with the exhibition of genitals and for nearly 20 per cent of the above group this was the only activity experienced. The remaining 80 per cent of pre-adolescent boys who reported any heterosexual activity carried it to the point of manually manipulating female genitals. Attempts to effect genital union were reported by half of the boys who were sexually active before adolescence.

About half of the adult males recalled homosexual activities in their pre-adolescent years, the mean age of the first homosexual contact being about nine years. Exhibition was the most common form of homosexual activity, and typically lead to the next step, the mutual manipulation of the genitalia. These two activities occurred in the play of two-thirds of all pre-adolescent males who reported any form of homosexual activity. For the majority of pre-adolescents homosexual manual contacts were incidental, casual, and usually without any recognition of their emotional possibilities. In only a small proportion of the cases did they lead to more extensive manipulation with heightened sexual arousal, possibly to the point of orgasm by the partner. Anal intercourse was reported by about one-sixth of the pre-adolescents who had experienced any homosexual activity. Pre-adolescent homosexual play was carried over into adolescent or adult activity in something less than half of all cases. A large proportion of the adults who were more or less exclusively homosexual at the time of interview dated the onset of their activities to the pre-adolescent period.

Before adolescence: girls. About one-quarter of the females questioned remembered being sexually excited before puberty; 4 per cent reported this as occurring before the age of five, 16 per cent by the age of ten. Reports of pre-pubertal orgasms were rather rare, reaching 9 per cent by the age of eleven, almost all being achieved during masturbation. It seems likely that most girls are capable of sexual excitement before puberty. Of the females surveyed 18 per cent reported purely homosexual contacts, 15 per cent purely heterosexual, and a further 15 per cent reported both hetero- and homosexual contacts—in all cases before puberty. Such childhood contacts were not always associated with sexual excitement and the majority were occasional and isolated. In a minority, the activity was more regular, but was mostly confined to short periods of time. The incidence of childhood sexuality in girls appeared to decrease with the approach of puberty, perhaps as parental restraint, fuelled by anxiety at the approach of the child bearing age, increased.

Mutual exhibition of the genitals was the commonest heterosexual activity in childhood (as it was for the boys), being reported by almost all the females who remembered sexual experiences at that age. Other behaviours were considerably more rare. In homosexual childhood games, the mutual exhibition of genitals again took first place. Manual genital contacts and vaginal insertions were much less frequent.

Adolescence: boys. The overall age for the first ejaculation was about 13 years and 9 months. By 15 years of age over 90 per cent of the males had experienced orgasm to ejaculation. (In sharp contrast, less than a quarter of the females of the same age had experienced orgasm.)

The causes of first ejaculation were, in order of frequency: masturbation (about two-thirds), nocturnal emissions (one-eighth), heterosexual coitus (one-eighth), homosexual contacts (one boy in twenty), with other causes occurring much less frequently.

Adolescence: girls. By 12 years and 4 months nearly 30 per cent had been aroused erotically by some sort of stimulation, under conditions which were subsequently recalled as definitely sexual. By 15 years of age half had been aroused, the figure reaching nearly 90 per cent by the age of 20.

About a third of the female sample had been first aroused sexually during heterosexual petting (the usual colloquial term for manual stimulation of female breasts), nearly as many by self-masturbation and a further third through psychological stimulation, chiefly through heterosexual social contacts. The percentage of females who had achieved orgasm rose with increasing age: 14 per cent by the onset of adolescence (average age 13), a quarter by 15 years of age and just over half by 20.

Adult experience: males. The major finding was that the maximum frequency of outlet was in the teens, when there was an average of nearly five orgasms per week. It fell to less than half that number by the middle forties and thereafter declined steadily still further. While Kinsey considers that the decline in sexual activity of the older male is partly, and perhaps primarily, the result of a general decline in physiological capacity, it might also be affected—in married males particularly—by a self-imposed limitation to a single source of stimulation, or by lack of opportunity. It cannot be assumed that environmental sanctions and opportunities are the same for all. A more precise test of the contribution of physiological factors to individual differences requires that the environment is held constant for those under study.

The number of sources of total outlet was highest in the 16 to 20 year age period, being 2.9 for the older teenage male; by 60 years of age the mean number of sources had dropped to 1.6. There was also a steady decline in erotic responsiveness with age and in the length of time for which an erection could be maintained during continuous erotic arousal and before there was an ejaculation—from an average of nearly an hour in the late teens and early twenties to seven minutes in the 60–70 year age group. The capacity to reach repeated climax in a limited period of time also markedly decreased in most males with advancing age, but there were considerable individual variations, some males retaining the capacity into the seventies.

A few individuals obtained 100 per cent of their total outlet from a single type of sexual activity, but most persons depended upon two or more sources of outlet, and a few used all six listed by Kinsey (masturbation, nocturnal emissions, premarital, marital and extramarital intercourse, and homosexual acts) within a short period of time. The mean number of outlets utilized by the males in the Kinsey survey was between two and three. A few males had gone for long periods of years without ejaculating (including one, who although apparently sound physically, had ejaculated only once in 30 years). Others had maintained average frequencies of 10, 20, or more per week for long periods of time. Nearly 5 per cent of those under 36 years of age had a total outlet which had averaged one in two weeks or less for periods of at least five years. Only 1 in 20 of this low activity group was in poor health but slightly over half were described by Kinsey as 'apathetic'. Following orgasm they might go for several days or weeks without further arousal. There seemed to be few, if any, psychological stimuli which excited them, and even when they deliberately put themselves into erotic situations, such as active petting, they might be unable to respond more than once in several weeks.

A further small group of 35 males (out of the total sample of around 5,000) started late but increased in rate sharply as soon as they made their first socio-sexual contact (involving another person). As later performance showed, their earlier rates were low only because their responses had not been aroused. There were many cases of males of average sexual capacity who were suddenly forced into relative inactivity by being deprived of opportunities; most seemed to be able to adjust to a lower rate. Kinsey argues that if one removes from the group of low activity males, those who were physically incapacitated, innately low in sexual drive, sexually unawakened in their younger years, separated from their usual sources of sexual stimulation, or timid and upset by their suppressions, there were simply no cases which remained as clear-cut examples of sublimation. However, as celibate priests were not included, such an assertion must be regarded as unproven.

Individuals with high frequencies (defined as seven or more per week) constituted about one in thirteen of the Kinsey male sample. High frequency was heavily associated with age. In the under 30 group there were four times as many high frequency males as in the over 50 group. Those who had reached puberty by the age of 12 were the ones who most often had the highest rates of outlet in the later years of their lives. Kinsey refers to a number of male prostitutes who were interviewed, some of whom ejaculated five or more times per day with regularity over long periods of years. It is not known whether a regular high frequency increases the likelihood of continued high frequency, or whether certain individuals are biologically predisposed to high levels.

Adult experience: females. As indicated above, nearly half the single females had responded sexually to orgasm at least once by the age of 20. The proportion rose to three-quarters, among the unmarried females, by 35 years of age. There was an increase in frequency of orgasm up to the age of 40 in single females, then a steady decline. The pattern was similar though less marked for the married females, but for the previously married females the general picture was one of decline from the point of the marriage ending. For all females, both the rate of increase to peak frequency of total outlet and the rate of decline from the peak, were much less steep than in the case of the males.

At all ages masturbation was the single most frequent source of outlet for the unmarried females in the Kinsey survey. A considerable proportion of the unmarried females between the ages of 36 and 40, nearly 30 per cent, were not experiencing orgasm from any source. The percentages were higher still in the older groups of unmarried females. Kinsey points out that many of these individuals were in positions of responsibility for the behaviour of other persons—school and college teachers, directors of organizations for youth, and members of state legislatures.

Coitus in marriage accounted for nearly 90 per cent of the total outlet of the married females aged between 16 and 35. After the middle thirties the importance of marital coitus decreased, falling to just over 70 per cent of total orgasms by the age of 50. Masturbation was the second most important source of sexual outlet for married females in the sample, providing between 7 and 10 per cent of the total number of orgasms achieved by the age groups from 16 to 40. During the next ten years the second place on the list came to be occupied by extramarital coitus which reached a little over 10 per cent, slightly more than the proportion accounted for by masturbation. Nocturnal orgasms provided between 1 and 3 per cent of the total outlet of the married females in each age group. Homosexual contacts (i.e. with another person as opposed to fantasy) never provided more than a fraction of 1 per cent of the orgasms in the total sample.

As in the case of the males considerable individual differences were found. About 2 per cent of females in the sample had never been aroused erotically at all, and some had been aroused only once, or a very few times, in their lives. At the other extremes were those who had been aroused almost daily, and sometimes many times per day, for long periods of years, with every variation between. Some individuals responded slowly or only slightly to external stimulation; others responded instantaneously and intensely, sometimes to orgasm. There were similar variations in the range of arousing stimuli, as well as the frequency of orgasm during marital coitus. Some experienced this on only 1 or 2 per cent of occasions; whereas others—40 to 50 per cent of the total sample—did so on almost every occasion. There were some who responded at an earlier stage but then ceased to experience orgasm, others who had responded all their lives. Some females obtained their entire sexual outlet from a single source, others had used all six of the possible sources at some stage in their lives.

Male–female differences. There were very marked differences in the proportion which had responded to orgasm among unmarried males and females. About one-third of the females interviewed had not yet done so by the time they were married. By comparison, *all* of the males had not only done so, but had already passed the peak of their sexual activity.

The development of sexual responsiveness was found to be markedly earlier in the male, coinciding with adolescence. The males reached their peak frequency of outlet within three or four years after the onset of adolescence; the females did not do so until their late twenties. The frequency of sexual response in the male declined after the late teens and early twenties and dropped steadily into old age. In females the frequencies of those sexual activities which were not dependent upon the initiation of socio-sexual contacts by males, remained more or less constant from the late teens into the fifties and sixties. Kinsey *et al.* (1953, p. 715) state: 'Nothing we know about the anatomy or physiology of sexual response, or about the relative significance of psychological stimuli in females and males, would account for these differences in the development of sexual responsiveness, and in the ageing patterns of the two sexes.' It should be noted that the differences between males and females are in terms of *averages*. Some females exceeded the majority of males in terms of many of the indices that have been discussed. Similarly some males fell below the majority of females in many indices. As in many other areas of life, the differences observed by Kinsey are declining as the social learning experiences of the two sexes become more similar. Recent evidence on this point will be cited shortly.

The major source of masturbation in the female sample was self-discovery, closely followed by spoken and printed material. In the male sample the most important sources were spoken and printed material, followed by observation and self-discovery. Among females 3 per cent learned through homosexual contacts as compared to 9 per cent of males. Whereas 93 per cent of the total male sample had experienced masturbation at some time, 62 per cent of the females had done so. In even sharper contrast, 92 per cent of the male sample had experienced masturbation by the age of 20, as compared to only 33 per cent of the female sample.

In males, the incidence of masturbation to orgasm *decreased* after the teens, whereas it *increased* to middle age in females. As might be expected it was higher in single than in married groups in both males and females. There was rather more individual variation in females than in males. A higher proportion of males (two-thirds) worried about the psychologically 'harmful' effect of masturbation as compared to half the females. The female sample used masturbatory fantasies less frequently than the men, the overwhelming majority of whom said that they almost always did so. (Few investigations study the rather important area of masturbatory fantasy and the use of imagery in sexual behaviour generally.) The time taken to reach climax by females in masturbation was about half of that taken during coitus. This very important point is further developed in our description of problems of sexual responsiveness in the next chapter.

Whereas nearly all males had had nocturnal *sex dreams*, with or without orgasm, only 70 per cent of the females had done so, the disparity being greatest in the younger age groups. The peak of activities for nocturnal sex dreams was in the teens to twenties for males and in the forties for females.

The incidence of *petting* increased with increasing age; about 90 per cent of both males and females had experienced it by the age of 25. There was no difference between the sexes in the *frequency* of petting to orgasm, but a very marked difference in the *percentage* of petting to orgasm, out of total outlet. In females this was 4 per cent below the age of 15, as compared to 1 per cent in males; similarly it was 18 per cent between 16 and 25 in females compared to 3 per cent in males. In females there was a strong relationship between decade of birth and both petting experience and petting to orgasm, between the ages of 21 and 25, such experience being more likely the later the decade in which the individual female was born.

There was a lower incidence of premarital coitus in females than in males. By the age of 20 only 20 per cent of the females had experienced premarital coitus as compared to 71 per cent of the males.

In the females, as in the case of petting, there was a very marked relationship between the decade of birth and the frequency of premarital coitus (two or three times as frequent for those born after 1900 as those born before 1900) and the percentage of total outlet it comprised. There was no relationship between either frequency or incidence of premarital coitus and the age of onset of adolescence. In both the Kinsey and the Schofield samples (see below) a significant number of the females engaged in premarital coitus did so with their intended marriage partner, in the period immediately prior to marriage. In the Kinsey sample over half the married women questioned reported having had one premarital partner, usually their fiancé; a third had between two and five partners, and one-eighth six or more partners.

In the Kinsey survey virtually all of the married couples reported coitus at one degree of frequency or another. There was a decrease with increasing age, although at the age of 50 over 90 per cent of couples still reported that coitus took place. The weekly frequency of intercourse in young couples averaged 2.8, gradually decreasing with age. In the first year of marriage up to 25 per cent of married women reported no orgasm (from any source); after 10 years this was reduced to about 10 per cent and from then on remained constant. Some married females achieved orgasm with men other than their husbands, in petting, or during self-masturbation. There was a correlation between premarital experience and a marked capacity for orgasm. Masturbation and petting raised the capacity for marital orgasm as much as did premarital coitus. Kinsey considered that women had to learn to reach an orgasm, and that a certain amount of practice was necessary. (An additional explanation would be that females have to learn to overcome social inhibitions against female sexual gratification.)

For females there was a marked increase in percentage of married coitus leading to orgasm for those born after 1900 as compared to those born before 1900. There was very little difference between the sexes in the frequency of multiple orgasm at the younger ages, but a very much higher incidence in females at the older ages (14 per cent compared to 3 per cent), suggesting again the importance of either practice or the time taken to overcome learned inhibitions.

The Kinsey data suggest that about half the married men, and about a quarter of the married women, had extramarital experiences by the age of 40. The incidence of orgasm in extramarital coitus was 85 per cent in females (very markedly higher than in marital coitus). The frequency of extramarital coitus increased with increasing age in females but decreased in males. Similarly, the percentage of total outlet occupied by extramarital coitus increased in females with increasing age, whereas with males there was little change.

In females the incidence of extramarital coitus increased with decade of birth (as did petting, premarital coitus, and marital coitus to orgasm). It was also higher in males with more recent decades of birth, except for those who had attended college. There was little relationship in either sex to the age of onset of adolescence. Women with premarital experiences had extramarital contacts twice as frequently as those who were abstinent before marriage (40 per cent of all cases as compared to 20 per cent).

Sexual orientation. The Kinsey workers developed a seven point scale of sexual orientation, from 0—exclusively heterosexual—to 6—exclusively homosexual. Between 60 and 70 per cent of single females were rated as Kinsey 0, varying with age, as compared to between 53 and 78 per cent of the single males. The figure for married persons was about 90 per cent for both sexes. In the male sample the proportion who were rated as Kinsey 6 (exclusively homosexual for at least three years prior to interview) varied between 7.4 per cent at age 15 to 1.8 per cent of the total sample for the male group. The major finding was that 4 per cent of the white males surveyed were exclusively homosexual throughout their lives from the onset of adolescence. The corresponding figure for females was little more than 1 per cent.

About 50 per cent of males and 30 per cent of females had experienced some sort of homosexual arousal by the age of 45. Among single individuals 22 per cent of males had experienced homosexual behaviour to orgasm by the age of 20 and 40 per cent had done so by the age of 40. The comparable figures for females were 3 per cent and 10 per cent respectively. The homosexual percentage of total outlet in single individuals before the age of 40 showed a gradual increase with increasing age in both sexes—as might be expected; heterosexuals tend to marry, homosexuals tend not to do so. The number of partners of those females who were homosexually active was smaller than for males.

Social Variables

Educational level. Among the *male* respondents the highest frequencies of *total sexual outlet* were those reported by the high school group. This held true for both married and single males and for every age group up to 40. Kinsey expected it to hold true for older ages but had insufficient numbers of subjects for firm conclusions.

The educational backgrounds of the unmarried high school and college *females* in the sample had no consistent effect on their total outlet.

In females there was a steady rise of the accumulative incidence of *masturbation* to orgasm from the group which left school at 14 (34 per cent of the group reported the behaviour) to the group which had successfully completed college (63 per cent). In both males and females masturbation occupied a higher percentage of the total outlet among college educated individuals than other groups, but the disparity between the college educated and the other groups was much larger for females.

There was no relationship between *nocturnal orgasms* and educational level in females but a rather close one in the male group, the highest incidence occurring in the college educated group.

There was a steady decrease in both males and females in *premarital coitus* before the age of 20 according to the level of education. After the age of 20 there was no relationship between the incidence of premarital coitus in females and educational level, whereas the relationships mentioned above persisted in males.

Frequency of *marital intercourse* bore no relationship to educational level for either sex. Orgasm was experienced more frequently by the better educated than by the less well-educated females.

Before the age of 25 there was no relationship between educational level and the incidence of *extramarital intercourse* in females; in males it was higher in the less educated. After the age of 25 the incidence was higher in the better educated females and was unrelated to educational level in males.

Homosexual contacts to orgasm by the age of 30 showed a steady increase in females according to educational level (from 6 per cent of those leaving school at 14 to 14 per cent of those who proceeded to beyond their first degree). In males the figures were higher for all groups and were unrelated to educational level.

Religion. Generally speaking, acceptance of the teachings of a church was associated with sexual frequencies in *males* which were two-thirds or less than the frequencies found among males of the corresponding age and educational levels who were not actively connected with a church. As Kinsey points out, this was either the direct effect of church teachings, or else those individuals who had become actively associated with a church were a self-selected group who would not, in any event, have had high frequencies of outlet. Similarly, religious background of any kind consistently reduced the total sexual outlet of both single and married *females*.

There were also some differences between males and females. Masturbation, as a percentage of total outlet, was higher in the more devout than in the less devout females, but was only slightly higher in the more devout than in the less devout males. The frequency of nocturnal orgasms bore no relation to religious activity for either males or females.

Petting to orgasm bore little relationship to religious activity in either males or females. (This means that religion served as a barrier to starting this activity; once started, religious affiliation played no part in level of activity.) Premarital coitus was markedly less frequent in the devout than in the less devout in both males and females. In females there was no relation between frequency of marital coitus and religious activity, but in males the less devout had a frequency one-quarter higher than the more devout. The less devout females were more likely to experience orgasm after marriage.

Extramarital coitus was higher among the less devout in both males and females. Generally, in both males and females homosexual contacts were more frequent among the less devout.

Studies in Other Cultures

There are two studies which were carried out in the Middle East at about the time of the Kinsey survey. A project concerned with Israeli sex life was reported by Klausner (1961a). His research comprised the two major ethnic elements of Israeli society—European and Middle Eastern. In this study about half of the males interviewed had experienced sexual intercourse by the age of 18, and all had done so by the age of 22. Of the females only 10 per cent had such experience by late adolescence, and about one-third by the age of 22. (This enormous discrepancy between the sexes prompts the question: with whom did the males have their experience? It is the kind of question which must always be asked whenever a survey reveals a large apparent discrepancy between the sexes. The answer would appear to be one or more of the following: many males resort to prostitutes; those females who are sexually active are extremely active, or some males are exaggerating while some females are denying.)

The Israeli survey also looked at female masturbation, finding that two-thirds of the girls had begun to masturbate by the age of 16 and by 22 almost all had done so. Kinsey found that by age 15 only 20 per cent had begun to masturbate and 33 per cent by age 20. Yet the figure for heterosexual intercourse in the American survey exceeded, for females, that found in the Israeli survey. It may well be that a high incidence of female masturbation is associated with a lower rate of coital experience or, more likely, that Israelis *mores* allow the former but not the latter, particularly in Israelis of Middle Eastern origin.

Klausner (1961b) also carried out a study in Iraq. By the age of 20 less than 12 per cent of Iraqi males had experienced sexual intercourse with a female friend. On the other hand, by their early twenties, three out of four had visited prostitutes. Klausner states that the strong sanctions throughout the Middle East against premarital heterosexual behaviour result in a high incidence of both male and female homosexual behaviour, but gives no figures to support this assertion.

MODERN STUDIES OF SEXUAL BEHAVIOUR

Schmidt and Sigusch (1972) summarized a number of studies carried out in Western countries during the present century. They identified two general trends, both in sexual attitudes and sexual behaviours. For the 30 years between 1930 and 1960, the incidence of premarital intercourse rose only slightly. However, in the 1960s, there was a sharp rise in premarital intercourse, at any rate among college educated persons, in the USA, Denmark, and Sweden. There were associated changes in attitudes to premarital sexual behaviour which became more permissive in the 1960s.

Schmidt and Sigusch (1972) also reported a series of studies that they carried out in West Germany. They included the adolescent as well as the young adult age groups and made direct comparisons (for the higher educational level only) between sexual behaviours in the 1950s and 1960s. They report a slight yet continuous reduction in the age of first masturbation for higher educational level boys over the full 20-year period (1950 to 1970). The incidence of masturbation for 13–16 year old boys rose in both decades by about 10 per cent. The accumulative incidence of masturbation during the ages of 13–16, in high educational level girls, was unchanged over the 1950s but by 1970 was double that of 1960. However, the changes were largely in respect of a willingness to 'try' the experience, not to repeat it frequently. There was little change during the 1950s in the age of first intercourse for any group, but marked changes during the 1960s, particularly for the more educated groups of both sexes, in the direction of an earlier age at first intercourse. Both male and female teenagers who went on to university and who were born in 1953, had had as much experience of intercourse by the age of 17 as those born in 1945 had acquired by the age of 20. The changes in the less educated between the 1950s and the 1960s were similar, but less marked.

The same kind of change in recent years in the United States is indicated by the *Redbook* (1975) survey of 100,000 females. Despite the caution that needs to be exercised about a non-random sample, several comparisons with the Kinsey data are of interest.

1. The average age of first sexual intercourse is several years earlier. This is confirmed by another large-scale American study by Udry *et al.* (1975).
2. The comparative figures for premarital intercourse before the age of 25 are 33 per cent for Kinsey and 90 per cent for *Redbook*.
3. The restraining influence of religion continues but seems less powerful than in the Kinsey period—75 per cent of the 'strongly religious' reported premarital sex before 25, against 96 per cent of the 'non-religious'.
4. Education beyond 18 still plays a restraining role but again the gap is narrowing.
5. As in the Kinsey sample, premarital intercourse increased the probability of extramarital intercourse. This was more true the younger the first experience of premarital intercourse. Extramarital sex was reported much more frequently than by the Kinsey sample and at a younger age. The highest incidence—nearly half—for extramarital sex was reported by working wives.
6. Satisfaction with marital sex exerts a mildly restraining influence on extramarital sex.

7. A detailed comparison was made between wives who 'experimented' extramaritally, despite reporting themselves satisfied with marital sex and those, equally satisfied, who remained 'monogamous'. The differences were rather few: the monogamous wives were somewhat more likely to experience orgasm on most occasions of intercourse, and less likely to practise oral sex, to have had sexual experience with another woman, or to masturbate. The major differences may lie in the social rules which govern the marriages of those surveyed, the rules for the 'satisfied extramarital' couples being more relaxed, as *Redbook* suggests. No data were collected on this point.

8. Despite the considerable percentage reporting extramarital intercourse, only 4 per cent reported 'mate-swopping'—defined as 'you and your husband exhanging partners with another couple for the purpose of having sexual relations'. A similar result was obtained by Spanier and Cole (1975) who surveyed a carefully constructed sample of a town in the Mid-West of the USA.

9. Kinsey and *Redbook* agree on the small percentage of women reporting homosexual experience—only 3 or 4 per cent of the married women in both samples.

10. Combining the data overviewed by Schmidt and Sigusch with the *Redbook* survey, it is clear that both the sexual behaviour and the subjective experience of the contemporary young woman is somewhat different from that of her mother. She begins sexual intercourse earlier, expects to enjoy it and more often does so, and, despite her greater likelihood of marital pleasure, is more likely to engage in extramarital sex. The sexes seem to be converging on the pattern termed 'permissiveness with commitment' (Schmidt and Sigusch, 1972). The change is associated with the general emancipation of women taking place throughout the Western world. Some sexual differences between men and women do appear to be biologically based and are likely to survive social changes; on average women proceed to orgasm during sexual intercourse more slowly, but have greater capacity for multiple orgasm. Others can now be seen largely to be socially determined: the former higher age of first intercourse and the apparently lower responsiveness to sexual stimuli. However, the fact that some differences between the sexes can now be seen to be socially, rather than biologically, determined, does not undermine the general importance of biological factors determining individual differences *within* the sexes.

THE DEVELOPMENT OF SEXUAL BEHAVIOUR

The Sequence

The Kinsey data implied that sexual behaviour develops sequentially, from arousal to a sexual stimulus through to sexual intercourse. In a more systematic manner, Schofield (1965a) charted the accumulative incidence of sexual experience. This was defined as the percentage of people in his sample (described

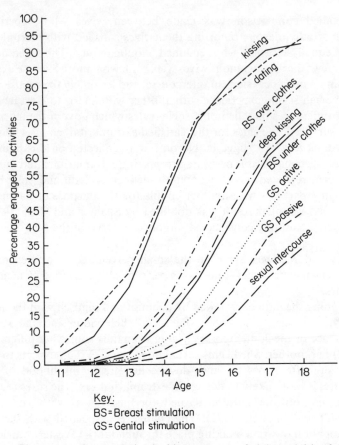

Key:
BS = Breast stimulation
GS = Genital stimulation

Figure 4.1   Accumulative incidence curves of eight activities for
boys. (From Schofield, 1965a)

earlier) who had experienced an activity by a given age. The accumulative
incidence curve of eight activities for the boys is shown in Figure 4.1 and for the
girls in Figure 4.2. From these figures it can be seen (for example) that 15 per cent
of all boys will have experienced deep kissing (the tongue of one partner
entering the mouth of the other) by the age of 14, and by the age of 17 the figure
is 61 per cent. Among the girls aged 15 one in ten had allowed a boy to touch their
genitals, but by 18 nearly half (46 per cent) had experienced passive genital
stimulation. By taking any point along the horizontal line, one can estimate the
number of boys and girls who are expected to be experienced in a particular
activity between the ages of 11 and 18.

Of the boys aged 15 to 17 and of those aged 17 to 19, 22 per cent and 7 per cent,
respectively, had never been out with a girl. By contrast only 9 per cent of the
younger girls (15 to 17) and 4 per cent of the older girls (17 to 19) had never gone
out with a boy. Of the younger boys who had never been out with a girl one-third
said they would like to do so, as compared to half the younger girls who had not

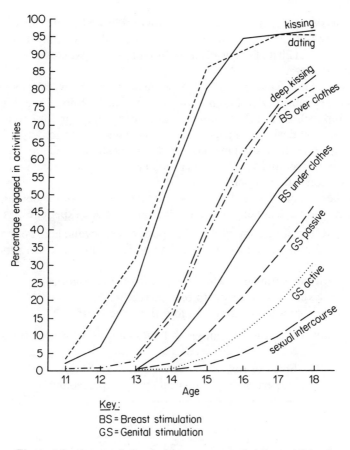

Figure 4.2   Accumulative incidence curves of eight activities for girls. (From Schofield, 1965a)

been dated. More females than males had experienced deep kissing; 72 per cent of all the girls compared to 54 per cent of all the boys. However, only 10 per cent of the younger girls and 14 per cent of the older girls said they liked it very much, compared to 16 per cent of the younger boys and 27 per cent of the older ones, respectively.

Of the older boys 37 per cent had experienced active genital stimulation as compared to 28 per cent who had passive experience. Among the older girls 33 per cent had had passive experience but only 20 per cent had active experience.

Eleven per cent of the younger boys and 30 per cent of the older boys had experienced sexual intercourse at least once, as compared to 6 per cent of the younger girls and 16 per cent of the older ones.

These detailed figures make it clear that the initial activities occurred earlier for girls than boys. Thereafter, the boys caught up with and passed the girls as activities later in the hierarchy were reached, and the gap gradually widened until there was a difference of 14 per cent in those who had experienced intercourse by the age of 19. In general, development was rapid and continuous. It can be concluded that if the lines shown in Figures 4.1 and 4.2 continued at the same rate, by the age of 20 half the boys and a third of the girls would have experienced sexual intercourse.

Differences in sexual behaviour between cultures, between groups within cultures at the same period of time, and between different decades of time for the same group, will be largely concerned with the average age for commencing a given activity, and with the proportion commencing a given activity by a certain age. The *sequence* of development is largely universal; what differs is the *rate* of development. Eventually, almost everyone has experienced sexual intercourse, but some sooner than others.

In further refining his analysis of the sequential nature of the development of sexual behaviour, Schofield described five stages of sex experience, as follows:

Stage 1.   Little or no contact with the opposite sex beyond going out on a date.
Stage 2.   Limited experience of sexual activities, including kissing and limited petting.
Stage 3.   Sexual intimacies which fall short of intercourse.
Stage 4.   Sexual intercourse with one partner.
Stage 5.   Sexual intercourse with more than one partner.

The situation for Schofield's sample (all ages combined) was as follows:

Stage of sex experience	Boys: percentage	Girls: percentage
1	16	7
2	35	46
3	29	35
4	5	7
5	15	5

In the older boys, the difference between educational levels was more pronounced than among the younger ones. Those who went to non-selective schools had the most sexual experience, the selective and private school boys had the least. Non-selective school girls passed more quickly from stage 2 to stages 4 and 5 than did selective or private school girls who seemed more likely to remain at stage 3 for a longer period. These findings suggested that the better educated girls were prepared to allow sexual intimacies as long as they stopped short of full intercourse.

Schofield studied a number of differences between the sexes. He found that girls were more likely than boys to sustain their relationship at each level of sex activity (i.e. to maintain the partnership for a longer period of time). At the more advanced levels of intimacy the boys had more partners than the girls, but the girls were sexually more active (more frequent sexual intercourse, but with the same—presumably older—partner). In general, the girls preferred the more permanent type of relationship in their sexual behaviour, but there was also a small group of girls who engaged in more casual relationships.

Fourteen per cent of the girls who admitted to sexual intercourse did so with casual partners. In the majority of cases if the relationship was at a fairly superficial level then the girl was less likely to go on to intercourse. She was more likely to do so if she saw the boyfriend as a future husband.

Once again, as in the Kinsey survey, it is clear that there were some girls who were more sexually active (even at the level of intercourse) than were many of the boys. Conversely, there were many boys who were less sexually active than were the majority of girls. The picture is one of considerable overlap between the sexes, as in most areas of human behaviour. General statements, intended to apply to *all* members of either sex, are quite inappropriate.

Table 4.1. Sexual Experience Questionnaire Results from Three Separate Studies

	Experience	Brady and Levitt (1965)	Podell and Perkins (1957)	Bentler (1968)
A.	Kissing with tongue contact	16	15	16
B.	Manual manipulation of clad female breast	15	16	15
C.	Manual manipulation of nude female breast	14	14	14
D.	Manual manipulation of female genitalia	13	12	12
E.	Oral contact with female breast	12	13	13
F.	Manual manipulation of your genitalia by a female	11	10	11
G.	Heterosexual intercourse: ventral–ventral	10	11	10
H.	Oral contact with your genitalia by a female	9	9	8
I.	Oral contact with female genitalia	8	8	9
J.	Heterosexual intercourse: ventral–dorsal	7	7	7
K.	Manual manipulation of your genitalia by a male	6	—	—
L.	Manual manipulation of another male's genitalia	5	—	—
M.	Oral contact with your genitalia by a male	4	—	—
N.	Penile–anal penetration of another male	3	—	—
O.	Oral contact with male genitalia	2	—	—
P.	Penile–anal penetration by another male	1	—	—

A Scale of Sexual Activity

This is based on the notion, strongly supported by the Schofield study described above, that the repertory of sexual experience increases in a sequential manner. The most appropriate type of measurement was developed by Guttman (1950) and is known as a Guttman scale. It comprises accumulative items which form a sequential pattern so that if one knows an individual's total score on the scale one can reproduce with a fair degree of accuracy that person's complete pattern of item responses. This type of scale has been used in the sexual field by Bentler (1968).

A similar technique was used by two other sets of workers, Brady and Levitt (1965) and Podell and Perkins (1957). The results for the various samples, all of which comprised unmarried college males, are shown in Table 4.1. The numbers which are inserted in the body of Table 4.1 represent the order of probability of experiencing each of the items. Hence, if any individual had experienced item E it was very likely that he would also have experienced items A, B, C and D. Similarly, if he had experienced item J, he will have experienced all the earlier ones. It should be noted that in the section of Table 4.1 dealing with the Brady and Levitt data, the fact that an individual has checked an item on the homosexual section of the scale (K to P) does *not* imply that he has experienced the heterosexual items.

A survey carried out by Eysenck (1971), which is referred to in detail later in this chapter, used as subjects 231 male and 379 female students in the United Kingdom, all unmarried. Among other questionnaires he administered a 19 item version of the Bentler scale (see Table 4.2). In Table 4.3 the results are shown for nine of these items, for males and females separately, and for the age groups 18, 19,

Table 4.2. Sexual Experience Questionnaire. (From Eysenck, 1971)

1. One minute continuous lip kissing.
2. Manual manipulation of male genitals, over clothes, by female.
3. Kissing nipples of female breasts.
4. Oral manipulation of female genitals.
5. Sexual intercourse, face to face.
6. Manual manipulation of female breasts, over clothes.
7. Oral manipulation of male genitals, by female.
8. Manual manipulation of male genitals to ejaculation, by female.
9. Manual manipulation of female breasts, under clothes.
10. Manual manipulation of male genitals, under clothes, by females.
11. Sexual intercourse, man behind woman.
12. Manual manipulation of female genitals, over clothes.
13. Manual manipulation of female genitals to massive secretions.
14. Mutual oral manipulation of genitals to mutual orgasm.
15. Manual manipulation of female genitals, under clothes.
16. Mutual manual manipulation of genitals.
17. Oral manipulation of male genitals to ejaculation, by female.
18. Mutual manual manipulation of genitals to mutual orgasm.
19. Mutual oral–genital manipulation.

Table 4.3. Percentages of Male and Female Students of Different Ages Who Have Participated in Certain Types of Sexual Activity (Activities Represented by Each Item Number are Listed in Table 4.2). (From Eysenck 1971)

Item:	Males:				Females:			
	18	19	20	21	18	19	20	21
1	96	94	95	93	80	91	93	92
6	96	92	91	92	69	78	82	79
12	83	73	78	85	44	67	73	71
16	62	66	71	83	30	61	68	78
8	53	49	55	58	28	50	60	65
18	30	41	42	48	17	30	34	43
11	9	15	26	21	4	19	26	30
19	13	16	18	19	9	17	24	27
14	9	10	5	14	2	6	5	13

Table 4.4. Percentages of Four Subject Groups with Experience of the Ten Items in the Short Form of the Bentler Sexual Behaviour Inventory. (From Kolaszynska-Carr, 1970)

Item	Male homo-sexual group	Male hetero-sexual group	Female homo-sexual group	Female hetero-sexual group
1. One minute continuous lip kissing, partner of the opposite sex	50.0	98.3	72.3	98.3
2. Manual manipulation of female breasts under clothes	43.1	96.5	67.7	96.7
3. Kissing nipples of female breasts	31.0	93.1	49.2	95.0
4. Manual genital manipulation of male by female	32.8	87.9	49.2	93.3
5. Mutual hand manipulation of genitals with a female/male	31.0	89.6	33.8	93.3
6. Successful heterosexual intercourse	19.0	91.4	27.6	85.0
7. Heterosexual intercourse, male using rear entry to vagina	5.2	70.7	10.8	61.7
8. Oral manipulation of male genital by female	8.6	70.7	21.5	70.0
9. Mutual oral manipulation of genitals with a male/female	6.9	62.1	9.2	65.0
10. Mutual oral manipulation of genitals with a male/female to orgasm	3.5	31.0	3.1	28.3

20, and 21 within each sex separately. The figures given represent the percentage of the samples who claim to have carried out each practice at least once. It can be seen that, by and large, the data form a Guttman scale.

Kolaszynska-Carr (1970) carried out a detailed questionnaire study of many aspects of sexual behaviour, particularly concentrating on the heterosexual experiences and attitudes of homosexual individuals. Her study, which was carried out in Britain, concerned four groups of individuals, with about 60 in each—homosexual and heterosexual, males and females respectively. It will be referred to again in more detail in Chapter 6. One section of the questionnaire consisted of ten heterosexual behaviour items—the short form of the Bentler Sexual Behaviour Inventory. The results obtained are shown in Table 4.4.

Once again, it is clear that for the heterosexual males and females these ten items formed a scale. The male and female heterosexual control groups (MC and FC, respectively) have a much higher proportion of their numbers experienced at every level than the homosexual groups (MH and FH). The disparity, as might be expected, becomes larger as one proceeds from the more frequently experienced items to the less frequently experienced ones.

Thus there is ample evidence that sexual experience operates in the form of a scale, so that if an individual has experienced one of the less usual items he will also have experienced all of the more usual ones. With increasing age higher points are reached on the scale of experience.

BIO-SOCIAL INTERACTION

We can now set out a number of tentative ideas on the ways in which biology and social learning interact. A comprehensive theory of human sexual behaviour must await further research, but any such theory must be based on the concept of *interaction* between biological and social learning components.

1. The age of first sexual intercourse. The basic requirement is that the individual has achieved the appropriate level of biological development. There are

Figure 4.3   Biologically determined upper limits of sexual outlet

considerable individual differences in the rate at which this occurs. Over and above such biologically based differences there are socially learned restraints, the most important of which have been related to being female, practising a religion, and staying in education after the minimum leaving age. Thus in the Kinsey sample, the highest mean age of first intercourse was reported by the actively religious, highly educated, females. The recent data, surveyed above, make it clear that such social restraints are much less powerful than in the past. Individual differences of course remain, but are less affected by social factors. 2. The same is true for the total frequency of sexual outlets of all kinds. The Kinsey data provided powerful evidence for major individual differences in total frequency. Differences within each sex were much greater, on average, than those between the sexes. Today sex differences have diminished even further, but we can expect considerable differences between individuals within each sex to remain. Such differences will be due both to biological and to social factors. We can represent the interaction as follows, for three male individuals, A, B, and C (Figure 4.3).

The heavy lines in Figure 4.3 represent the biologically determined upper limits of frequency of total sexual outlet per week for persons A, B, and C. For person A this is 20, for B about 10, and for C about 1. Social learning factors (previous experiences and their outcomes and current situational stimuli and restraints) will determine how close the actual frequency of outlet for A, B, and C will approach their theoretical maxima. With equal social learning histories and equal current exposure to situational stimuli and constraints, the order of frequency will be first A, then B, then C. The possible range of variation for A is clearly greater than for B or C. The last is biologically determined to have a low frequency of outlet almost irrespective of social learning factors. Conversely, rather powerful social constraints will be required to lower the frequency of outlet of A below that of B, and it is difficult to conceive of it falling to the level of C. It should be noted that the figures given above are rational and illustrative and that the general argument is tentative only.

If social factors continue to decline in importance, the considerable individual differences which will undoubtedly remain will more and more be attributable to biological influences.

PERSONALITY

To what extent are individual variations in sexual behaviour related to well-established measures of personality? We begin with a study which made broad comparisons between the parental and social influences exerted on those who began sexual intercourse relatively early as compared with those who had not yet begun. Next we review research which has related differences in sexual behaviour and attitudes to scores on personality measures.

Experienced and Inexperienced Teenagers

Schofield (1965a) compared those who had begun sexual intercourse (termed the experienced) with those who had not yet done so (the inexperienced). Being strongly influenced by other teenagers was significantly associated with sex experience for both boys and girls. There was an associaton between good looks and sex experiences for both boys and girls, but rather less so for the latter. While there was no association between experience and verbal fluency for girls, there was for the boys.

Many features *failed* to distinguish between the experienced and the inexperienced boys. The experienced boys came from all social classes and from all sections of the community. Their position in the family had no effect, nor did it make any difference if they came from a church-going home. Experienced boys were not more likely to come from broken homes (where the father was dead or absent). The parents' marital happiness or the number of times they had moved home had no effect. Mothers who went out to work and relationships with father were not important; only where there were poor relations with the mother were the boys more likely to be experienced (which suggests that a *close* relationship with the mother might inhibit heterosexual development—see Chapter 6 for a related view concerning the development of a homosexual orientation). Experience was related to type of school only slightly, nor was it related to whether the school was day or boarding, or to level of formal sex education. Youth clubs did not have much effect, nor did time spent watching TV or owning a car or a motor cycle. There were few signs in early childhood which could be used to predict the later sexual behaviour of the male teenager.

Several features successfully discriminated between experienced and inexperienced boys. The parents of inexperienced boys knew where they spent their leisure and insisted that they return home in the evenings at a definite time. Experienced boys tended not to go to church and to have less satisfactory school careers. They disliked school, had more school problems, and many left school as soon as they could. Even controlling the age of leaving school, the experienced boys seemed to have had more jobs than the other boys. Despite their frequent job changes the experienced boys tended to earn more money than the inexperienced ones, and Schofield speculates that this may be connected in some cases with physical energy and strength, another indication of which was that the inexperienced boys were less likely to be interested in sport. There was a positive association between the age of reaching puberty and degree of sexual experience, and a strong relationship with the degree of conformity to the teenage culture—experienced boys were more likely to be against adult standards and outsiders of any kind. They were sceptical about adult moral standards and opposed restrictions. Not only did the experienced boys go to bars more often, but they appeared to get drunk more often.

Many of the features which discriminated the sexually experienced boys were the same for the *girls*, but some were different. There was no difference in the number that came from broken homes, moved homes more often, whose mothers were working, whose parents went to church; nor were religious denomination, position in the family, or social class, discriminating features. In general, the experienced girls did not have less favourable backgrounds than the other girls, but experienced girls more often reported poor relations with *both* parents and there were more reports of marital difficulties among parents. As opposed to the experienced boys, experience was related to antipathy to family loyalty, dislike of home restrictions and preference for friends' advice. Schofield (1965a, p. 206) comments: 'Experienced girls have gone much further than experienced boys in rejecting family influences. Relations with both parents were often strained and they were less likely to receive advice on sexual matters from their parents. When they did get this advice, they were more likely to reject it.' For teenage girls to be sexually experienced represented a greater degree of social deviance (at the time of the study) than it did for boys..

In matters of parental discipline the experienced girls were like the experienced boys, as they were in religious influence, school records, jobs, and rate of physical development. They began dating and kissing earlier than the experienced boys and they were more likely than the boys to have a steady boyfriend than were the latter to have a steady girlfriend. There was a strong tendency among the experienced girls, as among the experienced boys, to go for advice to friends of their own age, rather than to parents or other adults. The gregariousness found among the experienced boys was not quite so apparent among the experienced girls. The important difference for girls is the person they go with; experienced girls were much more likely to go to cinemas etc. with a boy than with another girl. Like the boys they went to bars more often, got drunk more often, and smoked more cigarettes than their less experienced sisters. They went to more unsupervised late night parties, often when most of the other people there were adults. Although far fewer girls than boys had ever been in trouble with the Law, those who had appeared before a Court were more likely to be sexually experienced. They were in favour of intercourse before marriage, for both sexes. The main difference between teenage boys and girls who had sexual experience was that girls, in general, were subject to greater attempts at control by the family. Hence, there were more family pressures to overcome and more family loyalty to be derogated. Apart from this, female permissiveness is considered by Schofield to be essentially a personality characteristic, as in boys, but it was combined with an 'outgoing hedonism' in boys, and a 'rejection of family influences' in girls.

Schofield's findings suggests that male/female differences are at least partially related to the greater social pressures exerted on females. It would be expected that as the social training influences which are brought to bear on boys and girls, and the behaviour expected of them, become more similar, so will their sexual behaviours and attitudes. Thus the differences, found on average, between individuals according to *gender* would decline—as we have found to be the case in recent years.

Personality and Sexual Behaviour

Schofield (1965a) argues that a degree of extraversion is a prerequisite for premarital sexual experience, basing this on the Eysenckian notion that the learning of social rules is easier for introverts than for extraverts. As one of the social rules, according to Schofield, is the avoidance of premarital sexual intercourse, it would follow that introverts would learn this more easily than extraverts. In general, Schofield suggests that extraversion is likely to be associated with a more active sexual life, but he also implicates such purely situational factors as the opportunity for contact with the opposite sex and the facilities to make use of that opportunity.

Eysenck (1971) took up Schofield's suggestion that extraversion will be related to sexual behaviour. He studied several hundred male and female students by means of questionnaires. One was a version of the Bentler scale of sexual behaviour, described earlier in this chapter, and the other was the then most recent product of Eysenck's work on the questionnaire measurement of personality, the PEN which provides measures of three dimensions, psychoticism, extraversion, and neuroticism. Eysenck's theory of personality (e.g. Eysenck, 1967) expects that individual differences in the three major dimensions, P, E, and N, all of which are considered to be largely biological in origin, will relate to many areas of complex behaviour from cigarette smoking to motor skill learning. He and his colleagues have produced a vast number of studies over the past 30 years.

Eysenck derived the following predictions from his general theory of personality: extraverts will have intercourse earlier than introverts; they will have it more frequently; with more different partners per unit time; in more diverse positions than introverts; and will indulge in more varied sexual behaviour. On the whole he expected correlations with neuroticism to be negative. High N scorers are deemed to be characterized by a labile autonomic nervous system, and thus are susceptible to fear and anxiety to a degree which may make them less likely to indulge in sexual behaviour, particularly premaritally, than those low in N. He notes that features such as hostility, impersonality, and cruelty play a major part in the dimension of psychoticism (P), but found it difficult to make specific predictions, although he expected positive correlations with those items which were related to an impersonal view of sex.

There were very few significant relationships with either P or N, but a rather large number of significant ones with E. However, it should be noted that the correlations obtained, though usually in the predicted direction, were still rather small so that the majority of variation between individuals in sexual experience was not accounted for by extraversion scores.

A major criticism of Eysenck's study is that no data were provided on the rate of return of the questionnaires sent out. A low return rate is always grounds for scepticism. In the case of those who did return their questionnaires, it is possible that extraverts may admit more than do introverts, whenever the behaviour in question is subject to some degree of social disapproval (the questionnaires used by Eysenck were of course self-report scales).

However, some support for Eysenck's prediction is derived from findings obtained by Giese and Schmidt (1968), cited by Eysenck (1971). They used shortened scales for the measurement of E and N and administered questionnaires of sexual behaviour to over 6,000 German students, both male and female, most of whom were unmarried. The rate of development of sexual behaviour was greater for extraverts than for introverts, as was the median frequency of intercourse per month, and the number of partners in the past 12 months. The results were more clear-cut for the males than for the females.

Personality and Sexual Attitudes

The predictions which relate sexual behaviour to the Eysenckian view of personality have already been outlined. The sample used by Eysenck (1970) to study the relationship of sexual attitudes to personality was that described above in connection with the study of sexual behaviour and personality (Eysenck, 1971). In addition to the PEN and the Bentler inventory all subjects filled in a sexual attitude inventory consisting of about 100 items. The inventory is shown in Table 4.5, as are the percentages of 'Yes' answers obtained from the male and female subjects respectively. The subjects were divided into three groups, for each personality dimension in turn (e.g. high P, average P, and low P; of course, some individuals might be in the high group for the P measure, the average group for the E and the low group for the N, and so on).

Table 4.5. Inventory of Attitudes to Sex. (From Eysenck, 1970)

THIS QUESTIONNAIRE IS ANONYMOUS, TO ENCOURAGE TRUTHFUL ANSWERS

Read each statement carefully, then underline the 'yes' or the 'no' answer, depending on your views. If you just cannot decide, underline the '?' reply. Please answer every question. There are no right or wrong answers. Don't think too long over each question; try to give an immediate answer which represents your feelings on each issue. Some questions are similar to others; there are good reasons for getting at the same attitude in slightly different ways.

Percentage 'YES' answers

	Male	Female
1. The opposite sex will respect you more if you are not too familiar with them.	38	59
2. Sex without love ('impersonal sex') is highly unsatisfactory.	49	80
3. Conditions have to be just right to get me excited sexually.	21	43
4. All in all I am satisfied with my sex life.	40	60
5. Virginity is a girl's most valuable possession.	16	24
6. I think only rarely about sex.	4	13
7. Sometimes it has been a problem to control my sex feelings.	46	44
8. Masturbation is unhealthy.	7	21
9. If I loved a person I could do anything with them.	55	46
10. I get pleasant feelings from touching my sexual parts.	61	37
11. I have been deprived sexually.	25	8

Percentage 'YES' answers

	Male	Female
12. It is disgusting to see animals having sex relations in the street.	5	6
13. I do not need to respect a woman/man, or love her/him, in order to enjoy petting and/or intercourse with her.	43	12
14. It is alright for children to see their parents naked.	64	74
15. I am rather sexually unattractive.	10	5
16. Frankly, I prefer people of my own sex.	3	2
17. Sex contacts have never been a problem to me.	35	41
18. It is disturbing to see necking in public.	12	23
19. Sexual feelings are sometimes unpleasant to me.	11	16
20. Something is lacking in my sex life.	50	26
21. My sex behaviour has never caused me any trouble.	43	36
22. My love life has been disappointing.	39	23
23. I never had many dates.	36	26
24. I consciously try to keep sex thoughts out of my mind.	2	7
25. I have felt guilty about sex experiences.	29	41
26. It wouldn't bother me if the person I married were not a virgin.	68	73
27. I had some bad sex experiences when I was young.	15	13
28. Perverted thoughts have sometimes bothered me.	28	18
29. At times I have been afraid of myself for what I might do sexually.	19	26
30. I have had conflicts about my sex feelings towards a person of my own sex.	16	9
31. I have many friends of the opposite sex.	71	80
32. I have strong sex feelings but when I get a chance I can't seem to express myself.	23	12
33. It doesn't take much to get me excited sexually.	66	31
34. My parents' influence has inhibited me sexually.	30	25
35. Thoughts about sex disturb me more than they should.	12	7
36. People of my own sex frequently attract me.	4	4
37. There are some things I wouldn't want to do with anyone.	53	47
38. Children should be taught about sex.	94	97
39. I could get sexually excited at any time of the day or night.	88	69
40. I understand homosexuals.	44	35
41. I think about sex almost every day.	84	52
42. One should not experiment with sex before marriage.	7	21
43. I get excited sexually very easily.	60	27
44. The thought of a sex orgy is disgusting to me.	18	65

Percentage 'YES' answers

	Male	Female
45. It is better not to have sex relations until you are married.	6	31
46. I find the thought of a coloured sex partner particularly exciting.	24	3
47. I like to look at sexy pictures.	61	8
48. My conscience bothers me too much.	18	26
49. My religious beliefs are against sex.	7	13
50. Sometimes sexual feelings overpower me.	32	27
51. I feel nervous with the opposite sex.	25	15
52. Sex thoughts drive me almost crazy.	6	2
53. When I get excited I can think of nothing else but satisfaction.	24	15
54. I feel at ease with people of the opposite sex.	66	80
55. I don't like to be kissed.	2	3
56. It is hard to talk with people of the opposite sex.	12	6
57. I didn't learn the facts of life until I was quite old.	26	23
58. I feel more comfortable when I am with my own sex.	24	16
59. I enjoy petting.	92	78
60. I worry a lot about sex.	22	13
61. The Pill should be universally available.	84	65
62. Seeing a person nude doesn't interest me.	11	43
63. Sometimes thinking about sex makes me very nervous.	16	20
64 Women who get raped are often partly responsible themselves.	57	53
65. Perverted thoughts have sometimes bothered me.	26	18
66. I am embarrassed to talk about sex.	9	8
67. Young people should learn about sex through their own experience.	34	23
68. Sometimes the woman should be sexually aggressive.	88	64
69. Sex jokes disgust me.	4	22
70. I believe in taking my pleasures where I find them.	44	7
71. A person should learn about sex gradually by experimenting with it.	52	42
72. Young people should be allowed out at night without being too closely checked.	68	54
73. Did you ever feel like humiliating your sex partner?	20	12
74. I would particularly protect my children from contacts with sex.	5	9
75. Self-relief is not dangerous so long as it is done in a healthy way.	74	56
76. I get very excited when touching a woman's breasts.	57	45
77. I have been involved with more than one sex affair at the same time.	32	14

Percentage 'YES' answers

	Male	Female
78. Homosexuality is normal for some people.	74	70
79. It is alright to seduce a person who is old enough to know what they are doing.	73	35
80. Do you ever feel hostile to your sex partner?	37	40
81. I like to look at pictures of nudes.	63	10
82. Buttocks excite me.	42	8
83. If you had the chance to see people making love, without being seen, would you take it?	41	12
84. Pornographic writings should be freely allowed to be published.	59	32
85. Prostitution should be legally permitted.	62	32
86. Decisions about abortion should be the concern of no one but the woman concerned.	52	47
87. There are too many immoral plays on TV.	6	13
88. The dual standard of morality is natural, and should be continued.	32	26
89. We should do away with marriage entirely.	9	2
90. Men marry to have intercourse; women have intercourse for the sake of marriage.	7	3
91. There should be no censorship, on sexual grounds, of plays and films.	63	39

PLEASE UNDERLINE THE
CORRECT ANSWER

92. If you were invited to see a 'blue' film, would you: (a) Accept (b) Refuse	80	37
93. If you were offered a highly pornographic book, would you: (a) Accept it (b) Reject it	76	40
94. If you were invited to take part in an orgy, would you: (a) Take part (b) Refuse	61	4

95. Given availability of a partner, would you prefer
   to have intercourse:
   (a) Never   (d) Twice a week
   (b) Once a month   (e) 3–5 times a week
   (c) Once a week   (f) Every day
                                (g) More than once a day

96. Have you ever suffered from impotence?
   (a) Never   (d) Often
   (b) Once or twice   (e) More often than not
   (c) Several times   (f) Always

97. Have you ever suffered from ejaculatio praecox
   (premature ejaculation)?
   (a) Very often   (d) Not very often
   (b) Often   (e) Hardly ever
   (c) Middling   (f) Never

98. At what age did you have your first intercourse?

This large number of items were subjected to successive factor analyses, the result being two clear-cut factors, which were almost identical for the two sexes. Factor 1 combined several aspects of sexual problems and sexual deprivation and was termed *Sexual Pathology*. The second factor combined permissiveness and active sexuality and was entitled *Sexual Libido*.

Sexual pathology was correlated primarily with N (0.40 for the women and 0.47 for the men). The correlations with P were very small. Those with E were negative and not very large (-0.23 for the women and -0.17 for the men). Sexual libido was positively correlated with P (0.40 for the women and 0.19 for the men). Neuroticism was also correlated with libido but the correlations were of interest only for the women (0.29 as opposed to only 0.06 for the men). Perhaps the most disappointing finding in terms of the general theory was that extraversion was correlated with sexual libido only very slightly (0.13 for the women and 0.15 for the men).

These results are rather less impressive than were the relationships between sexual behaviour and extraversion. The sizeable correlation between N and the factor termed sexual pathology could be explained by an increased tendency for high N individuals to be aware of their own problems, to reflect on them, and to report on them more frequently than individuals who are low on N.

It is important to remind ourselves that Eysenck's theory of personality is essentially biological; all three dimensions are considered to be genetically based. This relates to our general emphasis on the importance of biological variables for human sexual behaviour.

OVERVIEW

Although the processes, social and biological, of sexual behaviour are universal there are vast individual differences in a number of key aspects, particularly in frequency of outlet and the range of outlets experienced. Major American, British, and European surveys have shown that differences within each sex are greater than those between the sexes. The latter gap continues to diminish as socio-sexual opportunities for females become more equal to those for males. A current survey might not find the striking age gap in maximum frequency of outlet found by the Kinsey workers over 20 years ago: mid to late teens for males and late twenties for females.

A small proportion of the population is solely homosexual throughout the life span; a somewhat larger proportion has experienced both homosexual and heterosexual outlets with a tendency to polarization with increasing age. Both religious practice and higher education tend to slow down the rate of development through the sequence of sexual behaviours from dating through to sexual intercourse with a series of partners and the use of a variety of positions.

Biological and social influences combine to produce the details of individual variation; a full account of sexual behaviour requires that due weight is attached to both factors. There are some relationships between individual differences, social and sexual behaviour and standard measures of personality such as extraversion, neuroticism, and psychoticism, although the correlations are not very powerful.

CHAPTER 5

Problems of Sexual Response

Sexual behaviours bring great pleasure to many people: but they bring distress to others, because of a number of problems which either prevent the behaviours occurring except in a minimal fashion, or which limit the satisfaction experienced by one or both participants. In this chapter we discuss the most common of these problems. We do so in the context of heterosexual behaviours between couples, but in principle, we can expect some of them to affect equally participants in homosexual encounters. However, the overwhelming weight of work by researchers and therapists has been concerned with the heterosexual context.

The monumental studies of treatment by Masters and Johnson have been published in the past ten years, a period which has seen also a flood of popular articles seeking to bring information about what has been called 'the new sex therapists' to the general public. We shall describe the elements of sexual encounters which are subjectively reported as satisfactory, the major types of problem which prevent or reduce satisfaction, some tentative explanations for their development and the major methods of treatment.

For sexual intercourse to occur at all requires dissimilar contributions from the two sexes. The male must develop and retain an erection long enough to enter the vagina and ejaculate. All that is required on the part of the female is the absence of vaginal spasm so that penile penetration can occur. However, for the subjective experience of intercourse to be reported as fully satisfactory by both partners a great deal more is necessary: the sexual arousal of the female as well as the male, and the maintenance by the male of his erection without ejaculation long enough for the cycle of female sexual response, described in Chapter 2, to proceed to a point at which orgasm is more or less inevitable. At this point both partners may complete their orgasm. Over a period of time a mutually satisfactory sexual relationship for any given couple means that the actual frequency of intercourse corresponds to the preferred frequency of both partners, that they use methods of heightening sexual arousal acceptable to both, and that orgasm is achieved by both partners in a significant proportion of attempts at intercourse (arbitrarily defined as 50 per cent by Masters and Johnson). Sexual intercourse is a skilled performance, the success of which requires training and practice, as do all skilled performances. In addition it usually requires mutual subjective attraction and appropriate circumstances, such as privacy. Its success is impaired by many factors, as we shall see, including the general social attitudes held concerning sexual behaviour and specific prior learning experience, as well as various physical causes.

DESCRIPTION

Introduction

Problems occur at all major points along the sequence of events which comprise sexual intercourse. In the case of the male they include the development and maintenance of his erection and the timing of his ejaculation. Those of the female comprise both the initial entry of the penis and the sequence of responses termed the orgasm. It is most important of all to note that the problem is often that of the particular *couple*, rather than that of either partner alone. Key related concepts are those of the *timing* and the *matching* of the entire sequence of mutual acts and consequent responses.

Problems of the Male

Male sexual problems consist of abnormalities of erection and abnormalities of ejaculation in the context of sexual intercourse. Abnormalities of erection are divided into acute and insidious onset impotence; abnormalities of ejaculation into premature ejaculation and delayed or absent ejaculation.

Impotence. This is defined as a persistent inability to obtain an erection sufficient to allow orgasm and intravaginal ejaculation (Loewenstein, 1947; Hastings, 1963). Problems of impotence are divided by Cooper (1968) into those of (a) *acute (quick) onset* and those of (b) *insidious (slow) onset*. Ansari (1975) has suggested that those of slow onset may be further divided into two groups; the first in which there is long-standing anxiety about the partner's sexual response, with marked difficulties in the relationship, and the second in which a decline in sexual powers is accompanied by anxiety or relationship difficulties.

Table 5.1

	Group 1 Acute onset	Group 2 Slow onset (marital discord group)	Group 3 Slow onset (physiological group)
Age at first inter-course	18.7 years	18.4 years	23.8 years
Frequency of SI/week 2nd year marriage	3.5	3.5	3.0
1 year prior to impotence	3.0	1.5	0.5

Acute onset impotence tends to occur in young males (mean age 29.0 years in Ansari's (1975) study). The problem, which is mainly manifested by failure of erection, begins suddenly in response to a clear physical or psychological event. People with acute onset impotence show evidence of a normal sex drive—their frequency of intercourse one year prior to the onset of impotence is closely comparable with their rate in the second year of marriage. These data differ from those of the slow onset groups as can be seen in Table 5.1 (Ansari, 1975).

Problems of ejacualtion are divided into those in which ejaculation occurs much too early for the partner and those in which it occurs too late or even not at all. The former is much more frequent.

Premature ejaculation. This is a problem in which orgasm and ejaculation persistently occur before, or immediately on, penetration of the vagina (Shapiro, 1943). The mean age of onset of premature ejaculation is similar to that of the acute onset impotence group, being approximately 27 years. Clients usually complain because of the female's frustration at her inability to achieve orgasm. As masturbators during adolescence this group have strong rapid erections with rapid ejaculations. Clear signs of anxiety are common when these individuals find themselves under stress.

Delayed or absent ejaculation. This refers to the persistent delay of ejaculation, well beyond that of the partner's orgasm and in some cases the complete absence of ejaculation. Masters and Johnson (1965b) term the overall problem ejaculatory incompetence. The mean age of onset of the problem is similar to that of slow onset impotence, being about 28 years, and the sequence of development of the two problems is also similar.

Problems of the Female

Full enjoyment by the female is impaired both by vaginal spasm and difficulties in achieving orgasm, even if penetration occurs.

Vaginal spasm (vaginismus). This is a spasm of the muscles of the lower third of the vagina. It may be present in various degrees and when fully developed it renders vaginal penetration by the penis impossible. Anxiety, pain, and vaginal spasm form the components of a vicious circle.

Problems of the orgasm ('orgasmic dysfunction', 'frigidity'). Frigidity is an older term which is rapidly being replaced by Masters and Johnson's term 'orgasmic dysfunction'. It can be defined as an impairment of a woman's capacity for genital sensory pleasure and related emotional experience. The definition implies the capacity for orgasm, but it should be remembered that sexual intercourse is a complex emotional and behavioural sequence which makes different initial requirements on the couples but which requires sexual arousal in both partners for the completion of mutual orgasm. It is possible for the male to experience 'satisfactory' sexual stimulation and orgasm without the female being brought to orgasm or indeed to any state of sexual arousal. However, sexual intercourse does require the absence of vaginal spasm. In his review of female sexual behaviour, Kinsey (1953) reported that 95 per cent of self-masturbation led to orgasm, but 25–30 per cent of his sample had impaired orgasmic response to sexual intercourse. He concluded that masturbation was the most effective form of sexual outlet for women. Masters and Johnson (1966) in their work on the direct laboratory observation of the sexual response in females, also concluded that masturbation produced the most intense orgasmic experiences. They found that intercourse produces a less intense orgasm than both self-masturbation and masturbation by a male; these findings may not hold good for sex play in private away from a laboratory situation and are in any event only group averages from which there will be wide individual variation.

Despite their marked potential for orgasm many women have orgasmic difficulties in intercouse. Kinsey (1953) reported that 22 per cent of married women between 16 and 20 years, 12 per cent aged 21–25 years and 5 per cent aged over 30 years had never achieved orgasm. Masters and Johnson (1970) define *primary orgasmic dysfunction* as the state of never having achieved orgasm by *any* method of stimulation, and *secondary orgasmic dysfunction* as a failure to achieve coital orgasm with any partner or a specific partner after already having experienced masturbatory orgasm. The Kinsey results suggest that secondary orgasmic dysfunction occurs in 25–30 per cent of women, while primary dysfunction occurs in 5–22 per cent of women, depending on their age. Such figures are specific both to the time of a particular study and the population taking part and are always affected by the way the questions are asked, by whom and in what circumstances. Nevertheless, it can be assumed that substantial numbers of women, even today, have either never experienced orgasm, either alone or with a partner or have done so at some time in the past but are no longer doing so at present.

EXPLANATIONS

Problems of the Male

Failures of erection (impotence). Erectile impotence has a number of causes, more than one of which may be involved for any particular individual: organic diseases and consequences; the first experience of sexual intercourse; unfavourable outcome of specific sexual encounters and an exceptionally high level of general anxiety. The most common specific *organic* causes are as follows: the effects of surgical operations; vascular, neurological, endocrine, and metabolic diseases; certain medications such as antidepressant drugs. A further organic or biological cause is the general low level of sexual drive frequently associated with the slow onset group which shows a gradual, progressive, fall-off of sexual responsiveness over many months or years. Cooper (1968) suggests that in this group associated anxiety occurs *after* coital failures and not before as in the acute onset group. Anxiety is thus seen as a consequence of the impotence rather than its cause. In Table 5.1 group 3, termed physiological, showed a gradual waning of sexual drive and potency without any evidence of major failures of the general relationship between the couple. Racey *et al.* (1973) measured serum testosterone in impotent men and found that the level in the physiological group was lower than in the other two groups, in both of which impotence is of psychological origin. Cooper *et al.* (1970) reported markedly reduced urinary testosterone in chronically impotent men. In this group erections in response to fantasy are very rare and early morning erections—normally associated with a full bladder—are also infrequent. The evidence to date therefore strongly suggests that among the slow onset impotents there is a subgroup in whom there is evidence of waning physiological powers of erection and an absence of psychological causes for their impotence.

The *first sexual intercourse* is often marked by exaggerated expectations and limited skills on the part of both partners; the frequent result is a failure to maintain the erection, followed by much self-blame and increased anxiety before the next attempt. If this fails also, the chances of still further failure are heightened. Such examples of erectile impotence are likely to occur quite frequently, and most seem to improve without any formal help, perhaps due to a more relaxed and hence relaxing partner. In some instances the problem will continue with the partner, the ability to maintain an erection to orgasm being confined to self-masturbation. A continuation of the problem is also more likely if the person concerned has only limited access to more skilled partners and/or he habitually rehearses his failures, particularly sexual failures. The occurrence of erectile impotence after a period of satisfactory performance may also be due to psychological factors, such as the sudden or gradual withdrawal of affection by the partner, or of the partner's approval of his performance, particularly if she makes very clear, whether verbally, non-verbally, or both, his current failure to satisfy her sexually. The effects of such feedbacks of failure may be immediate (acute onset group) or gradual (slow onset, psychological, group). The effects depend on such variables as the intensity with which the feedback is conveyed, the ability of the individual to attribute his failure to causes less related to his self-esteem, such as drinking alcohol immediately beforehand, as well as the general importance he attaches to the approval of his partner. Eventually the various features of the situation in which unsatisfactory intercourse occurs become cues for failure. The anticipation of failure means that fewer attempts are made—the individual may try to rationalize this by stating that his 'drive' is less than it was (a biological attribution) or that he is 'less interested' (psychological attribution). The outcome is a continued decline in attempts at intercourse with his partner, and continued failure when intercourse is attempted.

Premature ejaculation. Johnson (1964) reported that his group of premature ejaculators reached puberty earlier than did males with other sexual problems and also had a higher frequency of masturbation before marriage and of intercourse during the early years of marriage. He suggests that this indicates a high level of sexual arousability. Although high arousability does not in itself inevitably result in premature ejaculation, it is likely to make it more difficult for the individual concerned to delay his ejaculation until the partner has reached the stage of orgasmic inevitability. Masters and Johnson rightly point out the difficulties in defining the problem because of the variability of the partner's sexual responsivity and the different levels of skill which both partners bring to the problem of coping with the differing rates of arousal in males and females. They emphasize the learning element in the development of premature ejaculation, pointing out that many of their patients had early 'secret' sexual encounters when speed of ejaculation was important, both so as to avoid detection and to reduce guilt. The behaviour of premature ejaculation is thus developed, in response to a particular situation, by an individual predisposed to be highly and strongly aroused. It then generalizes to another situation in which speed or the avoidance of guilt are no longer relevant. The common factor in the two situations, responsible for the generalization, is sexual arousal to a partner. Unless the current partner is aware of the difficulty, and can help him to adapt to the new, more relaxed situation, formal help may be needed. It can thus be seen that premature ejaculation has both a biological basis and important learned components.

Delayed or absent ejaculation. The problem is relatively infrequent compared with the other male sexual problems—Masters and Johnson (1970) report having seen only 17 cases in 11 years. They concluded that psychological factors played a major role in development. Any explanation must account for the fact that the sequence of sexual response seems to proceed appropriately up to the point at which ejaculation would normally occur. At this point the sequence either stops or is so delayed as to lag well behind the partner's orgasm. Some cases gradually develop secondary impotence (Cooper, 1968), that is they become unable to maintain an erection. Whether this is due to a biologically based gradual reduction in sexual arousal is not clear. Alternatively, for some of these individuals, the effect of increased anxiety, consequent on criticism by the partner, whether real or apparent, is to inhibit the ejaculatory mechanism, rather than affecting the earlier-occurring erection. In other cases, there may be not much more than a problem in timing the sequence of responses—it is the female member of the pair who is quicker to orgasm rather than the male, as is more often the case.

Problems of the Female

Vaginal spasm. Haslam (1974) states that pain caused by attempts at penile penetration of either the vulva or anus is a common finding in the clinical history of women with frigidity and vaginismus. Dyspareunia (pain on intercourse, often associated with perineal spasm) is an important factor related to female sexual dysfunction because it can lead to a conditioned anxiety response to sex, and pain directly inhibits sexual arousal. Dyspareunia is either superficial or deep. Superficial dyspareunia has a number of causes including infections, low circulating oestrogen, use of vaginal deodorants and failure of vaginal lubrication. The causes of deep dyspareunia are almost exclusively related to conditions which cause cervical pain.

Problems of the orgasm. First it is important to point out that temporary difficulties with the orgasm are very common and are associated with a wide range of life-events not in themselves of a sexual nature. These include temporary physical ill-health, such as viral illnesses, and depressions. The weeks immediately after the woman has given birth, particularly if it was a traumatic one, or the new infant is exhausting, are also associated with temporary loss of interest and difficulties with the orgasm.

The two major theories of longer term orgasmic difficulties, as is the case with theories of behaviour in general, can be termed biological and psychological. Masters and Johnson (1966) claim that orgasmic ability is not related to the size or the position of the clitoris. Even so their treatment does include exercises designed to strengthen the muscle tone of the pubococcygeus muscle and the activity of this muscle may produce clitoral stimulation. Deutsch (1968) reported that the Masters and Johnson exercises produced improvement in 65 per cent of secondary non-orgasmic women. It seems clear that the anatomy of the pudendum and the function of the pubococcygeus muscles are factors which should to taken into account in cases of orgasmic dysfunction and exercises designed to increase muscle tone in the genital region may be useful.

Another biologically based view argues that there are two types of female orgasm, one due to stimulation of the clitoris, the other to stimulation of the vagina. It was thought until recently (e.g. Kinsey, 1953) that the latter was rather deficient in nerve endings, so that vaginal stimulation was much less likely to lead to orgasm than clitoral stimulation. It would follow that all that was required was that the partner should stimulate the clitoris for orgasm to follow. However, the perineal muscles of the vagina are well endowed with proprioceptive nerves so that this particular biological explanation must be rejected.

The view of most sex therapists and researchers is that most orgasmic difficulties in women are likely to be due to social learning experiences. Indeed, Runciman (1975) asserts that 97 per cent of all problems of female orgasm are psychological in origin. Masters and Johnson (1970) have proposed a theory of orgasmic difficulties based on the volunteers for their studies on sexual response and on clients who had sought their help. Neither sample is fully representative of the population at large and as yet there has been no research carried out on the sexual difficulties of those who have not asked for help from sex therapists. Masters and Johnson conceptualize sexual behaviour as involving two interacting systems, first the biophysical system—essentially the biological apparatus used in sexual behaviour—and secondly the psychosocial system—a set of values and attitudes relating to sex. Strong negative signals from either system cause orgasmic dysfunction. For women most of the negative signals come from the psychosocial system, due to the generally negative attitudes concerning female sexuality in our culture. Sex is therefore seen as being frequently punished, and women are rarely honoured or unreservedly praised for being sexual. These learned attitudes cause sexual feelings to be denied. Masters and Johnson propose different psychological causes for primary and secondary dysfunction. For example, primary orgasmic dysfunction is often caused by, or associated with, strong religious prohibitions, or with the woman regarding her partner as in some way second best and not matching up to her value system. Secondary dysfunction is related to such factors as masturbatory guilt, change in attitude towards the partner, or to an acquired homosexual preference.

A General Approach to the Explanation of Sexual Problems

1. Failure to achieve arousal. If one partner is not initially aroused by the other, the most skilled sexual technique may well prove ineffective. There are a number of possible explanations for this initial failure of arousal. First, one partner may never have liked or been in love with the other. Nevertheless, the early period of their relationship was marked by strenuous attempts to 'please' the other because this was seen to be appropriate early in marriage. For example, the female simulates orgasm, or the male maintains his erection by thinking of other, more desirable, partners. At a later stage one or both give up these attempts to simulate emotions they do not actually feel. A second possibility is that although the partners were emotionally aroused by each other earlier in the partnership, both enjoying sexual intercourse, one or both no longer loves their original partner or has fallen in love with another partner. Once again both may continue to give pleasure to each other by thinking of the new lover during intercourse, but eventually this device proves ineffective or unsatisfactory and 'frigidity' or 'impotence' develops.

In addition to the initial and eventual attitudes to the particular partner we have described above, there are other attitudes which reduce the probability of achieving orgasm by either partner. Such general attitudes exert their effect either by themselves or in combination with the attitude to the particular partner. They include the following: general disgust relating to sexual activities; fear of being seen or heard during sex; sexual shyness; fear of failure to satisfy any partner; general dislike of being touched by males; dislike of the opposite sex either sexually or in general; pain on intercourse (dyspareunia); fear of specific body parts being seen naked, perhaps because of a belief that the particular part is strange or unusual in some way (sometimes termed dysmorphophobia); phobias of contamination with body fluids; fear of pregnancy. Such general anxieties have their origins in particular social learning experiences which include one or more of the following: social training that sexual arousal is disgusting, or that sexual intercourse is unpleasant—such training may be given by parents, friends, the Church, school, and indeed the full range of social influences to which everyone may be exposed. Next there may have been particular personal experiences. These include one or several unpleasant sexual encounters with a desired but in fact rough or insensitive partner, sexual assault by an unwelcome partner, detection and punishment during a forbidden act of sexual intercourse, and pregnancy, possibly with damaging effects on career and social life. Finally, there may well be a combination of several of the above explanations. An initial expectation that sexual intercourse will be unpleasant increases the probability that actual sexual experiences will turn out badly. In turn these outcomes reduce the possibility of an enjoyable sexual life with even the most skilled partner. When both partners have gloomy initial expectations, negative earlier experiences, poor techniques and little love for each other, a mutual failure for sexual arousal to occur is almost inevitable.

In addition to the above psychological causes for failures of sexual arousal, it also seems to be the case that a number of men and women never experience sexual arousal from any source (Kinsey, 1947, 1953). The explanation is likely to include the following factors, existing separately, or in combination: an exceptionally low level of biologically based sexual arousability (drive); infrequent or absent exposure to sexual stimuli or sexual learning experience; extremely unpleasant social training concerning sexual behaviour given *before* exposure to real life sexual stimuli.

2. Failure of arousal to reach orgasm. In this case both partners have experienced an increase in sexual arousal from one of a number of sources: a partner, their own thoughts, or external stimuli such as pictures or films. Probably the most important reason why arousal occurs but orgasm does not, is a difference in the time taken by the two partners to achieve orgasm. Most men reach orgasm after penetration markedly faster than do most women. This means that in the case of many couples the male has completed his sexual response cycle while the female is still at an early stage of hers. Because the male has ejaculated and entered the refractory stage he usually ceases to stimulate his partner so that there is a much reduced possibility of her achieving orgasm. Repeated experience of this unpleasant cessation of stimulation is likely to lead

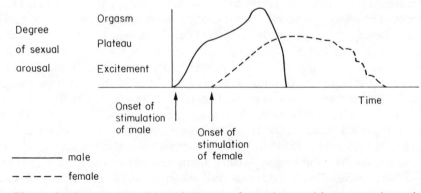

Figure 5.1 Incorrect matching of the rate of sexual arousal between males and females

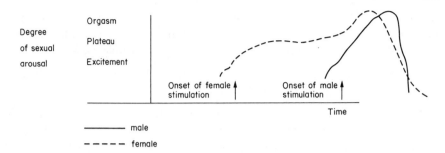

Figure 5.2 Correct matching of the rate of sexual arousal between males and females

the female increasingly to avoid further attempts at intercourse. In addition, her expectations of those attempts which are made are of failure rather than success, expectations which increase the chances of failure. Thus the vicious circle ensues of repeated failures, fewer attempts and more certain failures on those attempts. Figures 5.1 and 5.2 illustrate the difference between incorrect and correct matching of the rate of sexual arousal between males and females.

Figure 5.1 illustrates the situation in which the gradient of female arousal is slower than that of the male and the male time to orgasm is too short to take the female past the plateau stage to orgasm.

Figure 5.2 shows the graphs superposed, with the female curve moved to left. In this situation orgasm is achieved for both partners because the female has been stimulated for a longer period of time than she has in Figure 5.1 and so has been able to reach orgasm. The male has adjusted his behaviour towards the female so as to give her the maximum rate of arousal and to maintain this until she reaches the stage of orgasmic inevitability. At this point the male begins vigorous intromission to orgasm.

Masters and Johnson (1970, p. 74) summarize their view as follows: 'Sexual dysfunction is marked by specific levels of sensory deprivation that have their origin in fear and apprehension of sexual situations, denial of personal sexual indentity, rejection of partner or circumstance of sexual encounter, or lack of sexual awareness often lost originally through emotions of physical fatigue or preoccupation.'

We would add that the greatest personal distress may be experienced by those with a high level of sexual arousal, initially positive expectations and the actual experience of failure with a loved and loving partner. Such couples may be those most likely to seek help. It is to the methods and results of helping attempts that we now turn.

TREATMENT

The development of relatively effective methods of helping people with sexual problems has occurred in the past 10–15 years. In the rest of this chapter we set out the methods and results of these recent developments. We begin with the major treatment methods for psychological problems of all kinds, discuss some of the procedural and ethical difficulties general to such treatments and then proceed to the methods and results specific to sexual problems.

Methods

The major methods of changing behaviour can be considered under three headings: physical, environmental, and psychological. In the area of sexual problems it is mainly the latter two which have been used. Physical methods in psychological medicine such as electroconvulsive therapy (ECT), antidepressant drugs, and the minor and major tranquillizers have tended to be applied to the problems to which sexual problems may be secondary or unconnected, such as depression and schizophrenia. The methods described below apply to all the types of sexual problem which figure in Chapters 5, 6, and 7. In addition, there are others which are specific to a particular kind of problem. They are described in the section devoted to the problem concerned.

Environmental Methods

These include all techniques which are aimed at altering the social context within which the individual functions. (The fact that attempts to manipulate the environment are made does not necessarily imply that it is some defect in the environment which has been partially or solely responsible for the development of the particular problem.) Environmental methods include help and advice with regard to housing, occupation, family, and recreation. They may also include a planned attempt systematically to alter the ways in which any of these areas of the individual's daily life were organized.

Psychological Methods: The Psychotherapies

These include many variations, from simple reassurance to full scale psychoanalysis. Although the many psychodynamic approaches vary in their techniques and therapeutic aims as well as their explicit theoretical formulations, they all rely on verbal communication of some kind, although this may be carried out individually or in a group setting. The most ambitious and intensive form of psychotherapy is represented by *Freudian psychoanalysis*. This may last up to several hundred one-hour sessions, administered four to six times per week for several years. The intention is to afford the individual insight into the unconscious motivation of his behaviour and to allow the development of a 'healthy' personality structure. The aim is not the removal of the symptom, rather it is to solve the unconscious problems which have led, according to the underlying theory, to the development of a particular symptom. The major technique is that of free association, in which the individual is asked to say everything which comes into his mind without any effort to select or suppress. This material, together with the individual's reports on his dreams, is then explored and interpreted by the analyst. One of the major points to make about the method is that it can be available to only a very few individuals because of the amount of skilled manpower involved. Hence, psychotherapeutically oriented therapists have developed shorter methods which would still embody the major therapeutic principles of psychoanalysis. Thus, analytically oriented psychotherapy may, although seeking the same ends as full psychoanalysis, take a much shorter time, because the therapist plays a much more active role in directing the content of the treatment session to those areas that are thought to be the most significant in understanding the underlying sources of the patient's problem.

Perhaps the best known of the other schools of psychotherapy is that of Carl Rogers—termed *client-centred* therapy. The therapist is supposed to be active but non-directive and the aim is to allow the patient to resolve his own problems by the use of the 'healthy' part of his personality. There is much evidence, cited by Bandura (1969), that Rogerian therapists influence, by verbally reinforcing the appropriate comments of the individual in therapy, the psychological direction in which he proceeds. Such evidence supports the view that far from the individual in treatment choosing the therapeutic goal, the therapist makes the choice which itself tends to arise from the particular theoretical orientation of the therapist concerned.

A considerable body of evidence has been marshalled by Rachman (1971) which throws doubt on the therapeutic efficacy of the various forms of psychotherapy. There is a move towards regarding the psychotherapeutic situation, whether it involves the individual patient and the individual therapist, or a therapist and a group of patients, as lying within the overall ambit of experimental social psychology, so that work on inter-personal attraction, attitude change, and social influence all become highly germane (Goldstein et al., 1966). This development is likely to continue with increasing emphasis in future years.

Psychological Methods: The Behaviour Therapies

The aim is to modify the current, behavioural problems ('symptoms') of the individual. Principles derived from the psychology of learning are used to account for the development of the problem behaviour as well as to design techniques of modification. The major behaviour therapy techniques are: desensitization, in which anxiety is managed by gradually bringing the patient into contact with the stimuli of which he was previously fearful; operant conditioning, which for the most part employs positive reinforcement; aversive techniques (usually classical or instrumental conditioning) in which the individual learns to avoid the previously attractive but personally damaging stimulus. A conservative view of the very short history of the behaviour therapies (the major developments started only in the 1950s) would be that their therapeutic efficacy is encouraging, particularly for the more clear-cut problems, such as phobias and obsessions, and for sexual difficulties. Excellent high-level overviews of the behaviour therapy approach are provided by Bandura (1969), and more recently by Craighead *et al.* (1976). A very valuable handbook, which reviews both the psychotherapies as well as the behaviour therapies, is that edited by Garfield and Bergin (1978).

The very success of the behavioural approach to psychological problems has stimulated a vigorous debate concerning a variety of ethical issues. Essentially, ethical questions are concerned with what is *desirable*, rather than what is *true*. Feldman (1976) has suggested that the major issues are as follows.

1. Who are the interested parties (that is, those who should have a voice in crucial decisions relevant to therapy)? They include the obvious individuals—the client(s) and the therapist(s), but a case could be made for others also, including the family or legal guardians of the client(s), friends and employers, the employers of the therapist, his professional association and the law-making and enforcement agencies. In addition, various political and other pressure groups may claim an interest. The interested parties are concerned with one or more of the following questions:

(a) *The problem.* This has three aspects, the most important of which is whether there *is* a problem. (If the interested parties can agree that there is not, no further action need be taken and hence no other ethical issues arise.) If the parties decide that a problem exists, the next two questions are what is the problem and who has it (that is, whose behaviour requires change to bring about the results judged desirable by those who sought help)?

(b) *The objective of treatment.* The most relevant questions are: What are the current actions being carried out by the client(s) (including covert as well as overt behaviours) and which of these are to be maintained—perhaps even strengthened—and which changed? In the case of the latter the next decision concerns which behaviours are to be substituted. Often there are a number of alternatives. An important requirement is that the range of alternatives is explored fully. Not all will be equally desirable either to clients or to therapists. Both are affected by numerous constraints including their own subjective evaluations.

(c) *The method.* Sometimes several methods are available to achieve the agreed objectives relevant to easing an agreed problem. The choice of method by the interested parties is influenced by considerations of efficacy (how well the various methods work), efficiency (how much they cost), and subjective factors such as the pleasantness or unpleasantness of the various alternative procedures.

Feldman (1976) has argued that it is desirable for therapists to act so as to: (a) increase the access of the client to consequences the client decides are good; and (b) protect the client from consequences the client decides are bad. Ideally both (a) and (b) are desirable, but if one is not possible the other should still be aimed for. The client takes first place in the key issues of problems, objectives, and methods and deserves also to be given as full and accurate information as is possible relevant to the issues.

There are various constraints on the therapist. These will be legal (the law of the land and the code of his profession), technical (there is no method available to attain a particular objective), emotional, and those due to particular pressure groups. In the next chapter we discuss the important pressure group termed Gay Liberation. Finally, therapists, like clients, are children of their time. At present, particularly in the USA, there is much discussion of the desirability of involving surrogates (substitute but skilled partners) in the treatment of certain sexual problems. Twenty years ago the question would have been quite unthinkable. In most parts of the world this is the case still.

2. What is the particular relevance of the above set of basic questions and guiding principles to the problems of sexual response?

(a) *Is there a problem?* The initial description of the problem presented by the client/couple, together with the aspirations that they express, will help to answer this. The problem may be one which dominates and distorts their entire pattern of life—both their sexual and their non-sexual relationship may be seriously disturbed. On the other hand the couple's complaint may relate to a rather specific, even somewhat esoteric, sexual issue. For example, they may have read in a popular magazine that the average couple has intercourse every night and that the wife always has multiple orgasms. Their own experience is that sex occurs two or three times per week and that the wife enjoys an orgasm on most but not all occasions. A brief interview establishes that their pattern of sexual activity is entirely within normal limits for that age group and that it is generally pleasurable. In any important sense there is no problem.

(b) *What is the problem?* The extent of the couple's distress and the dislocation caused to their daily lives make it clear that there is indeed a problem but in what area—and hence what should be the focus of the attempt to help? In the case of problems of sexual response the emphasis of many therapists, following the general view of Masters and Johnson, has been that it is the sexual relationship which has broken down, or has never been established effectively, so that this should be the focus of attention. It is asserted that if an improvement can be brought about in the sexual area, the same improvement is very likely to follow in the non-sexual area.

(c) *Who to help?* This is a question which arises whenever the problem affects more than one person, whether directly or indirectly. In the sexual context it is very often a member of a well-established partnership who seeks help, but unattached individuals also consult therapists. In that case, the question *should* help be offered and if so how this is to be accomplished is very relevant. As indicated above the possible use of surrogate therapists is becoming an important ethical issue for sex therapists. In the case of a couple who seek help the apparent focus of help may be either the male or the female, depending upon the apparent problem (e.g. 'impotence', or 'orgasmic difficulties') but more often it is the couple itself which is the true focus. Certainly this is the case so far as the actual method of treatment is concerned. This is well illustrated in the following summary account of Masters and Johnson's approach. The sensate focus technique is particularly to be noted.

The basic assumption is that sexual enjoyment will follow if fear can be eliminated. The treatment is carried out on the co-therapy principle: a male–female couple is treated by a male–female team of therapists, the assumption being that men understand men and women understand women. An important requirement is that the couple abstain from any sexual activity until the therapists advise that it is desirable.

The intensive version of the programme lasts for two weeks and the couple meet with the therapy team each day. In less intensive versions of the Masters and Johnson approach the meetings are spaced more widely but the emphasis on the dual (often called co-therapy) team remains. The early part of the programme is the same regardless of the particular problems. Two days are spent in taking a complete social and sexual history: a detailed physical examination ensures that any organic basis for the problem can be detected and dealt with. Existing sexual attitudes are assessed and if necessary changed so as to enhance the likelihood of successful treatment. In Chapter 3 we pointed out the relevance of the initial attitudes to any subsequent attempt to change the behaviour concerned. If, for example, one partner has a firm belief that sex is to be the price paid for marriage rather than a potentially enjoyable experience, no therapeutic approach is likely to help the couple enjoy their sexual relationship until this initial attitude has been dealt with.

Next the therapists set out their explanations about the development and maintenance of the problems revealed in the initial interview, emphasizing the problems of the couple, rather than those of either partner. It is pointed out to both partners that rehearsing ('worrying') about their performance only reduces the likelihood of performing effectively.

The couple are then asked to practise the 'sensate focus' technique, the core of the Masters and Johnson approach. Effective practice requires that they choose an appropriate time and place to undress and give mutual pleasure by touching. One partner is selected to 'touch', the other to 'enjoy' but not necessarily in a, sexual way—thus no stress is placed on the 'performance' of either participant. Attempts at intercourse are forbidden. Next the roles are reversed. The sensate focus proceeds along a gentle hierarchy of increasing intimacy from touching in non-sexual areas to breast and genital touching so that the two learn how to give each other pleasure and how to indicate to the partner the effects of his/her attempts to give pleasure.

At this point the treatment becomes specific to the presenting problem. We will describe below the Masters and Johnson approach to a number of problems as we cover in turn the relevant methods and results particular to each.

In the area of sexual distress as in other psychological problems generally, there is great pressure on therapists to produce quick answers. But unless such answers are evaluated carefully the result may only be to raise false hopes. There is no substitute for the slow accumulation of reliable knowledge by the application of the scientific method.

There are two stages in the evaluation of a treatment method. The first stage requires a sufficiently clear description of the method for it to be used by therapists other than the group which originally developed it. The second consists of a controlled evaluation of the method. There are several ways of achieving this. One is to make a comparison between the new method and one which has been in use for some time. This requires that a group of clients reporting themselves as having the particular problem are assigned at random to one of the two methods. The two treatments are then carried out and their results evaluated as objectively as possible in terms of clearly defined outcomes. Either these outcomes should be evaluated by researchers other than those who carried out the treatment, or the measurement of outcome should be so objective that the inevitable bias towards a particular outcome by the researchers concerned cannot exert a significant effect. Satisfactory research can also be carried out on single cases but very considerable experimental control is required for reliable conclusions to be drawn.

At present, the field is characterized by much vigorous development and description of methods, particularly those of the behavioural type. Only a few attempts have been made to carry out controlled studies of carefully described treatments using either group or single-case methods.

Male Problems

Impotence. The management of impotence requires first an accurate assessment of each client. His sex drive is of particular relevance. This is assessed by taking a history of the frequency of all sexual outlets before the onset of impotence, for example for the first year of the current partnership, including the ability, or lack of it, to have multiple orgasm in a limited period of time. This ability is constant for any particular male but declines with increasing age (Kinsey *et al.*, 1948; Hastings, 1963). The level of sex drive is an important limiting factor which must be taken into account when treatment goals are being set.

In the case of the acute onset type of impotence there is virtually always a precipitating event which can be elucidated and discussed. The aim of these discussions is to reduce both partners' anxiety concerning erection and intercourse.

Penile erection is mediated by the parasympathetic system and increased sympathetic activity tends to impair it. Consequently anxiety, anger, disgust, and shame tend to be associated as instigators of impotence. Relaxation skills are taught to the patient as a stratagem which he can use at any point in his treatment when anxiety occurs. Masters and Johnson (1970) counsel both partners that no attempt will be made to teach the male to achieve erection. They teach relaxation and mutual sexual approach behaviour with intercourse banned in order to reestablish sexual arousal and concomitant erection. It is stressed that erection is a normal event in the context of effective sexual stimulation.

When the male can achieve and sustain a strong erection intercourse is allowed. It is usual to find that patients and their partners have some difficulties with their relationship and require sex education as well as psychotherapeutic explanation, reassurance, and encouragement. For example patients often have incorrect knowledge of male and female anatomy and restricted views of what is 'normal' or permissible sexual behaviour.

It is important for the couple to achieve an optimum sexual environment for the treatment of impotence. Such a state requires a fully co-operative female and the therapist must make a major effort to achieve this. This may involve conselling directed at the female partner before the couple can be instructed in techniques such as the sensate focus to produce and control the rate of pleasuring and sexual arousal. The promotion of frank verbal and non-verbal communication and a mutual understanding is vital. Masters and Johnson (1970) used a combination of the sensate focus technique with added stimulation by the wife using non-vaginal stimulation of the penis. After successful masturbation to orgasm has been achieved on a number of prior occasions rapid vaginal intromission is effected by the female when she has brought the male to the stage of ejaculatory inevitability. This is performed in the female superior position. Cooper's (1968) therapeutic aims for slow onset impotence and delayed or absent ejaculation were 'to remove or modify as far as possible psychological factors which were judged as inhibiting the male from responding to his sexual capacity' (p. 724). Cooper applied four main treatment principles in a flexible way according to each case. These were progressive muscular relaxation, the provision of an optimum sexual environment, sex education, and psychotherapy. He based the need for relaxation on the idea that anxiety and anger may be associated with over-activity of the sympathetic component of the autonomic nervous system leading to failure of erection. He saw relaxation as increasing the relative activity of the parasympathetic nervous system which in turn produced a reciprocal inhibition of the over-activity of the sympathetic system. His patients were trained in relaxation for periods of 30 minutes at a time; once the technique had been learned his patients were asked to relax while their partners sexually stimulated them. Intercourse was delayed until the patient could acquire and sustain strong erections for several minutes while feeling relaxed and confident. By optimal sexual environment Cooper meant frank communication by the male to his partner of those behaviours which most aroused him. The communication of 'needs' is similar to Masters and Johnson's sensate focus, 'give to get' formulation. Cooper added education in sexual techniques, female sexual anatomy and physiology, and acceptable sexual practices. Finally he gave superficial psychotherapy consisting of explanation, reassurance, and encouragement. He varied all the four components of his regime to suit different cases; for example in those where long-standing inter-personal conflict seemed to be the primary cause of the impotence he changed his psychotherapy to an analytical and interpretive form.

Cooper treated 54 cases of impotence in all. Twenty-three were slow onset impotence and 13 problems of ejaculation. Six out of the 23 slow onset group improved as did 6 of the 13 problems of ejaculation. Both these groups did much worse than the acute impotence group of whom 7 out of 8 improved. Cooper's treatment was given over a year and he makes the important point that if improvement is going to take place it does so relatively quickly (within 5 to 10 sessions). Cooper's overall outcome figure was an improvement rate of 37 per cent. This is similar to the improvement of 33.3 per cent obtained by Johnson (1965b).

It is clear that the outcome for problems of potency is poor when biological causes are important. It is of interest that Johnson (1965a) showed that a group of impotent individuals was more female in body build than a control group, and he found that the improvement rate in the former to be far below that for psychological problems in general (Johnson, 1965b), the implication being that the cause is not to do with social learning experience but with basic biological predispositions. Masters and Johnson also report a greater failure rate for what they term primary impotence than for secondary impotence. It is likely that 'primary' corresponds to 'slow onset' and 'secondary' to 'acute onset'. Thus it would be wrong to be optimistic in expecting favourable results in the treatment of slow onset impotence or of delayed or absent ejaculation. The outlook is better for acute onset impotence than for premature ejaculation as well as for those longer term impotent individuals for whom inter-personal factors are both important and can be modified.

An important element in the treatment of male sexual problems is the 'squeeze' technique. Semans (1956) described a technique of stimulation of the male by the female which was interrupted when the male signalled that he was about to enter the stage of ejaculatory inevitability. Masters and Johnson have added to and improved this technique by instructing the female member of the couple firmly to squeeze the penis around the *corona glandis* just before ejaculation and then to recommence masturbation. When ejaculation is regularly delayed controlled intromission is introduced without pelvic thrusting. In this way vaginal containment is achieved without the runaway arousal to orgasm which was the pre-treatment pattern. The penile squeeze technique can be applied by the female during intercourse (which takes place in the female superior position) by the female raising her body from the penile shaft and squeezing the penis for three to four seconds before re-insertion. Masters and Johnson claim success with the squeeze technique in 182 out of 186 men. It is of interest that Cooper (1968) could improve only 1 out of 10 premature ejaculators by Seman's technique which is inferior to that of Masters and Johnson, but group instruction reduces the therapeutic time so that a combination of the two may have some merit.

Mechanical aids have also been used in the treatment of impotence. Small *et al.* (1975) have developed the use of the Small–Carrion silicone/silicone sponge artificial aid. This is inserted surgically into the corpora cavernosa. They reported on the treatment of 31 cases of impotence associated with the following conditions: prostatectomy (4); priapism—a state of constant erection—(2);

psychogenic impotence (2); generalized arteriosclerosis (3); pelvic fracture (2); spinal cord injury (15); diabetes (2); congenital extrophy (1). Their paper reports excellent surgical results and they support their claims with photographs of 'erect' penises but they do not state whether or not post-operative intercourse was possible and, if so, whether it led either to arousal, or to orgasm. Furlow (1976) has reported on 36 patients who received an inflatable penile prosthesis by surgical implantation. Thirty-five of them had a functioning prosthesis at follow-up and 34 reported satisfactory intercourse with orgasmic sensation.

There is a small group of men of all ages who have sustained organic lesions which render them impotent and for whom such restorative operations are psychologically and physiologically important. The return of penile copulatory function is also of great importance to their partners, again for physiological and psychological reasons. We would expect surgical techniques in this area to improve and extend in their scope both because of the patients' greater ability to express their sexual problems and because of the increasing number of men who survive spinal cord injuries from road traffic and similar accidents. The inflatable prosthesis has the double advantage of producing an erection when it is required and can be removed after intercourse and of being less likely to produce side effects due to prosthetic pressure on the penile tissues. At the present time this kind of mechanism suffers from a degree of unreliability greater than that experienced by the non-inflatable type although it does not have the problem of a permanent erection.

Males suffering from renal disease are often both impotent and have reduced sexual drive (Levy, 1973). Antoniou et al. (1977) have made the startling discovery that zinc significantly improves sexual performance in renal failure patients. Chronic renal failure is by no means a rare phenomenon and this work merits attention because of its contribution to helping renal failure patients to have a normal life.

A number of therapists have used drugs for the treatment of premature ejaculation. Kraft and Al-Issa (1967) successfully used intravenous methohexitone to desensitize two patients. They were given supportive psychotherapy and sex education and told to abstain from intercourse during the early part of the treatment period; it is not possible to draw conclusions about this technique other than that the methohexitone may have helped to produce relaxation. Melgren (1967) used thioridazine on 40 premature ejaculatory patients with success in 15. His work is of interest because it seems likely that the thioridazine reduced the sympathetic system's contribution to the arousal process by lessening the activity of the sympathetic ganglia. The general and specific Masters and Johnson techniques seem to us to be the methods of choice for premature ejaculation, but the addition of thioridazine-like drugs may occasionally be of help.

Female Problems

A major fault in the literature on female sexual dysfunction is the blanket use of the term 'frigidity' (Falk, 1973) which refers to a wide variety of different problems. Many reports are of uncontrolled single case studies or of series lacking control groups. Treatment successes are defined in different ways and most studies lack information on the subjects' actual sexual behaviour and functioning.

Sotile and Kilman (1977) have reviewed the literature on the treatment of female sexual dysfunction against the following criteria: (a) client characteristics thought relevant to outcome; (b) treatment method; and (c) the assessment of sexual functioning after treatment.

Psychological methods. Leckie (1964) treated dyspareunia, vaginismus and orgasmic failure by *hypnotic suggestion.* He treated 57 cases in all, starting with sex education and then going on to suggest under hypnosis to each woman that she would enjoy sexual stimulation during intercourse. Leckie's improvement rates were as follows: 17 out of 30 for dyspareunia, 13 out of 15 for vaginismus, 3 out of 12 for orgasmic failure. His follow-up varied from two weeks to two years and showed that all subjects maintained their improvement. However, the criteria for improvement were so vague that it would be difficult to repeat the study. Richardson (1963) used various combinations of hypnoanalysis, suggestion, and hypnopsychotherapy on 76 women suffering from a variety of problems. He claimed that 95 per cent showed improvement in sexual functioning, an improvement which included orgasm during all coital experiences for 58 per cent of the sample.

Many therapists use *couple re-education* in the treatment of female sexual dysfunction. Chapman (1968) treated 74 married couples in whom the dysfunction included vaginismus and primary and secondary orgasmic dysfunction. Therapy consisted of clarifying areas of sexual ignorance and training in the use of fore play. Couples were asked to indulge in fore play with a prohibition on intercourse until both partners understood the other's sexual needs. Eighty per cent of the clients recovered or were improved and a five year follow-up of a sample of 48 showed that 94 per cent had maintained their improvement. One crucial factor which emerged from this study was that positive involvement of the husband correlated positively with high levels of marital and sexual satisfaction. Chapman suggests that both sexual functioning and general marital adjustment should be taken into account when reports of treatment are being assessed. We return to this point later.

Lazarus (1963) used the conventional *systematic desensitization* procedure (Wolpe, 1958). Nine of Lazarus's 16 clients did well and he concluded that systematic desensitization is most effective in treating women whose sexual pleasure is inhibited by specific or clear-cut fears. Brady (1966) used intravenous sodium methohexital to achieve relaxation in five clients with dyspareunia due to vaginismus compounded by strong negative emotions towards coitus and a failure of orgasm. Four who remained in treatment did well after an average of 11.5 sessions. Orgasm during intercourse was achieved on a mean of 50 per cent of occasions and this improvement was still present at follow-up of between three and eight months. The data were corroborated by the clients' husbands. Jones and Park (1972) treated 69 patients with intravenous brevital in a modification of Brady's technique. Although Jones and Park did not include orgasm in their criteria of improvement 55 of their clients experienced pleasure and satisfaction during intercourse. These reports suggest that desensitization combined with an intravenous anaesthetic agent is a successful method of relieving dyspareunia due to vaginismus and aversion to intercourse. Having the husband present in the sessions seem to be an advantage.

Specific techniques: 'artificial aids'. Several authors report the use of graded *glass vaginal dilators* in the real life desensitization of small numbers of women complaining of vaginismus and dyspareunia (e.g. Cooper, 1969; Haslam, 1965). All the clients could engage in pleasurable intercourse after a mean of seven treatments and follow-ups ranging from one month to five years showed that the improvement had been maintained. Dawkins and Taylor (1961) treated 44 women with severe vaginismus. Thirty-three were treated by self-dilation, the others by other methods of achieving dilation. Forty-one could engage in intercourse after treatment, but no data are available on subjective satisfaction or the continued presence of pain on intercourse.

Specific techniques: vaginal exercises. Kegel (1952) and Hall (1952) described exercises for strengthening and increasing the control of vaginal muscles. Kegel claimed that a woman's ability to derive pleasure from vaginal stimulation is closely related to the condition of her pubococcygeus muscle and he invented an instrument for measuring its strength. This instrument, called the perineometer, consists of a pneumatic cylindrical diaphragm attached by rubber tube to a gauge. The diaphragm is inserted into the vagina and when the vaginal muscles are contracted the pointer of the gauge registers a measure of the contractile strength of the vaginal muscles. Kegel interviewed and examined over 3,000 women using his instrument. He reported that women with a contractile strength measuring 0–3 mm Hg on the perineometer commonly expressed indifference and dissatisfaction regarding sexual activity. Those who showed a contractile strength of 20 mm Hg or more expressed few or transient sexual complaints. Kegel then hypothesized that a female's sexual responsiveness could be enhanced by regularly exercising the perivaginal muscles with the aid of his perineometer. He claimed that 78 out of 123 women were able to achieve orgasm during intercourse as the result of treatment, but provided no information on client characteristics, length of treatment, or method of data collection and analysis. Hall (1952) proposed that vaginismus could be successfully treated by having a woman voluntarily contract and relax her vaginal muscles, thereby enabling her to locate the control centre of the muscles. He successfully treated 16 of 24 women complaining of dyspareunia due to vaginismus. However he did not set out the criteria for treatment success. We conclude that the evidence that vaginal muscle exercises can increase arousability and rate of arousal is important but that the method requires controlled evaluation. It seems likely that strong vaginal muscles reflect a great deal of sexual experience, which was repeated because it was enjoyable. Merely strengthening vaginal muscles may be a useful preliminary to the use of other sexual techniques but is unlikely in itself to overcome the many psychological barriers we have outlined earlier.

Combined approaches. The results of three studies suggest that a combination of desensitization and psychotherapy is helpful in removing anxiety associated with sexual stimulation, but is not very effective with female orgasmic dysfunctions. Brady (1966) described a case study of a woman complaining of anxiety rather than pleasure during intercourse. Treatment included the combination of his method of systematic desensitization under the drug brevital (Brady, 1966) with interpretive psychotherapy. After 17 sessions of desensitizations and 16 sessions of psychotherapy she experienced her first orgasm. A follow-up after two years found her to be orgasmic in 90 per cent of her attempts at intercourse and to enjoy general marital and psychological adjustment. Ellison (1972) and Friedman (1962) proposed that manual vaginal dilation be combined with supportive psychotherapy in treating women suffering from vaginismus. Ellison described four case studies of this technique and Friedman reported the treatment of 100 women. Two of Ellison's clients were cured of their vaginal spasms, but only one was able to achieve orgasm regularly following treatment. Friedman reported that 71 of his clients were cured of their vaginismus, but only 20 attained the ability to achieve orgasm regularly during sexual relations.

Obler (1973) compared the effects of conventional psychoanalytically oriented group therapy, a modified version of Wolpe's (1958) method of systematic desensitization, and a no-treatment control group in 64 females who showed primary or secondary orgasmic dysfunction. There were 22 in each of the desensitization and no-treatment groups, and 20 were treated with group therapy. All three groups were matched for type of problem, marital status, and duration of the problem. Obler used graphic aids to portray the anxiety hierarchy scenes. Each desensitization client also had four sessions of assertive training and confidence training. Group therapy subjects were seen in weekly $1\frac{1}{2}$ hour sessions for a total of 10 weeks. All desensitization clients were seen in weekly 45 minute sessions for a total of 15 weeks. Each person and her regular sex partner were required to keep records, independently, of their successful and unsuccessful sexual interactions as defined by a success experinces form supplied by Obler. The results showed that the combination of modified systematic desensitization, assertiveness training, and confidence training was an effective method of treating female orgasmic dysfunction. Neither the group therapy nor the control conditions produced significant improvement.

Extensive Retraining Programmes for Couples

Much the best known retraining programme is that of Masters and Johnson. They begin with their general approach to all types of sexual problems described earlier. When the sensate focusing exercises have proceeded satisfactorily, the next stage is for the wife to experience an orgasm, first by stimulating herself manually and then by manual stimulation by the husband under her explicit directions. Once she is experiencing pleasure in this way the next step is to transfer the source of pleasure from husband's hand to husband's penis. This is achieved by placing herself on top and then inserting the penis, not moving until she feels ready to do so. As always she is in control of events. After she has contained the penis for some minutes male thrusting may begin and orgasm is finally achieved. It is evident that in this, as in other psychological approaches, the social skills and inter-personal sensitivity of the therapists are of great importance both in maintaining the client in treatment and in persuading them to engage in activities of great therapeutic relevance but which have been a source of much distress, often for many years.

Masters and Johnson (1965b) reported the treatment of 342 couples, including 193 cases of primary orgasmic dysfunction, 11 cases of masturbatory orgasmic inadequacy, 106 of coital orgasmic inadequacy, 32 cases of random orgasmic inadequacy, and 29 cases of vaginismus. (All the women who were described as vaginismic were also included in one of the orgasmic dysfunction categories.) For a couple to be considered a success immediately after treatment, the criterion of the absence of the problems present at the beginning of treatment had to be met. To be considered a long-term treatment success, a couple had to maintain their improvement for a five year period following termination of treatment. Data on each couple's sexual functioning were collected immediately after treatment through extensive interviews conducted both conjointly and individually with both members. However, longer-term follow-up data were obtained only on couples who had originally responded successfully to treatment. Periodic telephone interviews were the main source of follow-up data. Two-thirds of the couples were interviewed during the follow-up period. The success rates for the various types of female sexual disorders treated by Masters and Johnson were as follows: primary orgasmic dysfunction—83 per cent, masturbatory orgasmic inadequacy—91 per cent, coital orgasmic inadequacy—80 per cent, random orgasmic inadequacy—62 per cent, and vaginismus—100 per cent. Of the couples followed up, only five females (spread evenly throughout the disorders) showed a reappearance of their original problems. Masters and Johnson's treatment regime is quick and effective in relieving sexual dysfunctioning in highly motivated, well-educated, middle-class couples.

The criteria for improvement and cure used by Masters and Johnson in the treatment of female orgasmic dysfunctions make it difficult to interpret their outcome statistics. Only about 45 per cent of the couples treated for female sexual dysfunction were followed up and more importantly no follow-up data were obtained on any couple who originally failed to respond to treatment. Without adequate follow-up data, on both treatment successes and failures, it is impossible to assess fully the effectiveness of any treatment.

More recently, other therapists have reported on extensive retraining programmes. Hartman and Fithian (1972) described a programme that included the use of audiovisual aids for training purposes and the use of Gestalt techniques for the dual purposes of exploring each client's self-image and of examining a couple's method of interacting. They claim that their clients seemed to show improvement 'in approximately the same proportions as reported by Masters and Johnson'.

Lobitz and LoPiccolo (1972) described a programme for female sexual dysfunction modelled after Masters and Johnson's procedure. It included anxiety reduction, sexual skill training and improvement of communication between partners, but also had a particular distinguishing feature, namely an emphasis on masturbatory retraining in treating female orgasmic dysfunctions. The criterion for treatment success was that the 'female partner be satisfied in at least 50 per cent of (her) coital connections'. Using this criterion they reported success for all 13 cases of primary orgasmic dysfunctions (the classifications are those of Masters and Johnson, 1970). They reported that eight women who had never previously experienced orgasm were successfully treated using their masturbation programme. The criterion for success was that the woman be able to experience orgasm through concurrent coital and manual clitoral stimulation by her partner.

McGovern et al. (1975) using the same techniques as Lobitz and LoPiccolo reported their results on 12 orgasmically dysfunctional women. Table 5.2 presents a summary of their data on sexual arousal and stimulation. All the clients completed a background information inventory, a sexual interaction inventory, and a marital adjustment test before and after treatment. Their results indicate that the secondary dysfunction women were the more dissatisfied with their marital relations prior to treatment and that the sexual satisfaction of both groups was improved by treatment. This study does not permit any definite conclusions to be drawn because of the small numbers involved but the data suggest: (1) both groups of women could eventually achieve orgasm by self-masturbation; (2) the primary group could be brought to orgasm by partner masturbation after treatment; (3) the secondary group's orgasmic response in

Table 5.2. Mean Percentage Frequency of Orgasm during Sexual Stimulation. (McGovern et al., 1975)

	Self-masturbation		Masturbation by partner		Intercourse	
	Pre-treatment	Post-treatment	Pre-treatment	Post-treatment	Pre-treatment	Post-treatment
Primary n = 6 orgasmic dysfunction group	0	62.5	0	45.8	0	45.8
Secondary n = 6 orgasmic dysfunction group	66.7	70.8	35.0	41.6	16.7	16.7

intercourse was different from that of the primary group and was unresponsive to treatment. Thus their results suggest that there was no intrinsic difference between the groups in the responsiveness to self-masturbation, but an important difference in their capacity when the *partner* was involved in the stimulation. They conclude that primarily inorgasmic women respond best to therapy focused on sexual matters in contrast to the secondary inorgasmic women who require 'marital therapy' in addition to sexual help. They place great emphasis on teaching the women techniques of arousal by masturbation, but do not extend their ideas to teaching the male partner techniques of masturbation best suited to the female.

The emphasis placed above on the importance of the partner leads to a discussion of the relationship itself. Masters and Johnson make the explicit assumption that if the sexual life of the couple can be improved, their non-sexual relationship and mutual evaluation will also improve. However, it is likely that this conclusion is mistaken. The couples seen by Masters and Johnson were likely to be well satisfied in the non-sexual area of their lives. The evidence for this is indirect—their full-time attendance for two weeks in an expensive course of treatment—but is quite persuasive. Direct evidence comes from the McGovern *et al.* (1975) series described above (see Table 5.2). Contrary to expectations the secondary orgasmic group were less likely after treatment to enjoy sexual intercourse with the partner. This points clearly to the marital relationship itself in helping or hindering the course of a therapy in which attention is focused directly and solely on sexual behaviour. It is relevant, therefore, to consider recent developments in marital therapy which apply well-established behavioural principles to the problems of a mutually unsatisfactory marital relationship.

'Relationship Therapy'

An excellent account of the behavioural approach to marital distress—and marital therapy—has been given by Patterson *et al.* (1976). Although applied to marital relationships the analysis could be adapted readily to any other relatively long-term relationship (it is not dissimilar to the equity based view of intimate relationships set out in Chapter 3).

A central assumption of the behavioural approach is that relationships are maintained as long as both members continue to supply enough positive reinforcement to each other. It is further assumed that people marry or form a long-term intimate relationship in the expectation that this will increase the availability of such positive reinforces as sharing sexual and non-sexual activities and raising children. (However, so far as marriage is concerned the relationship may continue in spite of initial expectations not being met, due to legal, social or religious pressures to remain together as well as to what is expected to be the aversive experience of divorce.) A satisfactory marriage is one in which the mutual exchange of reinforcers is acceptable to both spouses. An unsatisfactory one is a marriage in which one of both spouses find the supply or reinforcers no longer adequate, either because it has actively decreased or because their requirements have increased or changed. How do people behave in response to these changes? First they may make reasonable requests for improvements or variations in the flow of reinforcers, but if their requests are not met the result may be that they continue to be made but in less and less reasonable form. Angry requests provoke angry responses which in turn evoke more anger and so on in a vicious circle of mounting aggression. An alternative pattern is that the partners avoid each other: long silences at dinner, few affectionate responses, only occasional joint activities, and long silent evenings in front of the television.

If the couple decide to seek help and find their way to a behaviourally oriented therapist, his intervention is likely to emphasize a number of key elements: pinpointing and discrimination training; improving communication skills; problem solving and negotiation training and contingency contracting.

Pinpointing means learning to describe exactly what the problem is—'we go to the cinema only twice a year', etc., rather than 'we have a dull life'. The therapist supplies the clients with a lengthy list of specific items and asks them to mark those that are pleasing or displeasing when carried out by the partner from whom they obtain positive reinforcement, rather than attending mainly to those experienced as negative. In fact, clients are encouraged to note the former and ignore the latter as far as possible. Noticing positive actions by the spouse encourages the other to reply in kind. Training in *communication skills* emphasizes listening actively to the spouse, rather than concentrating only on what they themselves are saying, sharing a dialogue rather than one partner dominating it, and reducing such aversive behaviours as sarcasm and ridicule. Next couples are taught how to *solve problems*, as a couple, the emphasis being on developing skills which can be applied to any situation. The key element here is that they learn that changes in each other's behaviour are negotiable and compromises are often necessary in order to achieve a mutually satisfactory outcome. Finally, having used their newly acquired problem solving, communication, and reinforcement skills to negotiate changes in each other's behaviour, the couple learn how to set contracts which will specify what is to be done by each, and what consequences will follow for compliance or failure to comply. Such contracts are termed *contingency contracts*. As always, the components of the contracts and their consequences are made as specific as possible. A simple *quid pro quo* version would be as follows: the husband agrees to take his wife out to dinner once a week if she washes his socks and irons his shirts once a week. A more complex version allows *independent* consequences—each receives a positive reinforcement for carrying out his or her side of the bargain. For example, if the wife did so, but the husband did not, she would still have an evening out, paid for by the husband. This helps to maintain the wife's behaviour change and keeps alive the possibility that her husband's will also change. Contracts sometimes include negative consequences for failure to comply—for example the husband would have to miss attending his favourite football game.

Finally, the therapist has to arrange gradually to fade out of the picture. He does this by transferring responsibility for planning contracts to the couple. Once this whole approach of 'giving to get' is well established, it tends to operate automatically, without conscious planning. Evaluative studies (e.g. Patterson *et al.*, 1975) suggest that this approach is very promising. Certainly it seems a most useful adjunct to the repertoire of the sex therapist.

OVERVIEW

Sexual intercourse may occur in the absence of female sexual arousal provided that penetration is not obstructed either behaviourally or by vaginal spasm. This dissymmetry between the partners in the sexual act, taken together with the significantly slower rate of arousal in females, is an important contributing factor in the genesis of sexual dysfunction in both men and women.

The problems of sexual dysfunction in the male include acute and insidious onset impotence, premature ejaculation, and absent ejaculation. Men with acute onset impotence in general have a normal level of sex drive whereas those with slow onset impotence have a low level of drive. This dichotomy is correlated with psychological problems in the former and an organic/physiological basis in the latter.

Most sex therapists and researchers view orgasmic difficulties in the female as due to social learning experiences. Failure of the female to achieve any degree of sexual arousal may derive from negative attitudes to sex in general, to elements of the sex act, or from negative attitudes to the partner specifically. The latter may have been present from early on in the relationship or have developed later on because of a number of different reasons.

Failure of female arousal to reach orgasm is usually due to an ignorance of the differential rates of arousal between males and females and an ignorance of sex stimulation techniques by the male. One of the most consistent findings by sex therapists relating to treatment of female sexual dysfunctions is a failure of communication between the couple at all levels including the emotional, but particularly concerning needs and 'feedback', before and during the sexual act.

Methods of treatment of sexual dysfunctions for both sexes are considered under three headings: physical, environmental, and psychological. Specific therapies for all the problems of sexual dysfunction are reviewed in the context of defining each couple's problem, the objectives of treatment, and the actual treatment method(s) to be used.

The following important points are stressed: analysis of the individual's problem, analysis of the partner's problem, analysis of the relationship of the pair, motivation and co-operation of the pair, treatment of the relationship, specific treatment of the sexual performance problem, and finally the place of the therapist during and after treatment.

CHAPTER 6

The Homosexual Preference

It is difficult enough to secure reliable information on heterosexual behaviour; it is even more difficult in the case of the homosexual preference, which if no longer illegal in many countries is often still socially censured. We shall survey what information exists and then set out what we consider the most promising explanatory theory of its cause. In doing so we shall draw on the same combination of biological and social learning influences that we have found helpful for sexual behaviour in general.

Definition

The least contentious definition is: sexual behaviour between members of the same sex, accompanied by sexual arousal, carried out recurrently and despite the opportunity for heterosexual behaviour. We thus exclude those who engage in homosexual activities only in prison, or other unusual settings. However, we include those who engage in substantial amounts of both homosexual and heterosexual activities. In this chapter we are talking about those whose preferred partner is an adult—that is someone who has already attained sexual puberty. In the next chapter we shall look at various other forms of sexual preference, including paedophilia—in which the preferred partner is a sexually immature individual, whether of the same or the opposite sex.

Classification

Homosexuals are not a homogeneous group, and several classificatory systems have been proposed. We consider the most valuable, both for purposes of description and of explanation, to be a division between primary and secondary (Feldman and MacCulloch, 1971). The distinction between the two groups may not be as clear-cut as the two terms imply; rather they may shade into each other, but for purposes of exposition it is convenient to retain the distinction.

Primary homosexuals are those who have never experienced heterosexual arousal at any stage in their lives. Heterosexual behaviour may have occurred occasionally; it will have been for appearance only, or in order to put their 'true' sexual preference to the test. Secondary homosexuals have experienced noticeable heterosexual arousal, usually together with some heterosexual activity. The two groups are not distinguished by their homosexual behaviour, although the primary group may more often adopt the passive role in sexual intercourse. The major distinction is in the heterosexual area. Most research studies have compared homosexuals with heterosexuals as if the former were one homogeneous group. If our dichotomy is broadly correct we would predict that many of the existing studies would report conflicting and confusing results on variables such as serum hormone levels.

Numbers

As yet there are no surveys of random population samples. It follows that the true number of those who prefer homosexual behaviour is unknown. Hence we do not know whether the proportion in the population is rising, falling, or remaining steady. Moreover, whereas the primary group is homosexual for the whole of their lives by definition, secondary homosexuals may in the past have been heterosexual, or may become heterosexual in the future. All one can talk about is the number of people having the homosexual preference at a particular point in time. The only large-scale surveys available are still those carried out by Kinsey and his colleagues and as we noted earlier, they have serious sampling problems. A rough analysis suggests that about 4 to 5 per cent of the white male sample in the Kinsey survey were of the primary type throughout their lives and over 12 per cent had been in the secondary group for at least three years between the ages of 16 and 55. About 20 per cent of the remainder had more or less incidental homosexual experiences. With increasing age, secondary homosexuals polarize, some become exclusively heterosexual, some exclusively homosexual, a decreasing proportion remain bisexual. Those who are exclusively homosexual in behaviour at the time of a research study will include both lifelong primaries as well as secondaries. Conversely a proportion of those currently exclusively heterosexual will have been homosexually active (secondary group) in the past.

The homosexual proportion of the Kinsey female sample was considerably smaller than that in his male sample. This may have been related to the generally lower level of self-reported female sexual activity at the time of the Kinsey survey. At least a proportion of the sexually inactive unmarried females might have adopted overt homosexual activity in a society more accepting of active female sexuality. We would expect a current Kinsey type of survey to indicate a much smaller discrepancy between the male and female homosexual proportions of the population.

DESCRIPTIONS

Most of the earlier research drew its homosexual samples from prisons and hospitals and the heterosexual sample from the population at large. More recent

studies have avoided this failing. Many homosexuals spend the maj
waking lives in more or less exclusively homosexual social settings.
discussing such settings.

The Homosexual Community

Homosexuals can be divided, very broadly, into those who live overtly
homosexual social lives and those who lead secret social lives (Leznoff and
Westley, 1956). The overt group tend to follow occupations which have
traditionally accepted homosexuals—the arts, interior decorating, and
hairdressing. This is not to say that such occupations are synonymous with the
homosexual preference. Homosexuals are to be found in every occupation and
trade. Overt groups have little contact with the heterosexual social world, and
may be highly organized socially, with a leader, sometimes termed the 'queen'.
Secret groups are loosely organized socially and their members maintain strong
contacts with heterosexual social groups. The overt/secret distinction does *not*
parallel the primary/secondary distinction.

Homosexual young males pass through a sequence of stages (Schofield, 1965b)
culminating in the full acceptance of a homosexual way of life. Not all reach this
stage, depending partly on the social acceptability of homosexuality in his
occupational group.

The fully developed homosexual community in such American cities as Los
Angeles (Hooker, 1967) and San Francisco (Achilles, 1967) lives in one specific
area of the city and frequents exclusively homosexual meeting places,
particularly clubs and 'gay bars'. The latter are the key social centres, both for
practical problems, such as finding a job or a place to live, and for obtaining
sexual partners, both for 'one-night stands' and more long-lasting relationships.
Youth is the key element in the sexual transaction, hence the emphasis on the
'cosmetic' self-appearance, dress, and body build. The bars also provide
'justification'—psychological support—for the legitimacy of the homosexual
way of life. The homosexuals who frequent them have the same sense of a
common fate as other minority groups, such as Blacks and Jews.

The female homosexual community tends to be less highly organized than the
male (Gagnon and Simon, 1967) and also places less emphasis on transient sexual
relationships. Loney (1972) found that female homosexuals much more
frequently made semi-permanent same-sex 'marriages'.

The social acceptance of homosexuals is greater among younger and more
educated than in older and less educated groups, being at its maximum on
university campuses. Even there, some disapproval is expressed. The acceptance
of the social setting in which he lives is closely related to the psychological
stability of the individual homosexual. Very recently, San Francisco has become
a particularly important centre for American homosexuals. This is so much so
that the gay community in that city has become a significant political force.

The majority of homosexuals attempt to conceal their sexual interests from
others at work. A minority of males, but a majority of females, try to imply an

interest in the opposite sex (Kolaszynska-Carr, 1970). The rise of Womens Lib. may reduce the latter finding. In general, the increasing development of homosexual communities and a tendency for individual homosexuals to identify themselves as such strengthens the probability that an individual homosexual will maintain his preference in exactly the same way as a member of any minority group, who spends most of his time with the other members of the group, is likely to remain a member.

Responses to Heterosexual Stimuli

We now survey responsiveness to heterosexual stimuli of all kinds, one of the major differences at the descriptive level between the primary and secondary groups of homosexuals.

The majority of homosexuals have had heterosexual advances made to them, as have almost all heterosexuals. A significant minority of homosexuals, presumably the primary type, have always taken strong evasive action (Kolaszynska-Carr, 1970) and report unpleasant subjective reactions, particularly fear and anxiety. In addition, some female homosexuals report marked anger and disgust when they find themselves exposed to heterosexual advances. Generally speaking male homosexuals get on better with the opposite sex than do female homosexuals, although less well than male heterosexuals, possibly because of the traditional notion that the male initiates sexual encounters. He is therefore more in control of the situation. However, both male and female homosexuals keep away from contexts in which sexual advances from a person of the opposite sex are likely, and they do so far more than heterosexuals (Ramsey and Van Velzen, 1968; Kolaszynska-Carr, 1970). There is good evidence that male homosexuals get on better socially with women significantly older than themselves than do male heterosexuals, and that this is because of the low probability of a sexual approach or demand from the female concerned (Kolaszynska-Carr, 1970). There is thus a clear picture of avoidance of heterosexual social stimuli by adult homosexuals (Bieber *et al.*, 1962; Kaye *et al.*, 1967) of both sexes. There is also good evidence that homosexuals show a decline in heterosexual arousal from adolescence to adulthood (Kinsey *et al.*, 1948, 1953; Kolaszynska-Carr, 1970). By definition, the decline is confined to the secondary group; the primary group has never experienced any arousal.

A number of objective measurement techniques have been used to quantify the self-description of a relative lack of heterosexual responsiveness. A very simple attitude scale, which measures a person's evaluation of his homosexual and heterosexual behaviour, the Sexual Orientation Method (SOM) has been introduced by Feldman *et al.* (1966) and further developed by Sambrooks and MacCulloch (1973). Prior to therapy aimed at changing sexual preference (see below), a group of homosexuals was discriminated from a group of heterosexuals on both the homosexual and the heterosexual scales, though with some overlap on the latter, due to the secondary group, as would be expected. Following therapy the successful clients (mainly secondaries) scored similarly to heterosexual controls; the unsuccessful ones (mainly primaries) were unchanged in their scores.

Another approach to the measurement of sexual interest is to show people pictures of males and females, dressed, nude or half-clothed, and record the time spent looking at the pictures. Those who are open about their sexual preference respond as expected, but it is very easy for those who are covert about their sexual preferences to fake their responses in a number of ways. One suggested solution to the problem of faking is to arrange for the slides to appear in response to a complex schedule of switch pressing carried out by the person under study, the pattern for each class of stimuli (heterosexual and homosexual) being subtly different and gradually trained (Cliffe, 1977). Nevertheless, the responses are still essentially muscular and hence under voluntary control, unlike physiological responses which are, in principle, largely involuntary. The problem of faking lies behind several attempts to index sexual preference by physiological responses to sexual stimuli. A method that seemed at first to be promising, namely the measurement of eye pupil response to sexually arousing homosexual and heterosexual pictures (Hess et al., 1965) has been repeated by Scott et al. (1967) who found that pupillary response was an index of general arousal rather than of sexual arousal in particular. The penile erection/vaginal blood response is much more satisfactory, being specific to sexual arousal. A penile plethysmograph was first described by Freund (1963) and more recent developments are summarized by Bancroft (1974). Once again, the possibility of faking, in either direction, cannot be ruled out entirely. Laws and Rubin (1969) showed that subjects, when instructed to do so, were able to inhibit previously maximum erection by 50 per cent in the presence of erotically simulating motion pictures. When instructed to develop an erection in the absence of a film subjects were able to attain 30 per cent of their previously recorded maximum erection.

Personality Assessment

The theory that the homosexual preference was an indication of psychological disturbance goes back at least as far as Sigmund Freud, who related homosexuality specifically to paranoia (a set of delusional beliefs, often concerning persecution). In a more general sense the view has been widely held that the homosexual preference indicated a neurosis, or a psychological instability of some kind. Indeed for many years the American Psychiatric Association included homosexuality in its list of psychological problems, along with various types of neurosis and psychosis. Of course, homosexuals may develop all kinds of psychological problems, as may heterosexuals, but the homosexual preference in itself is no longer thought to be an indication of personality disturbance.

A number of studies have compared homosexuals and heterosexuals on self-report questionnaires of personality. The general finding is that when the homosexual group is in some special and restricted setting—a psychiatric hospital or a prison—and the heterosexual group is living in a normal setting, the scores obtained by the former do indicate greater psychological disturbance. Because this difference is quite probably due to the variation in setting, rather than to differences in sexual preference, such studies must be interpreted with care. However, even when the comparison has been between groups both living in normal social contexts, the homosexual group tends to obtain scores indicating that they are more anxious than the comparable heterosexual group. This is an interesting phenomenon. There is increasing evidence that a major reason for this finding is the social rejection experienced by many homosexuals. One way to test this possibility is to ask samples of heterosexuals and homosexuals, both males and females, about their history of psychological problems. Kolaszynska-Carr (1970) asked members of these groups to attribute their psychological problems to a cause—sexual or non-sexual. Whereas there were no differences between the female groups, the male homosexuals were more likely than their heterosexual counterparts to have had a sexually connected psychological problem. When we remember that society is more hostile to male than to female homosexuality this result is entirely to be expected. Further evidence comes from studies of the relatively tolerant college environment. For example, Dean and Richardson (1964) found only a very small difference in psychological disturbance between student homosexuals and heterosexuals. It can be concluded that the presence or absence of a psychological problem is a most unsatisfactory method of distinguishing sexual preference. Providing that people are living in a social environment equally tolerant of both preferences, there is no reason to expect one group to be more disturbed than the other; the full range of psychological stability–instability will be found in both groups.

Physical Measures

Body build. The conventional view of the male homosexual is that his build is rather 'feminine'; the opposite stereotype is held of the female homosexual. What is the evidence for these popular beliefs? Once again, it is essential to study people living normal lives in the community and desirable to divide the homosexual group according to whether they fall into our primary or secondary categories. A report by Evans (1972) approaches these requirements. He compared 44 non-patient male homosexuals and 111 heterosexual men for body build, childhood behaviours, and a variety of biochemical measures. Half the homosexual sample was described as having been exclusively homosexual throughout their lives (corresponding to the primary group). The remainder reported occasional heterosexual activity (if we can assume that this had been accompanied by sexual arousal, they would correspond to the secondary group). Differences were indeed found for the body build measures; the homosexual group, despite being slightly taller, were significantly lighter, less muscular, and were longer in proportion to their bulk (termed linearity). Their physique was less masculine on a combined measure developed and standardized by Tanner (1951). Moreover, the range of scores was much greater for the homosexuals than for the heterosexuals—exactly what would be expected of a group containing two relatively different subgroups—whereas some homosexuals had body build scores as high (more masculine) as any of the heterosexuals, *none* of the latter had scores as low as some of the homosexuals. Evans also reported several interesting correlations between linearity and childhood behaviours (more effeminate in the high linearity subjects) which will be referred to later in this chapter.

Sex hormones. Early studies (Heller and Maddox, 1947) failed to show differences in endocrine levels between homosexuals and heterosexuals. The methods were technically crude and, in addition, these studies all compared heterosexuals with undifferentiated groups of homosexuals. The issue was revived by a report by Margolese (1970) who carried out an analysis of serum of androsterone and etiocholanolane in ten heterosexuals and ten homosexuals and found a clear separation in their values with no overlap, the levels of these hormones in the homosexuals being lower than in the heterosexuals. Evans (1972), testing the sample referred to in the previous section, and using refined methods of analysis, obtained significant differences in several biochemical indices between his groups. These included blood serum levels of testosterone and two of the products of androgen metabolism which are considered indicants of androgenic hormone levels, the values of all of which were lower in the homosexual group. Moreover, the *range* of scores was higher in the homosexual group, again suggesting, as did the body build data, the very varied nature of the homosexual group.

Other studies have both used refined biochemical methods and attempted a rough division of their homosexual samples which approximates to the primary/secondary distinction. Kolodny *et al.* (1971 and 1972) studied 30 male homosexual students between the ages of 18 and 24 who were interviewed and assigned Kinsey ratings. The mean testosterone levels when compared to a comparison group of 50 heterosexual males matched for age were significantly below the control mean for homosexuals who were rated as Kinsey 5 and 6, but not for homosexuals with Kinsey ratings of 3 and 4. Unfortunately this report did not detail the extent to which the Kinsey 6's had been solely homosexual for the whole of their lives. Nevertheless, the findings, which replicate those obtained in a smaller study by Loraine *et al.* (1970, 1971) are of considerable importance. Kolodny *et al.* point out that the depressed plasma testosterone levels of their Kinsey 5's and 6's could be the secondary result of a homosexual orientation (the relative absence of heterosexual activity might be the cause rather than the effect). One way to find out would be to carry out biochemical measures on continent males, such as monks, having established that their sexual preference was heterosexual.

However, more recent studies of hormones in male homosexuals have failed to support these earlier findings. Examples of these negative results include reports by Pillard *et al.* (1974) and Doerr *et al.* (1973). Between 1972 and 1977 there have been at least ten more studies on testosterone in male homosexuality which have been well reviewed by Meyer-Bahlburg (1977). He states that most of the homosexuals who have been investigated have normal testosterone levels which are indistinguishable from those found in heterosexuals. There are however a small number of studies which show high or low testosterone levels and only two studies which examined the levels of unbound (active) serum testosterone.

It is known that testosterone levels fluctuate widely both on a daily and a weekly basis (Parks *et al.*, 1974), so that it is quite possible that any real hormonal differences between groups of homosexuals and heterosexuals may have been concealed by these fluctuations. Clearly, more sophisticated methods of sampling for hormone assay are needed and the failure to subdivide homosexuals into primaries and secondaries may well be crucial to the exposure of serum hormone differences between homosexuals and heterosexuals (MacCulloch and Waddington, in press).

Meyer-Bahlburg (1977, p. 311) concludes that because of the inconsistency of the results on testosterone and the methodological shortcomings in many studies, it is 'premature to theorize on general mechanisms underlying endocrine deviations in adult homosexuals derived from individual studies . . . the data available make it seem highly unlikely that deviations in testosterone levels and production in adulthood can be held responsible for the development of male homosexuality in general'.

The results of studies on gonadotrophin levels in male homosexuals also lack uniformity or any coherence, although Kolodny *et al.* (1972) and Doerr *et al.* (1976) both found elevated levels of luteinizing hormone (LH), the former group with decreased plasma testosterone levels and the latter with raised testosterone. Some of Kolodny's subjects appeared to suffer from primary testicular dysfunction so that it is clear that the non-comparability of patient groups is almost certainly the reason for the generally confusing hormonal picture.

EXPLANATION

Introduction

The major explanations of the acquisition of homosexual behaviour will be considered successively in terms of the age at which the effects of biological influences or environmental events are said to occur, beginning with the view that homosexuality is genetically determined, and proceeding through intrauterine influences, early infantile experiences, to single-sex environments, and specific sexual learning experiences. Typically the explanations are intended by their supporters to account for the homosexual behaviour of *all* homosexuals. Thus at one extreme are the proponents of a biological view, and at the other extreme of an environmental view. Occasionally there is a hint of a biology–environment interaction, but in the main the views may be characterized as: the homosexual behaviour of all persons behaving in this manner is environmental in origin, or is biological in origin. By contrast, our approach is that there are two broadly distinct groups of homosexual individuals—the primary and the secondary. In general, and very cautiously, we expect future research to indicate the greater importance of biological influences for the primary group and of social learning influences for the secondary group.

Genetic Influences

The first, and still the largest sample of twins studied with respect to homosexual behaviour, was reported by Kallmann (1952a, b), who described the result of a study of 85 pairs of twins. Information on sexual behaviour was available for 37 of the 40 monozygotic (identical) pairs and 26 of the 45 dizygotic (non-identical) pairs. Whereas all the monozygotic pairs were concordant (similar) for homosexuality, this was true for less than half of the dizygotic group. Despite the apparent conclusiveness of this finding Kallmann's own conclusion was rather cautious: 'On the whole, adaptational equilibrium between the potentialities of organic sex differentials and consequent patterns of psycho-sexual behaviour, seems to be so labile that the attainment of maturational balance may be displayed at different developmental stages by a variety of disturbing mechanisms.' Thus, Kallmann seems to be hinting strongly at the possibility of gene–environment interaction in the causation of homosexual behaviour. A year later, Kallman (1953) considered the 100 per cent concordance between monozygotic twins obtained in his earlier study to be 'a statistical artefact'. In the same book he reported in the form of a footnote: 'A monozygotic pair, one of whom was both schizophrenic and homosexual, the other was neither' (p. 115).

Since this early work several authors (e.g. Rainer *et al.*, 1960; Klintworth, 1962; Parker, 1964) have reported pairs of monozygotic twins *discordant* for sexual behaviour, one being homosexual the other heterosexual. The report by Rainer *et al.* was concerned with two pairs of monozygotic twins, one female and one male, and in both cases the authors claim an early discrepancy in the maternal handling of the members of both pairs of twins. They emphasize the extent to which twins that cannot be easily distinguished induce maternal anxiety. The mother feels she needs to differentiate the twins. Consequently she accentuates, deliberately or otherwise, relatively small initial differences. A similar emphasis on differences in the way twins are handled was made by Parker in his report on three discordant homosexual pairs, two male and one female.

Heston and Shields (1968) report two sets of British data, the first being concerned with a family with a sibship of 14, which contained three pairs of male monozygotic twins. The second set of data consisted of all the twin pairs (12 in number) in the Maudsley Twin Register, which has been kept since 1948, in which at least one member of the pair had a 'diagnosis' of homosexuality. In the first set of data two of the three monozygotic twin pairs were concordant for homosexuality, and one for heterosexuality. All six individuals grew up in 'a severely disruptive environment'. Heston and Shields considered that both genetic and environmental factors were required to explain the aetiology of sexual behaviour in this family. Of the 12 male twins with a primary or secondary diagnosis of homosexuality 5 were monozygotic, and of these, 3 were concordant and 2 discordant (one of the latter two formed part of the series reported by Parker). Of the 7 dizygotic twins only 1 was concordant and 6 were not.

Despite the reports of discordant pairs it seems that concordance for sexual behaviour is more frequent in identical than in non-identical twins. This would be considered as supporting a genetic control of the behaviour in question. Nevertheless, so far as sexual behaviour, which is inevitably largely inter-personal, whether in overt behaviour or in fantasy, is concerned, some doubts must remain. Twins raised in the same home may have their first sexual experience with each other. By definition, identical twins are of the same sex. Given both the probable relative importance of the first sexual experience for later orientation, and the well-known closeness of identical twins, concordance for homosexual behaviour might equally well have an environmental as a genetic basis. It follows that even in those reports in which identical twins are more frequently concordant for homosexual behaviour than non-identical twins, one cannot conclude with confidence that this had a genetic basis unless the twins were separated very early in life and were subsequently reared apart in environments in which heterosexual behaviour was equally encouraged, or equally discouraged. In a study comparing separated and non-separated identical and non-identical twins, the genetic view of causation would be supported if the concordance for non-separated identical twins were as great for separated ones, and if it were greater in both than for non-identical twins of the same sex, whether reared apart or not. The difficulties of securing a sizeable sample of identical twin pairs reared apart are formidable and would be complicated by both the relative infrequency of homosexual behaviour and the reluctance of homosexual individuals to identify themselves. An alternative research design, which would employ the powerful statistical techniques developed in psychogenetic work on animals (Jinks and Fulker, 1970), might be possible using non-twin siblings, who would be much more easily obtainable.

MacCulloch et al. (1967) have described the case of a monozygotic twin pair discordant for sexual orientation, the homosexual twin being of the primary group. This appears to be one of the few reports in which there are sufficiently full data to assign the homosexual twin in a discordant pair confidently to either the primary or the secondary group. It is of interest that the homosexual twin patient of MacCulloch et al. was unaggressive and dependent as a child, in very marked contrast to his heterosexual co-twin. Because the twins were discordant a solely genetic explanation is ruled out, and an environmental contribution must be sought. The effects of the post-natal psychological environment provided by the twins' parents would have had to have been particularly powerful to produce such major and generalized differences in behaviour between the members of the twin pair and the possibility was therefore raised that the source of the 'environmental' contribution determining the primary homosexuality of the MacCulloch et al. patient was the intrauterine hormone environment in which the babies spent their first nine months after conception (see MacCulloch and Feldman, 1977). There does not have to be a sharp division between a genetic and an intrauterine view of the causation of primary homosexuality. It may be that there is a relative genetic predisposition, which then leads to differences in the intrauterine hormone environment of certain individuals: genetic predisposition does not have to be an all or none phenomenon. Below we consider the evidence concerning pre-natal hormonal influences.

Pre-Natal Hormones

It has been established that sex dimorphic behaviour in sub-human mammals is organized early in development, either pre- or perinatally, by sex hormones (Money and Ehrhardt, 1972). There are only a few studies in humans which relate to the effects of pre-natal hormones, but one significant work is that of Money and Ehrhardt (1971) who studied 10 cases of androgen insensitivity, all of whom were homosexual in relation to their chromosomal sex although they were phenotypically female. It is not possible to partial out the effects of hormones and rearing in this and other similar studies, e.g. Money and Ogunro (1974).

However, there is one significant hormonal indicator of pre-natal androgen deficiency which can be used in the adult human male. This potentially promising line of enquiry was opened up by Dörner and his colleagues in East Germany, who have carried out a good deal of animal work concerned with the role of hormones in the general process of brain differentiation described in Chapter 2. An important finding which underlines the study which follows concerns the successive influence of androgen and oestrogen. When normal female rats (i.e. *not* exposed to high androgen levels at a critical period of differentiation—prior to birth) are injected as adults with oestrogen, the result is an increase in the production of luteinizing hormone (LH). The effect on normal male rats (exposed at around birth to male levels of androgen) is the opposite; a lowering of LH. This *positive oestrogen feedback effect* is thought to be due to sexual differentiation of the brain. It suggests another way in which there could be hormonal differences between some homosexuals and all heterosexuals; differences in androgen levels could occur *in utero*, during the period of brain differentiation. In this case the *adult* levels of sex hormones of either group of homosexual males would not be expected to differ reliably from those of heterosexual males. However, at least one important chemical effect of the early presence or absence of androgen should be detectable in adults: the effect of injected oestrogen would be the female pattern of response for both heterosexual females and male primary homosexuals (the positive oestrogen feedback effect) in distinct contrast to heterosexual males and secondary homosexuals who should not show the same feedback effect. Dörner *et al.* (1975) investigated 21 homosexual, 5 bisexual and 20 heterosexual males. The two former groups correspond roughly to our primary and secondary categories. Whereas there was no difference in the serum testosterone levels of any of the three groups, there was a statistically significant difference in the oestrogen feedback effect between the 'primary' group and the combined heterosexual and 'secondary' groups. It may be that this result will not be repeated, thus experiencing the same fate as the earlier findings for simple androgen levels in the adult.

We have noted the equivocal results of studies comparing testosterone levels in adults, but there is one relatively consistent hormonal difference between homosexuals and heterosexuals which is reported in the literature; it is the androsterone/etiocholanolone ratio (Margolese, 1970; Evans, 1972; Margolese and Janiger, 1973), which is lower in homosexuals than controls and particularly so in individuals rated Kinsey 5 and 6. Margolese and Janiger (1973) have suggested that the altered ratio of androsterone/etiocholanolone in the adult may be a reflection of a shift in hormone metabolic pathways from a male pattern to a female pattern. We think that this is a particularly important suggestion because it is known that androgens masculinize the hepatic steriodogenic enzymes in the rat during a critical period of early development (Demoor and Denef, 1968). It seems quite likely that the functions of liver enzymes in the human foetus are influenced by circulating androgen and that a proportion, at least, of primary homosexuals have suffered a relative shortage of androgen *in utero* leading to changes in liver enzymes. Such changes would be reflected in adulthood by abnormalities in sex hormones and their metabolites; we would expect the changes to be more marked in those cases where foetal androgen levels had been very low.

Finally, a fascinating opportunity for an ethically acceptable test of the effect of hormonal influences during pregnancy was available to Yalom *et al.* (1973). Mothers-to-be who suffer from diabetes are often given large doses of oestrogen to protect their unborn children from certain medical consequences of the diabetes. The authors compared the six-year-old sons of diabetic mothers who had been given oestrogen during pregnancy with the sons of mothers who did not suffer from diabetes, and hence did not receive oestrogen. Differences were found on some measures of interest, namely for aggressive behaviour and athletic skills. However, the overlap between the groups was very considerable. Moreover, Yalom *et al.* failed to check the possibility that the diabetic mothers—who required special care during pregnancy—may have behaved more protectively by discouraging aggression, etc. in their sons' early years than did the mothers with normal pregnancies. In order to test biological explanations fully the alternative, environmental explanation, must always be borne in mind, and vice versa.

Child Rearing Influences

The notion that the quality of the relationship between mother and young son is responsible for the kind of sexual relationship the boy is able to make in adulthood has its origin in the psychoanalytic theory of personality development, and specifically the Oedipal situation, homosexuality being seen as the result of an unresolved Oedipal conflict. The normal resolution for that conflict would be that the boy identified with his father, and the girl with her mother. In behavioural terms, both would then learn appropriate sex roles, which would include heterosexual behaviour. The prediction is that an unusually close and intimate relationship with the mother will hinder the development of heterosexual relationships during adolescence and adulthood, and so lead to homosexual behaviour by both boys and girls. The process will be assisted by the behaviour of the father being hostile and rejecting.

The studies which follow have almost all been retrospective in nature, the source of evidence concerning his/her childhood being the recollection of the adult male or female homosexual. Only those studies which have used a comparison group of other adults, presumed to be heterosexual, will be cited.

O'Connor (1964) compared 50 non-homosexual neurotic patients serving in the Royal Air Force with 50 homosexual referrals. The homosexuals had a significantly higher frequency of close attachment to the mother, and poor relations with the father, as well as a history of long absence from father during adolescence. The extent of interviewer bias in determining the difference between the groups may have been quite large, as the same person interviewed both groups, so that the answers may have been affected by a theoretical preconception on the part of O'Connor. A similar criticism applies to a study by West (1959) which compared descriptions contained in hospital case notes of 50 overt male homosexual patients and 50 non-homosexual neurotic controls. The descriptions were independently rated for the nature of the relationship with the parents, and it was found that a combination of a very intense maternal relationship and an unsatisfactory paternal relationship occurred more commonly among the homosexuals than among the controls. Although once the descriptions had found their way into the case histories, they were independently rated, no such constraint was present on the original interviewer, whose questions, and impressions of the answers to them, may both have been influenced to an unknown degree by the theory which West was testing. In addition, the answers to such retrospective questions given by adult homosexuals may be influenced, possibly to a marked degree, by their own acceptance of the theory in question.

Bieber *et al.* (1962) examined the relationships between male homosexuals and their parents, as well as those between the parents themselves. The questionnaires were not completed by the subjects but their therapists. This raises the possibility that the latter, all psychoanalytically orientated, were biased in their reporting of supportive detail and also in their original selection of cases for investigation. It was concluded that: 'The homosexual son emerged as the interactional focal point upon whom the most profound parental psychopathology was concentrated' (Bieber *et al.*, 1962, p. 3).

The most common type of mother among the homosexual group ($N = 100$) and significantly more common than among the control group ($N = 106$, also in psychoanalytic therapy, but not for homosexual problems) was described as 'close binding and intimate'. All but five of the homosexuals' mothers were described as having had 'psychopathological' relationships with their sons. With regard to the fathers of the homosexuals, Bieber *et al.* (1962, p. 310) concluded: 'The father played an essential and determining role in the homosexual outcome of his son.' As a group, the fathers of the homosexuals were described as 'detached, hostile, minimizing and rejecting . . . not one could have been considered a normal parent'. The authors also considered that: 'A constructive, supportive and warmly relating father precludes the possibility of a homosexual son' (p. 311). In addition to the doubt concerning biased reporting raised above, the parental relationships described for the homosexual group were also widely found in the control (heterosexual) group, albeit to a significantly smaller extent, which tends to detract from their specific significance in the aetiology of homosexuality.

Evans (1969) used a 27 item questionnaire adapted from Bieber and administered it to a group of non-patient homosexual men and to a comparison group. The questionnaire was completed by the subjects themselves, and not, as in the Bieber *et al.* study, by the therapist on behalf of the subject. The results were very similar to those of Bieber *et al.*, despite the differences in technique and samples. Snortum *et al.* (1969) also adapted material from the Bieber interview schedule and converted it into a self-administered inventory of developmental experiences, which they administered to a group of male homosexual subjects about to be exempted from military service and to two control groups. While their results also confirmed the significance of a 'close binding' mother and a 'rejecting, detached' father in the aetiology of male homosexuality, both this and the Evans study are subject to the criticism that the answers to retrospective questions given by homosexuals may be influenced by their own acceptance of the theory in question (see earlier for the concept of *justification*).

Bene (1965a) compared 83 non-patient homosexuals with the same number of married (presumed heterosexual) males of roughly equivalent age and social class. Both groups were administered the Family Relations Test (Bene and Anthony, 1962) in order to ascertain the nature of their child–parent relationships. The results showed that homosexual men recalled unsatisfactory relationships with their fathers more frequently than with their mothers. Manosevitz (1970) compared a sample of 28 non-patient homosexual and 22 heterosexual males, matched for educational socio-economic levels. It was found that the parents of the homosexuals were more likely to be divorced or separated than were the parents of the heterosexuals at the time of testing. The conclusion was that homosexuals more frequently came from homes in which they experienced the effects of marital discord.

Apperson and McAdoo (1968) report that in their sample of 22 non-patient homosexuals and 22 heterosexual controls, they found the fathers of the homosexuals were more commonly reported as critical, impatient, and rejecting and that the mothers were less restricting than the mothers of the heterosexual group. In contrast to the above studies, Greenblatt (1966) found no difference between homosexual and heterosexual men on semantic differential ratings of the attributes of mother and father. Fathers of both groups were rated as good, generous, pleasant, dominant and underprotective. Mothers were also rated as good and pleasant, as neither dominant nor subordinate, as neither overprotective nor underprotective. Interestingly enough, Snortum *et al.* (1969, p. 770) concluded: 'The characteristics presently ascribed to the parents of homosexuals bear a striking resemblance to those that have been attributed to parents of schizophrenic patients.'

Studies of the childhood parental relationships of female homosexuals will now be considered. A comparable form of the questionnaire used by Bieber *et al.* was used by Kaye *et al.* (1967) in a study of 24 female patient homosexuals, compared with the same number of non-homosexual patients. The questionnaire was completed by the reporting psychoanalysts, and can therefore be criticized for the same reason as the Bieber *et al.* studies. Kaye *et al.* concluded that although the relationships the homosexual group had with their mothers were 'pathological', they did not differ significantly from those of the control group. The fathers of the two groups were, however, very different. Those of the homosexuals were described as 'puritanical', 'exploitative' and 'feared by their daughters', although the fear was not that of being physically harmed. 'He is overly possessive and is subtly interested in his daughter physically, yet tends to discourage her development as an adult' (Kaye *et al.*, 1967, p. 364).

Bene (1965b), using a group of 37 non-patient female homosexuals and 18 married heterosexual controls, carried out a corresponding study to that with male homosexuals described earlier. Her results suggested that although lesbians received less affection and felt more hostility towards their mothers than did the married controls, much more striking differences between the two groups were found in the feelings that were recalled about their fathers. The lesbian group were more often hostile towards, and afraid of, their fathers than were the married control subjects, and also felt that their fathers were weak and incompetent. In addition, Bené asked each subject whether her parents had wanted a boy when she was born. Significant differences emerged between the groups, which suggested that there might be a connection between the parents' wish for a son and the homosexuality of their daughter. Similar findings were also noted by Kenyon (1968) who carried out a postal questionnaire study of 123 non-patient female homosexuals and married controls. He found that three times as many lesbians as heterosexual controls (28 per cent versus 10 per cent) thought that their parents would have preferred a boy to them. Kenyon also noted that poor relationships were recalled more frequently with both parents in the homosexual than in the control group. This finding was confounded to some extent by the higher neuroticism scores.

Kolaszynska-Carr (1970) asked her subjects to describe the relationships they had with their mother and their father. The replies to these two questions were recorded verbatim and were rated by two independent judges into five major categories. When the overall ratings of the groups for relationships with the father were compared, only the two heterosexual groups were found to differ; the female group getting on less well with the father during childhood. The two female groups did not differ significantly from each other. The two male groups differed only in that more homosexual than heterosexual replies were placed in the 'not very well' category.

When the overall ratings of the four groups for their relationships with their mother were compared, differences were found only between the two homosexual groups; the female group getting on less well with the mother. The hypothesis concerning poor parental relationships for both male and female homosexuals received little support from this study. This is of some importance because Kolaszynska-Carr's study is probably the best designed and controlled yet reported.

What conclusions can we draw concerning the theory that inappropriate child–parent relationships predispose to adult homosexual behaviour? On the face of it, the majority of studies support the view that male homosexuals had more than usually close relationships with their mothers and less than usually close ones with their fathers. Female homosexuals tend to report a relationship with their father which was hostile and rejecting on the part of the latter. Before we can accept these conclusions at even a descriptive level we should note the higher scores obtained by Kenyon's (1968) homosexual group as compared with his heterosexual group on the Neuroticism Scale of the Maudsley Personality Inventory. The implication that disturbed individuals, seeking explanations for their present problems, are more likely to 'blame' the way they were handled by their parents than are other individuals.

Another such report, which casts doubt on the parental relationship theory, has been contributed by Siegelman (1974). He studied several hundred non-patient male homosexuals and heterosexuals and found that for the groups as a whole the homosexuals did describe less satisfactory family relations. However, when subgroups of those who scored low on a questionnaire measure of anxiety were compared, the differences in family relationships disappeared, suggesting that disturbed relationships are reported only by highly anxious homosexuals, and not homosexuals in general. This is always uncertain in retrospective studies, and is particularly so in the present case. It will be recalled that the homosexual sub-culture places heavy emphasis on the search for a justification of homosexual behaviour as something beyond the individual's own control, in terms of either biological or parental influences. Thus, even if a particular study has avoided biasing the outcome by administering a self-report questionnaire directly to the subjects, instead of via a psychoanalyst or some other intermediary, who might himself be in favour of the theory, bias might still enter because of the homosexuals' *own* acceptance of the theory. This might be particularly so for those who are more disturbed, a possibility suggested by Siegelman's results (see above).

An even more fundamental problem is raised by the possibility that parental rejection, or over-closeness, even if it did occur, was *in response* to an existing feature of the child, rather than responsible for a later homosexual orientation in a child not otherwise predisposed. Bell (1968) has cited considerable evidence for the view that children serve as stimuli for their parents; a child unresponsive to parental stimulation will fail to reinforce parental attention, thus extinguishing that attention. For example, the apparent association of an 'autistic' child with 'cool, rejecting' parents suggests the conclusion that the parents have 'caused' the autism. The reverse is, at least, equally possible. Applying this analogy to the present context, it is possible that a father who hoped for a 'manly' son might reject an 'effeminate' one (we shall shortly suggest that the primary homosexual is likely to have been relatively 'effeminate' in childhood). Faced with this situation, the mother might protect the boy concerned. The parental behaviour is thus in response to the child, rather than the reverse. Similarly, parents who wished for a son, but instead were granted a daughter, might respond with rejection. The findings of Bene (1965b) and of Kenyon (1968) mentioned above, support this possibility. A different kind of response would be to treat a girl *as if* she were a boy, by strongly discouraging feminine behaviour, including heterosexually oriented behaviour. The opposite case would be that parents who wanted a girl, but had a boy, might strongly discourage masculine behaviour.

However, we should not go to the other extreme, and completely discount parental behaviour as initiating behaviour in the child, as well as responding to it. For example, parents who convey strong disapproval of heterosexual activities, but fail to mention homosexual ones might, particularly in the context of a single sex environment (see next section), inhibit the use of heterosexual outlets, and increase the likelihood of homosexual ones. A particularly unpleasant father might lead a daughter to expect the worst from men in general—hence, they are better avoided. Other examples could be given. What is clear is that retrospective studies are quite unsatisfactory as methods of testing any explanation where the evidence is obtained by self-report and consists of evaluations of earlier events. This basic criticism applies both to the parental relationship theory and to the view that unpleasant heterosexual experiences are of major importance. The only completely satisfactory method is that of the prospective study. Our present conclusion is that the parent–child relationships are certainly worthy of investigation, but that we should view the relationship as an interaction, rather than a one-way process.

One way round the effects of bias on retrospective studies by adult homosexuals searching for justification is provided by the proposed primary–secondary dichotomy. If we can assume that neither group is more likely than the other to seek justification, it follows that neither is more likely to give biased retrospective accounts. Differences in parent–child relationships as reported by members of the two groups would then be of considerable interest. Unfortunately, the published reports to date of parent–child relationships do not allow the respondents to be divided into primaries and secondaries. In general, we would expect the nature of parent–child and parent–parent relationships to be largely irrelevant to the development of the primary homosexual. In contrast, an environment which inhibited the development of heterosexual behaviour, either through direct means or by poor parental modelling, would be more likely to be found in the childhood of secondary homosexuals than of both heterosexuals and primaries.

It is convenient to collect together at this point the occasional data on the childhood behaviour of homosexuals interviewed as adults. Once again, there should be no greater tendency for justificatory descriptions by primaries than by secondaries—in the sense of reporting childhood behaviour which suggested that they were 'inevitably' different. We expect primaries to report both sex-inappropriate behaviour and at least occasional expressions of a desire to be female, secondaries to report neither (or at least much less frequently than primaries and no more frequently than heterosexuals). Evans (1972) reported relationships between body-build, homosexual behaviour, and self-reported childhood behaviour. As mentioned earlier he found homosexuals to be higher on linearity, being longer in proportion to bulk, and lower on muscularity. Those males in the total group who were high on linearity and low on muscularity more often avoided physical fights, described themselves as frail and played with girls. Unfortunately, Evans did not compare his homosexual and heterosexual groups directly on the above childhood behaviours, let alone make separate comparisons for the two proposed homosexual groups, so that only an indirect inference is possible. However, these data do suggest a tendency towards childhood behavioural differences between adult homosexuals and heterosexuals. A similar inference can be drawn from data collected by Carrier (1971) on Mexican homosexuals divided by self-description into anal-active and anal-passive subgroups on the basis of the role they preferred in anal intercourse. Whereas 88 per cent of the anal-active group reported heterosexual contacts, only 32 per cent of the anal-passive group did so, suggesting a rough identification of the former as secondaries and the latter as primaries. Significantly more passive subjects reported playing with dolls and experimenting with female clothing as children, and as regarding themselves as effeminate, both as children and adults. Interestingly there were no differences between the groups in ratings of their parents on a scale of masculinity–femininity, suggesting that parental modelling was unlikely to account for the self-descriptive effeminate behaviour of the anal-passive group. Finally, whereas none of the anal-active group experienced 'a desire to be female at least once', 83 per cent of the anal-passive group did so.

Green *et al.* (1972a) compared the playroom toy preferences of 15 boys described by their parents as 'masculine' with those of 15 boys described as 'feminine', because of cross-dressing (i.e. in girls' clothing), preferring female playmates, and showing female gestures. Masculine boys played more with masculine toys, feminine boys played more with feminine toys. The 'feminine' group was considered to show the set of behaviours described by adult transsexuals as characterizing themselves in childhood. The authors refer to anecdotal evidence that adult homosexuals also report such childhood behaviour.

Single Sex Environments

There is considerable evidence to link the isolation of animals from access to the opposite sex with disturbed heterosexual behaviour and occasional homosexual behaviour. Although, in natural surroundings mammalian homosexual behaviour takes place when animals are sexually aroused, it usually does so only in addition to heterosexual behaviour. A copulatory preference for males in adult male rats can be induced by prolonged segregation from females (Jenkins, 1928). A proportion of the sample who were isolated continued for an indefinite period to prefer homosexual behaviour, even when allowed access to females. Similarly, Rasmussen (1955) showed that male rats given an electric shock when they attempted to copulate with females were discouraged from further attempts at heterosexual behaviour.

The concept of imprinting at a critical period of development (Sluckin, 1976) has been used to account for such effects. The degree of reversibility of imprinted responses appears to be related to the level of the maturation of the organism. Harlow (1965) showed that adult monkeys separated from their mothers during the first six months of life were relatively incapable either of sexual behaviour with the opposite sex, or of appropriate maternal behaviour towards their own first born offspring. However, there seemed to be some degree of recovery, because mating behaviour improved at a later age and their reponse to the second born offspring was also normal.

Human infants and adolescents are rarely isolated completely, so that it is difficult to separate out the effects of isolation from the opportunities to copy other youngsters who are behaving in a homosexual manner, which they in turn might have acquired from a particular sub-culture. Membership of a single sex sub-culture such as a boarding school, the norm in which was homosexual behaviour, would provide a powerful environment for the acquisition of homosexual behaviour through the imitation of models.

Unfortunately, there is very little evidence for or against such a hypothesized increase in homosexual behaviour in single sex environments, other than of an anecdotal or autobiographical kind (Lewis, 1955). Schofield (1965a) as a minor aspect of his survey of the heterosexual behaviour of adolescents, asked his subjects questions concerning their homosexual experiences. A very much higher proportion of those educated in single sex boarding schools reported such experiences than those educated in day schools, whether co-educational or single sex. However, Schofield did not question his subjects concerning their *present* preferred sexual orientation, and as his sample went up to the age of 19 years only, the persistence of the effects of school experience could not be assessed. West (1967) cites anecdotal evidence of the acquisition of homosexual behaviour by previously heterosexual males incarcerated in prisons or prisoner of war camps. He suggests that the post-confinement persistence of such homosexual behaviour is dependent upon whether it afforded a sexual outlet only or was associated also with emotional gratification, but supplied no quantitative data concerning the post-confinement effect.

Kolaszynska-Carr (1970) found that the proportion of each of her four groups who attended boarding school varied between 16 and 31 per cent. All intergroup differences were non-significant. However, certain significant differences were noted in the average length of time the subjects in each group had attended boarding school. The average length of attendance for the male homosexuals was 8 years, significantly longer than the average length of attendance (5 years) of the male heterosexuals. The average length of attendance of the male homosexuals was also significantly longer than that (4 years) of the female homosexuals. Other intergroup differences were not significant. Hence, the *length* of stay in a single sex environment during adolescence may be of importance for the development of homosexual behaviour in males.

Comparing homosexuals in psychiatric treatment with non-homosexuals in psychiatric treatment, Schofield (1965b) found no difference in the prevalence of homosexuality at the schools attended by the two groups (this is relevant to the modelling theory). He presented no data on the *type* of school attended by the two groups.

Positive and Negative Responses to Early Sexual Experiences

We begin with data relevant to the early experiences of heterosexual behaviour which might have had a negative effect. (It will be recalled that there is good evidence for negative heterosexual attitudes held by adult homosexuals.) Kolaszynska-Carr (1970) looked at relationships with the opposite sex during adolescence. Unfortunately she did not look separately at primary and secondary homosexuals. Nevertheless her data are of much interest. Differences between the homosexual and control groups in the frequency of dating were not found up to the age of 15 but were found from the age of 15 onwards. Considerable differences between homosexual and heterosexual groups were found in the number of subjects who had wanted to go out with members of the opposite sex in the age periods 10 to 15 and 15 to 20. Far fewer of the two homosexual groups reported this desire. Whereas for the heterosexual groups there was a significant rise in the second age period over the first in the number who wanted to date members of the opposite sex, there was no such rise for the two homosexual groups. Thus, while early differences existed they had been considerably amplified by the age of 20. Most of Kolaszynska-Carr's subjects who had experienced heterosexual attraction could recall clearly the first time they had felt sexually attracted to a member of the opposite sex. The mean ages at which the two groups of homosexual subjects had first experienced such attraction were significantly higher than the ages of the two heterosexual groups. In the cases of those homosexuals who had experienced heterosexual attraction, it had occurred less frequently, had been less strong, had more often ceased to exist, and had first occurred at a significantly later age, than among the heterosexuals. This finding may have considerable relevance to the explanation of homosexual behaviour. It seems that the secondary homosexuals begin their heterosexual life at a later age than do heterosexual individuals, perhaps because they have to overcome barriers against overt heterosexual behaviour learned in their home environments, as suggested earlier.

Significantly more of a lesbian group (40 per cent) than of a heterosexual group (25 per cent) remembered being frightened by the sexual behaviour of a man (Kenyon, 1968). Gundlach and Riess (1968) noted a significantly higher incidence of rape below the age of 16 among a homosexual group than among a heterosexual one. What does not appear to have been done is a study of the feelings of adult homosexual individuals about their early heterosexual encounters in terms of the extent to which they felt that this had reached their expectations and hopes. It is the discrepancy between the expectation and the return in heterosexual, as opposed to homosexual, encounters that is of particular interest.

Some data are available on the adolescent self-perceptions of adult homo-sexuals (Kolaszynska-Carr, 1970). No differences were detected between the homosexual and the heterosexual groups in the number who believed that they were unattractive to the opposite sex up to the age of 15, and from the age of 15 to the age of 20, nor were any differences found in the number of homosexuals and heterosexuals who had held the slightly more extreme belief that they would never be attractive to members of the opposite sex. The extent of feelings of rejection by the opposite sex because of personal unattractiveness appeared therefore to be very similar among all groups. However, the heterosexuals, both males and females, had met sexual interest from the opposite sex significantly more frequently than the homosexuals. Kolaszynska-Carr put forward two possible reasons for this difference: first, the homosexuals avoided the company of the opposite sex, thereby reducing the likelihood of such sexual situations developing; second, the opposite sex had perceived the sexual orientation of the homosexual subjects, consequently they did not show sexual interest or make physical advances as these were not likely to be reciprocated. A quarter of the male homosexuals and nearly half of the females had experienced successful heterosexual intercourse, as compared to almost all heterosexuals. More heterosexuals than homosexuals reported having attempted intercourse out of strong physical desire. Homosexuals, not surprisingly, often attempted in-tercourse to prove that they were not homosexual. Reports of impairment of performance or lack of responsiveness were common even from those homo-sexuals who had experienced successful heterosexual intercourse. For most heterosexuals, it was an enjoyable and satisfying experience, to be repeated; for the homosexuals it had been less often enjoyable and was an activity which they did not desire to repeat. As compared to the female heterosexuals, the female homosexuals reacted to heterosexual intercourse with panic and disgust.

The possibility of a *combination* of relatively pleasant homosexual, and relatively unpleasant heterosexual, experiences, in heterosexually arousable individuals is important for a social learning explanation of the secondary group of homosexuals. A relevant study has been carried out by Manosevitz (1970). He found that the total sexual activity before adolescence reported by his homosexual group (all interviewed as adults) was greater than for the hetero-sexual comparison group. Total sexual activity was no greater for homosexuals then heterosexuals during and after adolescence. He compared those homo-sexuals who had successful (leading to orgasm) heterosexual relations, with the heterosexual members of his sample. When asked how they felt about their first heterosexual intercourse experience the heterosexuals tended to rate it as very enjoyable, the homosexuals as only moderately pleasant. The groups were asked if they ever felt nervous, anxious or violent when sexually excited by females. Significant differences in the expected directions were obtained on all questions. Manosevitz considers that his findings suggest that the pre-homosexual child becomes sexually active earlier in his life than the pre-heterosexual individual. 'If a child's object choice is undifferentiated, that is, directed towards both males and females, and if he is sexually precocious while most of his social relations are with males, then it is possible that many of his early sexual experiences will be with same sexed partners. It is entirely possible that these early sexual experiences with males may affect the subsequent development and adult sexual preferences' (Manosevitz, 1970, p. 401). Kinsey *et al.* (1948) also reported an earlier sexual development in homosexual than in heterosexual individuals.

Performance

It can be seen that there are a number of possibilities for the initial acquisition of homosexual behaviour. The variables eliciting the performance of homosexual behaviours by those who have already acquired them are very similar to those eliciting heterosexual behaviours listed in Chapter 3. They will include those facial and bodily features reliably associated with sexual pleasure, a display of sexual interest by a partner viewed as both possible and desirable, the presence of social models responding to homosexual stimuli (e.g. at gay clubs, bars and parties, etc.), a relative lack of previous sexual activity, specific situations previously associated with sexual activity and opportunity variables such as privacy.

Maintenance

Once again, the factors maintaining continued homosexual behaviour are those which maintain heterosexual behaviour; external reinforcement (verbal and non-verbal by a partner or third party), physiological reinforcement (orgasm), and self-reinforcement. Positive outcomes maintain behaviours, negative ones diminish them. As with all types of behaviour, the schedule on which reinforcement is received is very important. The examples we gave in Chapter 3 apply equally to homosexual behaviours. Thus, a person with a well-established homosexual preference, but a consistent record of failure with actual partners is rather likely to avoid further attempts with other people, confining himself to homosexual acts in fantasy, the opposite being true for someone with a consistent record of success. Partial success again leads to continued efforts; how consistently it will do so depends on the individual's exact reinforcement history.

TREATMENT

Introduction: Ethical Principles

In Chapter 5 we preceded the section on methods of helping those with sexual problems with a discussion on the ethical issues which underline all the psychological therapies. These issues are particularly crucial in the context of help-seeking by homosexuals. Until recently such efforts have been concerned with methods of changing the sexual preference from homosexual to heterosexual, but improvements in legal status and in social attitudes and the rise of homophile organizations have combined to increase the probability of homosexuals coming to therapists to seek an alternative goal, namely an increased ease with being homosexual.

A symposium published in the *Journal of Homosexuality* explored the ethical issue very fully. On the one hand, Silverstein (1977) asserted: 'Under no circumstances should a therapist attempt to change the sexual orientation of a patient, including those circumstances where the patient requests such a change. Our position is based on ethical and moral issues that transcend the argument of the efficacy of various treatment modes, i.e. whether we can change sexual orientation, but whether we *should* change it' (Feldman, 1977, p. 241). Davison (1977), another symposiast, agreed, arguing that participation in therapy aimed at change condones current societal prejudices. Essentially what Davison and Silverstein were saying is that the homosexual client who seeks great ease should be helped, the one who seeks a change of preference should not; this rejection of clients' stated goals should extend (Silverstein) to withholding the names of therapists who might be prepared to offer help towards reorientation. But why should the homosexual client be treated differently from other clients in being given only one option? It might be argued that this is another instance of social deprivation suffered by the homosexual, but this time practised by those who would assert that they are most on his side.

Silverstein illustrates his view with the case of an English clergyman seeking change from a homosexual to a heterosexual orientation and successively refused help in England, Sweden, and Canada before coming to New York and telephoning Silverstein who also refused, not only to give the help requested but also to make a referral to someone who might. 'I do not believe that it is my responsibility to meet any demand on the part of the person seeking therapy that conflicts with my own principles and values' (Silverstein, 1977, p. 206).

One of us (Feldman) recently was referred a client whose story illustrates our approach. He was a professional man, married, with young children, living in a provincial English town. Since adolescence he had frequent 'one-off' homosexual encounters with young males, aged 14 to 19, usually in cinemas or public lavatories, the behaviour starting when he was in an all male boarding school, where homosexual models and opportunities were considerable. At the same time, he had been actively heterosexual and his only sustained emotional relationships had been heterosexual, culminating in marriage in his late twenties. Homosexual behaviour had been acquired by participatory modelling in a single sex environment, was performed in response to the widely present eliciting stimuli of public settings where willing partners were readily available and was maintained by the physiological reinforcement provided by orgasms. By contrast, heterosexual partners were much more uncertain and unpredictable in response. By the time he married, the homosexual behaviours were well established and so continued, despite enjoying with his wife a close emotional relationship and a reasonably satisfactory sexual relationship. He had wished, over the years, to be helped to become solely heterosexual in preference, but lacked information as to how to go about this. However, he finally sought help in his early thirties from a knowledgeable and competent therapist, working in a major centre, stating as his objective the totally heterosexual preference. Unfortunately, for the client, the therapist had adopted the Davison/Silverstein view and had argued him to 'accept his homosexuality', indicating that this was the only desirable goal and suggesting contact with gay organizations. Several months later he was arrested by the police and charged with homosexual behaviour with a 15-year-old in a public place. He was found guilty and heavily fined. The case featured prominently in the local newspaper with some consequential social disapproval and much personal distress, although both his business partners and his wife were most supportive. However, the wife felt unable to continue sexual relations with him. At this point he again consulted his own doctor who, by chance, had recently come across a medical press article on the availability of treatment aimed at reorientation and referred him for help.

Treatment took the form of anticipatory avoidance learning and directed masturbation (see below for both) together with the more recently developed cognitive self-control procedures (Mahoney, 1974). The result, at the time of writing, has been what the *client* sought; he has ceased visiting public places to find homosexual partners, and has only very occasional transient, and easily controlled, thoughts about homosexual stimuli. Sexual relations with his wife have been resumed and he is much more responsive to heterosexual stimuli in general than had been the case since his teens. With the *caveat* that the follow-up period is still brief, a long-term trend towards exclusive homosexual behaviour in a secondary homosexual has been halted and reversed in response to the client's wishes.

This person's experiences exemplify our general view of desirable therapist behaviour towards the homosexual who approaches a therapist for *some* kind of help: (a) explore the client's social context and social possibilities and the range of information, both accurate and inaccurate, currently available to him as to the homosexual and heterosexual preferences and settings; (b) fill in the gaps on information or place the client in contact with those best able to do so, such as the gay organizations; (c) offer a range of alternatives including reorientation to the heterosexual preference, greater ease with the homosexual preference, and an increase in heterosexual behaviour, coexisting with continued homosexual behaviour; (d) find out the client's current goals and attempt to achieve them.

Some therapists will find it personally, or professionally, difficult to offer the particular goal sought by the particular client. In that case the remedy is simple: refer to another therapist known to offer the form of help sought.

In practice, most behaviour therapists seem to agree with the broadly-based approach to treatment we favour, as well as our general view of homosexuality, namely that it is not a psychological problem in itself but simply one version of sexual behaviour, which the person concerned may or may not wish to continue. Davison and Wilson (1973) surveyed the attitudes to homosexuality of American and British behaviour therapists (86 respondents, 73 of whom had carried out behaviour therapy with homosexuals): '87 per cent denied homosexuality is *prima facie* evidence of psychopathology ... 91 per cent believed that it is possible for a homosexual to be happy and well adjusted.' In addition '87 per cent stated that they have either treated or would consider treating a homosexual with a goal of making him/her more at ease as a homosexual' (Davison and Wilson, 1973, p. 690). There seem to be no available data on the corresponding attitudes of psychotherapists.

Methods and Results

We now review some of the published results of attempts at treatment of homosexual behaviour. Unfortunately, very few workers have reported their homosexual clients in terms of our primary/secondary dichotomy, although inferences can sometimes be drawn from the data. The emphasis, until very recently, has been on reorientation of homosexuals but studies are now beginning to appear of systematic attempts to achieve the 'greater ease' goal.

Reorientation: psychotherapy, and psychoanalysis. The outcome of a number of series have been reported. Curran Parr (1957) compared 25 of a total of 100 privately treated homosexuals with 25 who had received no treatment. After an average follow-up of four and a half years there were no differences between the two groups. An improvement rate of about 20 per cent was found for two other British series (Woodward, 1958; Coates, 1962). No untreated controls were used for comparison purposes and outcome criteria were vague or unstated.

A large-scale and detailed study was carried out by Bieber *et al.* (1962). They reported a survey of 77 American psychoanalysts who had treated between them a series of 106 male homosexuals. The success rate (defined as a shift to heterosexual arousal and behaviour) was 40 per cent for a group analogous to the secondary category and zero for another group resembling the primary category. The overwhelming majority of those defined as successes received more than 150 sessions of treatment. Assessment of outcome was by the reporting therapist.

Reorientation: behaviour therapy. Many therapists have reported the use of *aversion therapy* which involves either pairing aversive stimuli with homosexual stimuli (pictures of nude males) or making the aversive event contingent on such responses as erections while viewing slides. Both apomorphine, a nausea-inducing drug and electric shock have been used as aversive stimuli. McConaghy (1969, 1970) compared apomorphine, aversion-relief (a variant of aversion therapy) and an untreated control group. Results at follow-up were somewhat encouraging for both of the two active methods but more in the direction of an improvement in heterosexual responding than of a reduction in homosexual responding.

The greater ease of control of electric shock has led to its much more frequent use. Several reports have appeared of comparisons with other methods (Bancroft, 1970; McConaghy and Barr, 1973; McConaghy, 1975). Essentially the results were rather modest, but again there was a suggestion that it would be useful to make direct attempts to increase heterosexual responding as well as to reduce homosexual responding.

A lengthy programme of research into an instrumental learning approach, *anticipatory avoidance learning* (AA), has been carried out by Feldman and MacCulloch (see 1971, for a comprehensive overview). The client views a slide of a male and avoids a shock if he switches it off. The removal of the male slides is associated with subjectively experienced relief and this in turn is associated with the appearance of a slide of a female. Variations in procedures are aimed at strengthening the response of 'avoiding' the previously attractive slide of the male and 'approaching' the previously less attractive slide of the female. Both 'male' and 'female' slides are introduced in a hierarchial sequence selected by the client. Two large-scale studies of AA have been reported by Feldman and MacCulloch. The first was an unselected series of 43 homosexual clients and resulted in a marked change both in self-reported sexual behaviour and in sexual attitude (SOM, see earlier) in the majority of the secondary homosexuals but a virtual absence of change in any of the primary homosexuals. The general distinction in outcome between primary and secondary emerged also in a controlled trial of AA, a classical conditioning avoidance method, and psychotherapy (also in Feldman and MacCulloch, 1971). Both avoidance methods were successful with the majority of secondaries, but failed with the primaries; psychotherapy fared badly with both groups, except for a distinct improvement in the heterosexual SOM scores of the secondaries.

This trial can be criticized, justifiably, for the psychotherapy group having been treated by MacCulloch—raising the question of experimenter bias. Nevertheless, the ineffectiveness of psychotherapy has been documented previously (see above) except in the Bieber *et al.* series (1962) and whereas AA consists of about 20 half-hour sessions the Bieber series had at least 150 one-hour sessions, a vast discrepancy in terms of skilled manpower.

Some support for AA is provided by reports by Birk *et al.* (1971) and Tanner (1974), but essentially the method should be regarded as only one component of a complete behavioural approach; the remaining components including training in self-control procedures to deal with the range of events which often elicit behaviours culminating in homosexual encounters such as sexual thoughts and transient mood changes in response to minor sources of distress, direct approaches to increasing heterosexual arousal, and training in heterosexual social skills (see below for the latter two methods).

Several reports have appeared of small series or controlled single case studies of *covert sensitization* (Cautela, 1967) in which both stimuli and responses are presented 'in imagination' by describing to the client a sequence of events in which he visualizes a potential homosexual partner, first as attractive and then as nauseously unattractive. As a 'relief scene' the client then visualizes a female. Callahan and Leitenberg (1973) reported some superiority over aversion therapy, the effect being greater for decreasing response to males then in increasing response to females (in contrast to the aversion therapy procedures).

Several other behaviour therapy procedures have aimed at increasing heterosexual responding. There have been occasional reports (e.g. Stevenson and Wolpe, 1960) of *systematic desensitization*, very widely used in the treatment of phobias. More direct approaches to increasing heterosexual arousal are those of *pairing* (e.g. Herman, 1972) and *fading* (e.g. Barlow and Agras, 1973). In the former, male stimuli are used to arouse the sexual response and this is then associated with the sight of female stimuli. In the latter, a slide of the female is 'faded in' as that of a slide of a male is 'faded out'. Marquis has used directed masturbation to male stimuli to associate sexual arousal with female stimuli which are 'faded in' appropriately. The methods hold out some promise, in that they may serve to restore the heterosexual arousal previously experienced by secondary homosexuals. None of the behavioural reports specifies the homosexual category of the client; it would be of value to assess heterosexual arousal techniques with primary homosexuals.

The possession of appropriate social skills is crucial in translating increased heterosexual arousability into successful heterosexual social behaviours. Some progress has been made in developing *social skills training* for people with a range of psychological problems (e.g. Trower *et al.*, 1978) but little has yet been applied in the homosexual area, partly because the basic research into the essential components of heterosexual social skills is still in its early stages.

Reorientation: concluding comment. Thus far the published reports of reorientation methods have tended to consist of *techniques*, applied to homosexual clients in general, as opposed to a careful behavioural analysis of the current behaviours, controlling events, and desired outcomes of the individual client. This latter general *strategy* is increasingly influential in the behavioural approach to psychological problems of all kinds. Techniques are employed not according to the label attached to the client, but as indicated by the initial behavioural analysis of the problem. A behavioural analysis approach allows important research questions to be tackled by controlled single case designs and is well represented in the area of sexual problems in general by Barlow (1973).

'Increasing ease'. At the time of writing there appears to be only one report of an attempt at increasing the ease with the homosexual orientation of those who wish to remain homosexual but feel troubled by the social consequences of doing so. Russell and Winkler (1977) studied the effectiveness of assertive training (aimed at helping the individual to select and carry out appropriate behaviours). They compared an assertive training group with a 'non-directive' group who were simply referred for help to a homosexual guidance service. Both groups seemed to improve and to much the same extent. It might be that training members of a homosexual guidance service (increasingly being set up by the gay community) in psychological methods, designed to increase ease, would combine the advantage of a behavioural analysis with the provision of relevant models of a successful adaptation to the homosexual social role.

OVERVIEW

Theories about the development of the homosexual preference have far outstripped the collection of reliable data, even concerning the proportion of the population preferring homosexual partners. This is due largely to the social stigma still attached to the homosexual preference. Partly as a consequence many homosexuals (used as a synonym for 'the homosexual preference') live much of their lives in partially separate homosexual settings and share a sense of common fate.

For more effective descriptive and explanatory studies we urge a distinction into primary and secondary homosexuals. The crucial defining difference is the life-long absence of heterosexual arousal (primary group) as compared to a past or continued response to heterosexual stimuli (the secondary group). Both groups respond to homosexual stimuli. When social settings are equally tolerant standard personality assessments fail to discriminate homosexuals from heterosexuals. The biological measures of body build and the oestrogen feedback effect may have some promise in discriminating the two hypothesized groups of homosexuals. Explanations of homosexual behaviour have implicated every stage of the development of the human adult, from genes to adolescent experiences.

There is much controversy over whether or not it is desirable to offer homosexuals treatment aimed at reorientation. We have argued that therapists should assist homosexual clients attain the goals they themselves select, including reorientation, increased ease with the homosexual preference and a combination of the two preferences. Most reports of treatment have concerned reorientation; the most promising results with the secondary group are achieved by a combination of methods to reduce homosexual responsiveness and to enhance heterosexual responsiveness, as well as increasing sexual knowledge and social skills. To date the results with the primary group have been far less hopeful. Programmes designed to enhance ease with the homosexual preference are likely to benefit from co-operation with the homosexual community.

CHAPTER 7

Other Sexual Behaviours

This chapter consists of two main sections; the first is concerned with sexual variations which are not in themselves illegal and the second with sexual behaviours which are still legally banned in the UK and the USA (sexual offences).

SEXUAL VARIATIONS

Fetishist Behaviours (Fetishism)

Definition. Fetishism refers to sexual behaviour when an object is the stimulus for sexual arousal. Fetish objects include boots and shoes, typically rubber articles and female clothing. In the case of female clothing, which is actually worn by the person concerned and who experiences sexual arousal, the behaviour is known as transvestism, or cross-dressing. Fetish behaviour appears to be confined almost entirely to males. Transvestite fetishism is to be distinguished very clearly from transsexualism, which is discussed in the next section, and involves the conviction, in the case of the chromosomal male, that the inner self is female and vice versa in the case of the chromosomal female. According to this view the male transvestite has no desire to be regarded as a female, or to 'change his sex'. However, it is also possible, first that there is a continuum between the heterosexual transvestite at one end of a scale and the transsexual at the other end, and second, the transvestite individual may, in the course of time, develop into a transsexual. For the present purpose it is simpler to regard them as two quite distinct groups of individuals. There is also the special case of the homosexual transvestite who wears female clothes to attract a male homosexual partner.

Explanation. Two papers (Rachman, 1966; Rachman and Hodgson, 1968) provide a rare example of experimental research into fetishist behaviour. He studied the possibility that sexual fetishism is a learned response, a suggestion which was originally made by Binet in 1888. (The bizarre nature of many of the sexual fetishisms suggests, *a priori*, that a chance conditioning of neutral stimuli

177

to sexual arousal might occur.) In his first experiment Rachman conditioned sexual responses (monitored by the phallo-plethysmograph) to slides of boots of various types (the conditioned stimuli—CS) which were displayed on a screen, immediately prior to the presentation of slides of sexually arousing nude females (the unconditioned stimuli—UCS).

All three volunteers reached the criterion of five successive plethysmograph reactions to the CS within a maximum of 65 paired trials. Rachman was also able to demonstrate extinction and spontaneous recovery. It is of interest that the person who took twice as long to condition as the other two showed the greatest resistance to extinction, and that all the volunteers displayed stimulus generalization to at least one other stimulus (low heeled black shoes) which had not been paired originally with the UCS. In a further study, Rachman and Hodgson (1968) conditioned five volunteers to give a sexual response to a slide of a pair of knee length boots (CS) which was paired with a UCS (again a slide of a nude female). In order to control for pseudo-conditioning a control condition was used in which the UCS was presented prior to the CS. While all five volunteers reached the criterion of five successive responses to the CS with forward conditioning, none did so with backward conditioning. Three of the five showed evidence of stimulus generalization, and the subject who showed the most generalization was the one who took the greatest number of trails to reach the criterion.

It should be noted that an attempt at a partial replication of these studies by Langevin and Martin (1975) achieved only limited success. But in any event it is unlikely that the chance association of a neutral CS with a sexual UCS is *sufficient* to account for the development of fetishism. The intensity of the UCS, or of the CS, or the sexual arousability of the person may be of major importance. The last possibility underlies the view of several research workers that the development of fetishist behaviour is associated with some form of cerebral dysfunction. Epstein (1960) suggested that increased cerebral activity provides the basis for increased responsiveness to sexual stimulation. The heightened arousal provides the basis for orgasm to occur more frequently and hence with an increased probability of being conditioned to neutral non-sexual stimuli. The fetishist then tries to achieve control over his hyperresponsivity and this ritualizes the fetishist act. Epstein supports his theory by citing ten cases which were reported elsewhere in the literature.

A similar view has been put forward by Wölinder (1965) who provided a review of reports relating cerebral dysfunction (particularly temporal lobe disorder) and various sexual deviations. He included several cases of concurrent sexual deviation and temporal lobe epilepsy in which both the convulsion and the deviation disappeared following surgical intervention. Wölinder also presented EEG data on 26 cases of cross-dressing. Of these, eight records were normal, six probably normal, two were borderline and ten abnormal. Six of the EEG records considered abnormal showed the site of the cerebral abnormality to be in one or both temporal lobes. No comparison group was used, and it is not known to what extent the analyses of the records were carried out blind. Further reports of an apparent association between temporal lobe lesions and sexual deviations have been provided by Davies and Morgenstern (1960) and Kolarsky et al. (1967). The latter study presented data on 86 male epileptic out-patients in an attempt to relate sexual deviations to the inferred site of the lesion and its age of onset. Nineteen of these 86 were psychosexually deviant, and 11 of the 19 had their lesion localized in the temporal lobe. Irrespective of the site of lesion, the lesions of the sexually deviant subjects had had an earlier age of onset than did those of the non-deviant subjects. While Kolarsky et al. do not hypothesize that all instances of sexual deviation have their origin in a brain lesion, there is a strong presumption that at least a significant proportion of examples of fetishism are associated with brain lesions. Such lesions, particularly of the temporal lobe, might predispose to the development of the behaviour, although they do not make it inevitable. The bizarre nature of fetishisms makes a combination of abnormal brain functioning and classical conditioning a useful explanatory theory, and further studies on these lines would be valuable.

The psychoanalytic theory of fetishism, as set out by Gillespie (1964), emphasizes fetishism as a means adopted by the individual of overcoming castration anxiety. The fetish remains as the sign of triumph over the castration threat and spares the fetishist any need to become homosexual by making the female into a tolerable sexual object. Gillespie also emphasizes the importance of identification in fetishism. Identification serves as a further defence mechanism, the identification being with a female figure. The criticisms which are frequently made of psychoanalytic theory in general (e.g. Rachman, 1963) apply equally to particular instances. However, the psychoanalytic theory of fetishism does highlight one of the most important facts in this area, namely that it is very rare among females—at any rate, in the absence of published reports, it can be said that females rarely *complain* of fetishist problems. Combining this with the earlier discussion on brain dysfunction and fetishism, it seems likely that early differences in cerebral development between males and females would be well worth investigating.

Once sexual arousal and orgasm have been associated with a hitherto neutral object the object concerned is more likely to evoke sexual arousal; it is no longer neutral. The probability that it will do so is strengthened by the physiological reinforcement provided by orgasm and further repetitions of the fetish behaviour are then likely, particularly if alternative outlets are difficult to obtain or are associated with unpleasant feelings due to experiences of failure or rejection. Thus, lonely, socially unskilled individuals are more likely to continue fetishist behaviours, once they are begun, than those with ready access to willing sexual partners. A further contributory factor is a well-established habit of frequent and intense cognitive rehearsal of sexual behaviours; cognitive rehearsal may be a potent factor in the maintenance of fetish behaviour.

Transsexualism

Introduction. From antiquity onwards many cultures have supplied anecdotes of men who dressed as females and assumed the female role; the reverse phenomenon is known, although to a lesser extent. A recent and well-publicized example is that of the book by Jan Morris (1974). Jan, formerly known as James, is a well-known and highly regarded journalist and writer. Morris dates the desire to change sex to the age of three, 'when I realized that I had been born with the wrong body and should really be a girl' (p. 9). The belief remained, with increasing intensity through boarding school, Oxford, the Army (9th Lancers), and journalism (including participation in the 1953 Everest Expedition).

Throughout school, Oxford, and the Army, Morris was 'pining for a man's love and was never short of protectors' and characterizes the company of males in those years as a 'substitute for girlhood'. There were 'emotional entanglements with both sexes' but overt sexual behaviour only with males (although Morris is throughout very reticent concerning such matters), until 'love rescued me', in the person of Elizabeth: 'we might have been brother and sister, . . . we looked rather alike . . . and were *en rapport*' (pp. 56–58). Although they had five children, sex was subsidiary and Morris asserts that they could have done without it.

The so-called 'sex-change' operation was achieving much publicity by the early 1960s and Morris decided, with Elizabeth's strong approval, to seek help. This took the initial form of several years of oestrogen tablets, resulting in a more female external appearance (increased breast development and smoother skin etc.). Finally, in 1972, Morris underwent surgery in Casablanca. During the years of hormone treatment Morris gradually changed 'his' social role, more and more frequently wearing female, instead of male clothing, altering his name, by deed-poll, from James to Jan and carrying through the change in such official documents as bank books and driving licence. Most friends, particularly close ones, but women much more so than males, were very accepting, even approving, as were their children. After the operation, the social transition was speeded up and completed. Elizabeth and Jan now presented themselves to newcomers as sisters-in-law, and travelled as two close female friends.

Definition. It was only relatively recently that transsexualism was clearly differentiated from transvestism. Benjamin (1953) considers the urge for the change of sex operation to be the best diagnostic sign of transsexualism. It enables the classification of transsexuals into two groups: those who hate their external genitals and wish them to be altered—the 'true' transsexuals—and those individuals who want to keep their genitals but dress in clothes of the opposite sex in everyday situations as opposed to doing so only in sexually meaningful situations—as in the case of homosexual transvestites. Kockott (1970) considers that the major feature of the transsexual is a complete identification with the opposite sex; the identification is a fixed idea and in the extreme form the wish to achieve the sex change operation becomes the only goal in life.

One of the most puzzling aspects of the problem of defining transsexuals is that, because they have a complete identification with the opposite sex even though their sexual interest is directed at their own physical sex, they do not consider themselves to be homosexuals. Benjamin (1953) argues that they cannot be called homosexual because they feel they 'belong' to the sex opposite to that of the chosen partner. Money and Brennan (1969) described a series of 20 physically male transsexuals who had undergone a 'sex change' operation, and reported that 9 of these had married physically normal males who were heterosexual. He puts this forward as evidence for the view that the male-to-female transsexual is not homosexual. However, he also reported that in all cases the 9 post-operative transsexuals had met their future marital partners in homosexual bars.

It does seem, on common-sense grounds, rather unlikely that a heterosexual male would seek as a marital partner a travesty of a heterosexual female and there are similar doubts about the likelihood of a female-to-male transsexual attracting a heterosexual female as a partner. Nevertheless, a study by Bentler (1976) lends support to Money's assertion. His sample of 42 male-to-female transsexuals, all of whom had had surgical operations, included a group predominantly homosexual, *and* a group predominantly heterosexual, both by self-report. That is, prior to surgery all the latter said they had been married 'as a male to a female, and almost all had enjoyed' 'pleasant and successful' sexual intercourse with a female. In contrast, none of the homosexual transsexuals answered either question in the affirmative. The 'heterosexual' group asserted their heterosexual preference strongly and consistently. But the consequence of their surgery was to reduce the likelihood, to put it mildly, that women would continue to consider them as appropriate sexual partners. (Surgery in this context typically consists of removal of the male external organs and the construction of an artificial vagina.)

So the puzzle remains. Its solution is assisted by a report by Barr (1973). He found that nearly 90 per cent of a group of transsexual patients (who were candidates for surgery) showed penile volume changes to slides of males and females similar to those shown by a group known to be homosexual in preference and very different from those whose preference was known to be heterosexual. If we can assume that objective measures of penile response to standard stimuli are a more accurate guide than self-report then considerable doubt is cast on Bentler's distinction between homosexual and heterosexual transsexuals. An alternative possibility is that the latter do exist but were scarcely represented in Barr's sample.

Individual features. Money and Epstein (1967) report intelligence test scores for male and female transsexuals and for 19 pre-pubertal 'effeminate' boys. All three groups showed significantly higher mean verbal than non-verbal scores. No information is provided by the authors on the social class background of their subjects, and as middle class individuals have on average higher verbal than non-verbal scores it is not possible to assign the reason for the obtained disparity to the transsexual or 'effeminate' nature of the sample. Dorbar (1967) reported a group of 34 male transsexual patients to whom were administered a number of cognitive, personality and perception tests. The distribution of Wechsler IQ test scores showed a preponderance towards the upper end of the scale. This supports the possibility that both Dorbar's sample and Money and Epstein's sample were drawn from a middle class section of the population. As Dorbar points out, transsexual patients are persons who have taken the initiative in seeking a solution to their problem by contacting agencies whom they hope will help them, suggesting a degree of sophistication more likely to be found in middle class than working class individuals.

Most of the personality data reported by Dorbar (1967) are concerned with the House-Tree-Person Test and only qualitative and anecdotal accounts of the results of this test are given. However, the finding that in not a single case was a body drawn naked might be of some interest. Dorbar also states: 'It is quite clear that these patients have an intense disgust for their own male bodies.' She reports that they took great care never to view themselves in the mirror and also employed a variety of means to make their true physical sex as inconspicuous as possible.

In general, it seems that the detailed psychological assessment of transsexuals has barely begun. Prospective developmental studies are indicated, particularly of 'effeminate' boys or masculine girls. Such studies are now being carried out particularly at the Gender Identity Research Clinic in Los Angeles. We referred to this work in Chapter 6.

Explanations. First, can the transsexual be regarded as suffering from some kind of psychological disturbance of which the desire for 'sex change operation' is the outward evidence?

Money and Gaskin (1970) discuss the female-to-male transsexual. They consider that in the 'idealized case' of female transsexualism, the patient has a childhood that resembles in obverse that of the male transsexual—whom they term the 'effeminate homosexual' type. She repudiates her female figure, seeking also a hysterectomy, so as not to be confronted with any internal or external evidence of her feminity. Finally, they attempt to distinguish the transsexual obsession from a delusion, considering that the obsession should rather be called a 'fixed idea'. Hoenig and Kenna (1974), who studied a very large number of British transsexuals, tend to agree and concluded a detailed attempt to fit the transsexual into the psychiatric classification by saying 'And so we have an orphan on our hands, whose relations cannot be found'.

Much the most influential earlier theory on the causation of transsexualism arose from studies on individuals who were physically intersexual, possessing internal organs or chromosomal constitutions which had characteristics both of the male and the female. The first survey of intersexuals was carried out by Ellis (1945) who abstracted from the medical literature all the cases in which both the glandular constitution and sexual preference of intersexuals were known. Of 39 intersexuals who were reared as males, 34 showed sexual desires of a definite type; in all 34 cases their desires were heterosexual. This was despite the fact that 23 of them had either mixed or female sex organs. It seemed that the sexual inclination of the majority of intersexuals correlated closely with their upbringing. In a study of a consecutive series of 100 patients with different types of intersexuality, Money and Hampson (1957) confirmed that, with an occasional exception, the behaviour of these individuals followed the sex of rearing. They considered that gender identity was firmly established by the age of two or three and that attempts to change either became increasingly difficult after that age.

One criticism of this approach concerns the great difficulty of generalizing from individuals who are intersexes to those who anatomically and physiologically quite clearly belong to one sex or the other. Certainly the major distinguishing feature of the transsexual, the fixed belief in the fact that he should have been born as a member of the opposite sex, was quite lacking in the intersexes. Hence, the possibility raised in Chapter 6, in connection with the development of homosexuality, concerning early hormonal influences on the development of sexual behaviour appears relevant.

The following summarizes this general approach and applies it to transsexualism. There are male and female hypothalamic brain centres which control sexual behaviour according to the way in which they are activated in foetal life. It has also been discovered, at any rate in animals, that a critical period exists when, in a genetically male foetus, activation of the masculine centre occurs, due to androgen production in the foeto-placental unit. In the case of a child who later becomes a male transsexual some process interferes with the production or the effects of androgen so that existing progestogen activates the female centre and produces a female brain. The 'female' brain determines the subsequent sexual behaviour and causes gender role disorientation. Conversely, in the genotypic female cerebral 'masculinization' occurs through an abnormal level of male sex hormones or by a failure of the progestogen protecting effect. Endocrine differences would not necessarily be expected in the adult precisely because the activation of cerebral centres is time-locked to the twelfth week after conception. Indeed, as we have seen (Chapter 6), earlier reports of such differences have not been consistently confirmed, although it is possible that some people have abnormal serum levels of sex hormones in adulthood.

A further suggestion is made by Money and Gaskin (1970) who implicate the 'possible disruptive effect of events in the social environment after birth'. They state: 'It is possible that a traumatic intensity of, or over exposure to, any form of social interaction in infancy or early childhood is potentially detrimental to the delicate process of gender-identity differentiation.'

'The effects of such detrimental social experience, if it occurs at a critical developmental period of gender-identity differentiation, may be permanent or near-permanent, and virtually ineradicable. In this sense it becomes an imprint and shares the indelibility that a genetic trait has, once it has expressed itself. The most likely explanation in the majority of cases of transsexualism, on the basis of today's knowledge, is that transsexualism is an extremely tenacious critical period effect in the gender-identity differentiation of a child with a particular, but as yet unspecifiable, vulnerability' (Money and Gaskin, 1970, pp. 252–253).

Bentler (1976) has combined a biological emphasis on pre-natal brain feminization with post-natal social learning experiences, such as the positive reinforcement of sex-inappropriate behaviour and lack of such reinforcement for sex-appropriate behaviour. In other words, boys biologically predisposed to be 'effeminate' are positively reinforced for showing 'feminine' behaviours but are not reinforced when they show masculine ones.

Sado-Masochism

The sadist derives sexual pleasure from inflicting pain, humiliation or violence on his partner, the masochist from submitting to such experiences. Little is known in any scientific sense about this form of sexual behaviour. Very few sadists or masochists seek help and there appear to be no studies on those who have not done so. Mayer-Gross *et al.* (1968) also point out that sadism may take forms that are not immediately identifiable as sexual, examples being the Nazi war criminals, who tortured and killed their victims, though without necessarily making any specifically sexual assault or deriving apparent sexual pleasure from their acts.

Henriques (1968) illustrates the extreme popularity of flagellation in the nineteenth-century London brothels. 'By the middle of the century London had become the flagellation capital of the world.' He cites authors of the time as indicating how the painful sensations ultimately underwent complete transformation into pleasurable ones. This appears to be the central element of masochism and will be returned to later. Henriques suggests that school physical punishment laid the ground for the later development of the behaviour. He also points out that respectable newspapers such as *The Times* and the *Telegraph* were prepared to take advertisements which, in effect, offered the services of a flagellator.

One of the very few scientific reviews of the field is that by Sandler (1964) and he deals, almost entirely, with animal work. However, he does give a useful definition of masochism: 'The crux of the issue rests on demonstrating the typically noxious effects of a stimulus, on the one hand, and the absence or modification of this reaction in the masochistic situation, that is, a change in reaction to what is typically regarded as a punishing stimulus. For our purpose, therefore, masochism will be regarded as having been demonstrated in those instances where an empirically determined noxious stimulus, defined in terms of a pain response (avoidance withdrawal, howling, leaping, etc.) does not reveal such effects in another intact member of the same species' (Sandler, 1964, p. 198).

Sandler points out the wide degree of agreement between theorists of very different schools. Skinner, one of the leading figures in behaviourist psychology, proposes two forms of masochism. In discussing how self-injury may be arranged, he states that individuals might expose themselves to aversive stimulation if, by doing so, they avoid even more aversive consequences. In the second form, aversive stimuli might be paired with the reinforcer which follows a given activity. The end result may be: 'The aversive stimulus becomes positively reinforcing in the same process' (Skinner, 1953, p. 367). This view is strongly in accord with psychoanalytic thinking. For example, Fenichel (1945) states as one of the several conditions under which masochism might occur: 'Certain experiences may have so firmly established the conviction that sexual pleasure must be associated with pain that suffering has become the prerequisite for sexual pleasure' (Fenichel, 1945, p. 357).

Drawing on experimental studies of animal behaviour Sandler lists the factors that must be present in order for the phenomenon of masochism to appear, as follows. The punishing event must be introduced only after a response has been established in the usual reinforcing paradigm; the punishment must be introduced in such a way that the response is not completely inhibited during acquisition; some attempt must be made to provide for the maintenance of punished, non-reinforced behaviour over longer periods of time. The last point very strongly implicates what is known about the enhanced resistance to extinction following partial reinforcement schedules (Lewis, 1960). There is no doubt that the appropriate scheduling of events has a powerful influence on response durability. Behaviour can be maintained over long periods of time in the absence of reinforcement through the use of training under intermittent stimulus and this technique has been responsible for high rates of response to self-aversive stimulation. Sandler (1962) studied five Marmoset monkeys and found that, when they were operating under intermittent reinforcement as well as the other conditions which were listed above, they showed continued responding in the face of repeated punishment. He points out that if observations of these subjects had been restricted to those periods of responding during which no reinforcement occurred (often as high as 95 per cent of the time) one might even conclude that these are 'truly' masochistic creatures. The animal studies cited by Sandler were concerned with non-sexual behaviours carried on for 'painful' rewards. The generalization of this model of acquisition to sexual behaviours is at the present time inferential.

Turning now to the sadist, once he has learned to obtain pleasure in a general sense from inflicting pain upon others, or at least has learned not to be distressed about inflicting pain upon others, this behaviour might serve as a basis to which sexual pleasure can then become attached. As the behaviour is not, in itself, illegal, and as sadistic individuals rarely, as far as is known, seek help, any systematic study of sado-masochism will be a difficult task.

SEXUAL OFFENCES

Introduction

We shall discuss only those sexual offences in which there is a *victim* (either non-consenting or below the legal age of consent), which do not involve an actual physical assault on the victim, and concerning which we have a reasonable volume of research findings. Thus we shall concentrate on rape, sexual relations between an adult and a minor (paedophilia), and indecent exposure (exhibitionism), and exclude homosexual relations and incest. Homosexual relations between consenting adults in private are no longer an offence in most countries of Europe. Changes in the law are also probable in the United States or have already begun to be enacted. In the future it seems likely that the law will become increasingly similar for homosexual and heterosexual behaviours between consenting adults. Incestuous acts (roughly, sexual intercourse between father/daughter, mother/son, or brother/sister) are prosecuted very rarely in

Britain or in the USA. As there is not usually a 'victim' in the usual sense of that word, complaints are unlikely to come from either participant, and in fact the true incidence is entirely a matter for conjecture. At present, quantitative research on any aspect of incest, whether causes or consequences, is very sparse, although it is now recognized that daughters may be their father's unwilling partners and in general the behaviour attracts much social revulsion.

The Social Context

Clinard (1968) points out that what is an unimportant sexual act in one social context may become a serious breach of law in another. He notes the different consequences of a pat on a waitress's rear by a truck driver in a transport cafe, a diner in a middle-class restaurant, and a man in the street who encounters her by chance. The first may be regarded as perfectly normal in the context, the second as an offensive display of bad manners, the offender being asked to leave, and the third, if reported to the police, may lead to a charge of sexual assault. Gebhard *et al.* (1965) gave the following definition of sex offence, combining both cultural and legal aspects: 'A sex offence is an overt act committed by a person for his own immediate sexual gratification which (i) is contrary to the prevailing sexual *mores* of the society in which he lives and/or is legally punishable, and (ii) results in his being legally convicted.' (Cited by Clinard, 1968, p. 345.)

Wheeler (1967) points out that the strongest legal sanctions are directed towards controlling the degree of consent in the relationship, with many states (in the USA) allowing the death penalty for forcible rape. Other bodies of sex law place limits on the nature of the object. For example, while there is an increasing tendency in different parts of the world to allow homosexual relations with a consenting adult, there is little serious move anywhere (with the possible exception of Holland) to allow them between an adult and a person under 14 (16 in Britain), even if he (or she) appeared to consent. There are parts of the USA in which legal restrictions are also placed on the nature of the sexual act, so that full legality is restricted largely to acts of heterosexual intercourse other than oral–genital contacts, digital manipulation, and anal entry, all of which are technically illegal, even when they occur by consent between a married couple. Finally the law attempts to control the setting in which the act occurs. Acts which are legal when they occur in private may be proscribed when they occur publicly.

Clinard (1968) cites a good deal of evidence to support the view that sexual offenders do not usually re-offend. For example in England, of a group of nearly 2,000 convicted sex offenders who had been released for four years, 85 per cent had no subsequent conviction (Radzinowicz, 1957). However, it is very difficult to know what to make of such figures. The majority of offences of most kinds are either unreported or remain undetected by the police. This is likely to apply with particular force to sex offences. Hence, it is very likely that the low apparent proportion of re-offending among convicted sex offenders considerably under-states the actual percentage which re-offend. The finding that a considerable proportion of convicted sex offenders do not attract a psychiatric label is of some importance because individuals who are disordered are likely to be less 'efficient' offenders (in the skills which avoid detection) than are less disturbed persons. It follows that those offenders who remain uncaught are likely, if anything, to be even less disturbed, on average, than those who are caught.

We can conclude that the findings about those who carry out the offences which follow are based on samples of offenders which are only tiny fractions of the total population of those actually carrying them out and may be very unrepresentative as samples. At the time of writing there appear to be no studies of *undetected* rapists, exhibitionists, and paedophiles.

Rape

Introduction. A physical assault which includes sexual intercourse is termed rape and if the accused is convicted the result is often a lengthy prison sentence. The overwhelming majority of rapes reported to the police are carried out by males on females and all the research to date has concerned male offenders. In Chapter 3 we discussed the complex relationship between sex and aggression. Rape by a conquering army has been noted extensively and an important research question, to which we return below, is the extent to which rape represents an indication of the low regard in which the victim is held, rather than a sexual act in itself. Whereas exhibitionists and paedophiles may obtain a high proportion of their total sexual outlets through their deviant preferences, there is evidence that this is not true of many convicted rapists, whose heterosexual activities with consenting partners may be at least average in frequency (Gebhard *et al.*, 1965).

Frequency. There are no reliable data on the true number of rapes, but it can be said with certainty that only a fraction are reported. In Britain in 1973, nearly 900 were reported to the police, twice as many as 10 years earlier. Does the increase indicate a true increase in frequency or simply a greater willingness to inform the police?

Social reaction. There is no doubt that a great many victims do not report what has happened, both because of their distress and shame and because of a very widespread expectation that the police enquiry and any subsequent court appearance will prove equally humiliating. Certainly there have been a number of instances, well documented, by such organizations as WOAR (Women Organized Against Rape), in which the court has seemed more sympathetic to the accused—even when found guilty—than the victims. Many big cities, particularly in the USA, now have a Rape Crisis Centre, manned on a 24-hour basis, to which victims can turn for immediate help and advice.

Features of offenders and explanations of rape. The most thorough study to date is by Amir (1972) but he is careful to point out that it includes only convicted rapists who may be a very biased sample. Amir found the rates of forcible rape by known rapists to be highest for young, single, lower socio-economic non-whites, exactly as for officially indexed crimes of violence in general. In addition, rape tended to be an intra-class racial phenomenon—the victim was also likely to be poor, and non-white. (It should be noted that Amir's survey was carried out in Philadelphia.) Thus Amir emphasizes a particular sub-culture as supplying a learning setting for crimes of violence including rape.

Obviously a certain proportion of any group of humans is likely to be psychologically disturbed, but is disturbance a particular feature of convicted rapists? Amir reports the majority of convicted rapes to have been planned and carried out by young heterosexually active males, often against someone they knew, however slightly. An alternative approach is to divide rape into those carried out by people who are sexually deprived at the time and those who are upset and angry at the time. This latter dichotomy was investigated by Howells and Steadman-Allan (1977) who studied the self-reported feelings, at the time of the rape, of a group of rapists and a group convicted of non-sexual assault. Whereas for many of the rapists sexual feelings were the most salient, for others negative emotions concerning the victim predominated—exactly as for those guilty of non-sexual assault.

A social learning approach to the acquisition of the behaviour would point to the importance of social models—young men who had already raped, the presence of others bent on rape, and the opportunity provided by suitable victims, as well as a probable lack of detection. Once carried out, the behaviour becomes part of the repertoire of the individual concerned. This account deals well with group rape, but does it cope as well with rapes carried out by individuals? It may be that the latter are more socially isolated, with less access to friends of either sex. Once again, the social learning approach makes a contribution. An examination of 'solitary' rapists suggests common features of both the victim and the circumstances. For example, the victims of a particular rapist may be young students living in single accommodation and his assaults are carried out after dark. By successful repetition, features of both the victims and the circumstances become habitual cues for the behaviour of sexual assault. Solitary rapists, particularly those whose rapes are reinforced by the distress of a victim (disliked for what she 'represents') rather than by the reduction of transient sexual arousal, seem likely to be influenced by prolonged cognitive rehearsal of the whole sequence of the act. Conversely, cognitive aspects seem less likely to be important for 'group' rapists and those solitary rapists aroused to rape by sexual stimuli.

Paedophilia

Introduction. In Britain heterosexual intercourse is illegal between a male and a female when either, or both, partners are under 16. Homosexual intercourse is illegal when either partner is under 21. In practice prosecutions tend to be brought more in the homosexual than in the heterosexual area and when one partner is an adult and the other under 16, than when both are adolescent. In such instances the adult concerned attracts the label 'paedophiliac' or 'pae-dophile'. There are no data on the proportion of the adult population whose preferred sexual partner is a pre-adolescent. Convictions reflect many factors including complaints by the 'victim'. It is quite unknown what proportion of habitually paedophiliac individuals are ever convicted. Even the definition itself is inconsistent between research studies. One of the few major surveys, that of Mohr *et al.* (1964), carried out at the Toronto Psychiatric Clinic (Canada), included all paedophiliac referrals (55 in number) between the years of 1956 and 1959. They defined paedophilia as 'the expressed desire for immature sexual gratification with a pre-pubertal child', where pre-pubertal meant before the development of secondary sexual characteristics. Because the average age of onset of puberty is well under 16, many of those in the sample would seek as partners children aged 13 and under. By contrast, another survey, carried out in Britain by Schofield (1965b), defined as paedophiliacs those whose preferred sexual object was under the age of 16. Hence some of Schofield's sample would not be regarded by Mohr *et al.* as paedophiliacs.

The behaviour. Whereas Mohr *et al.* emphasized 'immature' sexual gratifi-cation, meaning sex acts appropriate to the age of the victim (used throughout this section instead of 'partner', which may, or may not be, more accurate depending on the 'willingness' of the child concerned) such as mutual genital display, fondling, etc., Schofield made no such limitation. However, 6 of the 26 homosexual paedophiliacs in Mohr's sample used fondling as their major sexual act; by contrast in 14 cases the major acts consisted of undoubted overt adult sexual behaviour including fellatio, anal intercourse, and masturbation. In addition, Mohr *et al.* cite other studies, including that carried out by Radzinowicz (1957) in which only 9 per cent of the homosexual offences recorded consist of fondling, and a California study (California Department of Mental Hygiene, Sexual Deviation Research, 1954) in which the vast majority of paedophiliac acts consisted of overt sexual behaviour. In the case of heterosexual paedophiliacs only a minority of the acts with the victim involved 'immature' behaviour such as fondling or display. No definite generalization to the total population of paedophiliacs can be made from the samples of offenders seen in prison, or in psychiatric centres, as it may be that complaints are not made either by the victims or their parents unless sexual behaviour of a more active kind than fondling or display is involved.

Individual features. A majority of the paedophiliacs in the Schofield sample were married. However, there was a strong tendency for the marriage to break down, the same tendency being noted by Mohr *et al.* Both Mohr *et al.* and Schofield reported that homosexual paedophilia began relatively late in life. Mohr *et al.* described three peaks, one in puberty, one in the mid- to late-thirties, and one in the mid- to late-fifties, 'only a small minority being paedophiliacs from childhood onward'. Twenty-two of the Schofield series reported no sexual experience with boys until the age of 21, 15 of whom claimed none until the age of

30, and 6 none until well over the age of 50. By way of contrast, Feldman and MacCulloch (1971) found that all seven of the paedophiliac patients whom they treated by aversion therapy had an unbroken history of paedophiliac behaviour from adolescence onwards. The difference between the findings of the latter authors, and those of Mohr *et al.* and Schofield, may reflect the different degrees of thoroughness of interview used. Feldman and MacCulloch interviewed their patients, in hospital, for several hours in each case. Schofield's interviews were carried out in prison, and lasted no more than 50 minutes. Although the prisoners were assured that the information would be confidential, Schofield himself doubted whether the prisoners behaved as if they believed this assurance. Similarly, the Mohr *et al.* group had all been apprehended.

One of the few systematic reports concerning the personality of paedophiliacs is that by Fisher and Howell (1970) who administered to groups of homosexual and heterosexual paedophiliacs the Edwards Personal Preference Schedule (EPPS, Edwards, 1959). The EPPS consists of a number of scales designed to indicate the level of a particular 'need'. Both groups had been convicted (in California) of sexual offences against children. It was found that heterosexual and homosexual paedophiliacs were more like each other than either were like the heterosexual male comparison group (a large normative sample reported by Edwards, 1959). Both homosexual and heterosexual paedophiliacs were significantly higher on *intraception* and *abasement*, and significantly lower on *autonomy* and *aggression*. The heterosexual paedophiliacs were lower than the homosexual paedophiliacs on *heterosexuality*. The finding concerning heterosexuality casts doubt on the view that male paedophiliac behaviour is a substitute for heterosexual behaviour adopted by some middle aged men. In sum, both homosexual and heterosexual paedophiliacs tended to be rather more neurotic and introverted (to simplify the terminology of the EPPS) than the population at large. It is unknown whether these personality features preceded the beginning of paedophiliac behaviour, or were responses to the social disapproval of such behaviour.

Social reactions and individual outcomes. It is safe to say that the attitudes of the population in general range from extreme hostility to feelings that paedophiles are to be pitied and helped to become more normal. A recent development in Britain is the Paedophile Information Exchange, which aims to change such social attitudes. According to an interview with the ex-Chairman of PIE reported in the *Guardian* (1977) PIE aims to reduce the age of consent to four and to remove from the statute books all laws restricting children's sexual activities. In support of these aims PIE members cite evidence concerning the early sexual development of many young children and the loving nature of many adult–young child sexual relationships. Nevertheless such arguments seem essentially self-serving, as the *Guardian* writer (Polly Toynbee) points out: 'the true situation is one of adults initiating young children into adult sexual activities which they would otherwise not have encountered for some years, and then only with partners at or near to their own age.'

The actual extent to which the victims of paedophiles are affected by their experiences has been looked at by several authors. Mohr *et al.* (1964) review evidence to show that there is little tendency for the victims to show sexual problems as adults, of a gross kind, but there is a tendency for some to experience problems in their social and emotional adjustment. Unfortunately in none of the surveys cited by Mohr *et al.* were control groups used. Doshay (1943) followed up 108 boy victims of sex offenders aged from 7 to 15. In the whole group there was not a single instance of a paedophiliac offence when they themselves were adult. Similarly Tolsma (1957) followed a panel of 33 boys who had homosexual experiences with adults. All but 8 were married and did not continue homosexual practices. It should be noted that in both surveys the victims concerned were those whose experiences were known to the police. A further, unknown number, will also have had the same experience. Finally, Schofield (1965b) reports that three-quarters of a non-patient homosexual group had started homosexual practices before the age of 17, most of them with boys of the same age. Only a relatively small proportion (16 per cent) had a homosexual initiation by an adult. Once again the sample is hardly likely to be a representative one. It would be desirable to compare over a long period a true sample of the partners of paedophiliacs with other children, the two groups being matched for variables such as degree of psychological disturbance at the age at which the victims were first involved. In the meantime most parents will decide that while sexual encounters with adults may or may not do their children actual harm, they are rather unlikely to gain positive benefit from them and will endeavour to prevent them occurring at all.

Explanations. There are few reliable descriptive findings concerning paedophiliac behaviour, and hence little on which to base explanatory theories, which would enable the development of well-grounded methods of help. Nevertheless, the general finding that behaviour is maintained by its consequences and by the availability, or otherwise, of alternative behaviours, is likely to apply also to paedophiliac behaviour. The performance of the behaviour will be elicited by opportunity and appropriate instigating stimuli. The antecedent conditions for its initial acquisition are less obvious. Their specification will be assisted if the problem of the most usual age of onset of the behaviour can be cleared up. The central aspect of the behaviour seems to be the attraction of an adult to sexually immature persons, whether of the same sex or the opposite sex. Moreover, the attachment is frequently more than a solely sexual one. There may be a generalized and life-long inability to form emotional attachments to adult persons of the same age, but in that case why have some paedophiliacs married? There are no reported studies of the wives of paedophiliacs.

Concluding comment. Paedophiliac behaviour is most unlikely to be legalized and the courts will continue to have before them many hundreds, even thousands, of cases per year. Many will be sent to prison, where they are exposed not only to the criminalization experienced by prisoners in general, but also to the hostility and contempt reserved by their fellows for sex offences, particularly those concerning children.

Exhibitionism

Introduction. As far as the official statistics are concerned exhibitionism is one of the most frequently encountered sexual deviations in the United Kingdom. The offence 'indecent exposure' formed one-quarter (490) of Radzinowicz's (1957) total of 1,985 sexual offenders in his 1957 study, and represented approximately one-third of the sexual offenders found guilty in 1965. However, as pointed out by Schofield (1965b) the likelihood of the very much more common homosexual behaviour resulting in a conviction was so minimal prior to the change in the law as to be almost non-existent. Once again, one cannot argue from the frequency of a sexual behaviour in the criminal statistics to the frequency of the behaviour in the population at large.

In the case of exhibitionist behaviour, the only source of information is the complaint of the victim (used throughout this section as a less clumsy term than 'exposee'). The frequency of complaint will depend upon the degree of personal distress experienced by the victim and her previously learned manner of responding to exhibitionist behaviour: 'ignore it', 'report it', etc.

Definition. The simplest definition is 'The exposure of a part or whole of the body for sexual or non-sexual rewards' (Evans, 1970). A variation is given by Rosen (1964) who defines an exhibitionist as a man who exposes his genitals to someone of the opposite sex outside the context of the sexual act. Mohr *et al.* (1964) define exhibitionism rather similarly, except to add as an important feature: 'Not leading to an aggressive act'. The behaviour seems almost entirely confined to males, even in non-Western cultures (Ford and Beach, 1952). In those few societies in which women deliberately expose their genitals, exhibitionism appears to be a stage of courting behaviour.

Classification. Both Mohr *et al.* and Rosen (1964) divide exhibitionist acts into two groups. In the first, the act follows as the result of some rather obvious social or sexual upset, disappointment or loss, or as an accompaniment to a severe mental or physical illness. The second is associated with an obsessive-compulsive personality. The individual may try to resist the compulsion to expose himself, but finally gives way to it. Rosen describes two types of precipitating event. In the first there is an internal sexual excitement arising spontaneously, as in the adolescent, or instigated in the adult exhibitionist by sexually arousing visual stimuli. In the second type exposure occurs as a result of a non-sexual tension situation.

Description. Evans (1970) states that the act of exposure will vary according to the timidity or the boldness of the offender and the urgency of the compulsion.

Some expose from behind a curtained window or while seated in a parked car. At the other extreme the offender may totally undress and spring out before his victim. The act is, as often as not, carried out in a public place. Some exhibitionists expose repeatedly in the same spot.

Mohr *et al.* (1964) report that in only 4 of 54 cases were neighbours exposed to instead of strangers, and in 3 of these instances the neighbours were inadvertent victims. (However, exhibitionists may avoid exposure to neighbours because recognition and complaint are much more likely.) Both Mohr *et al.* and Radzinowicz (1957) report that exhibitionists exposing to adult females tended to expose to them individually, while those exposing to children were more likely to do so to groups of children. Some exhibitionists are extremely specific in their choice of victim—she must wear certain clothes, must appear educated and sophisticated, or have other virtues.

A central feature appears to be that no further relationship is sought between the offender and the victim. In only a few instances does exposure constitute a frank sexual invitation. For most exhibitionists the intended reaction of the victim appears to be of three kinds: fear and flight; indignation and abuse of the exhibitionist; pleasure and amusement. It is also true that a 'victim' who responds favourably is not likely to complain to the police. Once again, research has been confined to those who have been convicted. The usual age of onset of exhibitionism is at puberty and the peak period ranges between the ages of 15 and 30. Onset after the age of 45 is extremely rare except when it is the result of organic factors (Evans, 1970).

Individual differences. The intelligence scores of the Mohr *et al.* (1964) series were normally distributed, but there was some tendency to educational underachievement. However, as no data were provided on social class the specific importance of educational factors cannot be estimated. While the majority of the Mohr *et al.* series had good work records, the authors also state: 'They seem to have difficulty with their supervisors'; no evidence for this statement is supplied. Exhibitionists tend to marry, according to Mohr *et al.*, at a normal age, the majority being married in their early twenties, with the peak age at 22 to 23. In most series the proportion who were married varies between 50 and 60 per cent (Evans, 1970). Mohr gives an anecdotal description of the nature of the relationships with the wife and the personality characteristics of the wife; the latter are said to include considerable difficulty in the sexual area, but no clear data are supplied. The characteristics of the wife are said to involve dependence and ambivalence; again the evidence is anecdotal.

Mohr *et al.* cite personality assessments by Rickles (1950) to the effect that exhibitionists tend to be: 'Tense, compulsive, with a rigid control over emotions'. No quantitative data, or data for comparison groups are given, but there does seem to be general agreement in the literature that the exhibitionist act has the phenomenological quality of a compulsion (the 'urge' to perform a behaviour is first resisted, then the resistance is overcome). Rosen (1964), reviewing a series of 24 exhibitionists who received psychoanalytic therapy over a two year period, considered that there was a functional equivalence between exhibition and the expression of aggression. He drew this conclusion because: 'It was possible to deal indirectly with the sexuality of the patients a great deal of the time by discussion of their aggressions.'

Associated problems. Several organic conditions have been reported to be associated with a consequent exhibitionism. Evans (1970) sees some exhibitionist acts as a consequence of confusion and the loss of self-esteem and moral values present in conditions that involve damage to the central nervous system. Typical examples are brain tumours, presenile psychosis, senile arteriosclerosis, and general paralysis of the insane. Diabetics have exposed when their blood sugar is poorly controlled. Often an exposure occurring in a person with no previous convictions of any kind is a warning that something organic is wrong and, indeed, some cases appear in court before the true source of the problem is realized (Evans, 1970).

Explanations. The early childhood of the individual has been a favourite candidate for the explanation of almost any behavioural problem. One-third of the Mohr *et al.* (1964) series had fathers absent for prolonged periods of time and also claimed to have had more distant feelings for their fathers than for their mothers. In the absence of control data the relevance of this finding cannot be assessed. Evans (1970) pursues two lines of speculation. The first, which is behavioural in nature, is that the exhibitionist act is acquired by classical conditioning as a chance association with another behaviour and is then reinforced by masturbation to the deviant fantasy. Evans cites a case in which the individual was urinating in an alley when a young female chanced to pass and notice the act. This was followed by the individual becoming an habitual exhibitor. Evans thinks it likely that the act was reinforced by the ensuing pleasure of masturbation to orgasm to the recalled fantasy. He also cites a case, reported by Bandura and Walters (1963), in which observational learning in the home appeared responsible for the acquisition of the deviant behaviour. Once acquired, the behaviour is maintained by similar outcomes following subsequent exposures, and performance is in response to readily available instigating stimuli. The importance of both anticipation and subsequent cognitive rehearsal is suggested by the frequent reference to the obsessional nature of the thinking of exhibitionists. Cognitive rehearsal of the relevant deviant behaviour, particularly when combined with a lack of opportunity for alternative, socially acceptable behaviours, may help to maintain both paedophiliac and exhibitionist be-haviours, in combination with the reinforcement received for their overt performance. Alternatively, Evans speculates that exhibitionism may be under-stood in terms of the concept of displacement. This is well defined and understood among some animals. For instance, if animals are fighting, they will often break off the encounter and go through the motions of seizing food or copulating with the nearest female or other substitute. Energy displacement will thus 'spill over' from one basic drive to another, and particularly between the sex drive and aggression, which may be linked in the male. At present the best explanation is a combination of learning, obsessional thinking, and poor heterosexual social skills.

TREATMENT

Introduction

In earlier chapters we described the major methods of treatment for problems of sexual response and for those associated with homosexual preference. The same methods have been used in the treatment of other sexual variations and of sexual offences, although several additional methods have been applied to offences.

The general ethical principles we have argued for apply to the treatment of other sexual variations. Essentially the client is the major arbiter of goal and method. However, for sex offenders the situation is potentially more complex. The 'client' is also a legally defined offender—the possibility of treatment has arisen as a result of an appearance in court. The victim is therefore another interested party, represented by the legal authorities. Re-offending, for example, by a rapist, exhibitionist or paedophile is always possible. The conventional penal methods, such as imprisonment, are likely to have little or no effect in reducing the possibility of re-offending in these cases once the period of confinement is over and may even have a damaging psychological effect on the offender.

Should therapists then act as 'agents of society' and connive in the imposition of treatment on sex offenders whether they seek it or not? To some extent the ethical conflict can be avoided by the assertion that any treatment will fail unless the recipient is fully co-operative. Whether or not this is true most current opinion is strongly against treating sex offenders unless they have been fully informed of the consequences of accepting or rejecting the treatment and of the goals and methods involved and have consented freely. This means, for example, that the length of a sentence should not be conditional on 'willingness' to enter a course of treatment. Instead the legally prescribed punishment should take its course and, quite separately, towards the end of the sentence, perhaps even after its conclusion, the offender should be offered the opportunity of treatment. Acceptance or rejection then would be as much his own affair as it is for a non-offender. Moreover, it is undesirable merely to suppress a particular sexual activity; therapists should seek to provide an alternative behaviour acceptable both to the offender and to society in general. However, there is one crucial difference between sex offenders and other types of sexual problem; the former will be evaluated by an additional outcome measure—that of re-conviction.

Fetishism

The behaviour therapy literature on the treatment of transvestism and fetishism is largely restricted to single case studies. There are two reports of series of cases.

Feldman *et al.* (1968) described the treatment by anticipatory avoidance learning of a heterogeneous group of five cases of sexual deviation, two of whom complained of transvestite behaviour, and one whose sex object was females many years older than himself.

The technique of treatment was very similar to that used for the homosexual patients treated by this group of workers. In each instance a photograph of the deviant sexual stimulus was used as the CS. In the case of the two transvestite patients this consisted of a series of photographs of the patient wearing his transvestite clothing in a hierarchical order of attractiveness.

Relief stimuli consisted of photographs of the wife or girlfriend of the patient. Two of the above three patients improved completely in response to treatment; the partial improvement of the third was attributed by the authors to his wife being a most unwilling sexual partner, so that there was no alternative sexual outlet to the suppressed transvestite behaviour.

Much the most detailed report of the treatment of fetishist patients was provided by Marks and Gelder (1967) who described a group of five patients all of whom were treated as in-patients by electrical aversion. In the early stages of treatment the shock was delivered when the patient imagined himself in a sexually provocative and arousing situation which incorporated some features of his deviant behaviour. In the second stage of treatment the patients were shocked when they carried out the deviant behaviour in reality—such as putting on female clothing. The shock was delivered on an intermittent schedule—approximately one-quarter of all trials were non-shocked and the penile plethysmograph was used to monitor the progress of treatment throughout; further monitoring was made possible by the use of a version of the Osgood Semantic Differential technique.

Many interesting findings came out of this work. For example, with repeated exposure to the aversive stimulus, the patients reported increasing difficulty in producing their fetish image. The time taken to obtain the image increased, and in several instances the patients reached a point when they were unable to obtain the image at all. It was also shown that the change in ability to obtain the deviant sexual image was probably attributable to the effects of the aversive stimulation and not to simple habituation effects. With increasing time in treatment there was an increasing difficulty in obtaining an erectile response to the fetish stimulus. Finally, there was a remarkable specificity of the erectile changes in treatment to the particular stimuli which had been associated with the aversive stimulus.

Transsexualism: Sexual Reassignment

Money and Gaskin (1970) describe methods which aim to suppress those physical characteristics which are contrary to the individual's belief as to his 'true' gender identity. In the male, hormone therapy means the administration of oestrogens and progestins and in the female the administration of androgens. Hormone therapy for the male transsexual results in a decrease in erections and ejaculations, an increase in the amount of breast tissue and in the pigmentation of areolae and nipples, a redistribution of the subcutaneous fat towards the female pattern, a decrease in muscular strength, an increased hair growth on the scalp, and a decrease in sexual arousability. In the female transsexual, following hormone therapy, there is a decrease in menstruation, an increase in body hair growth, a deepening of the voice, and an increase in sexual arousability. The period of hormone therapy serves as a stage leading towards the final step of surgical sex reassignment by enabling the patient to test out his adjustment to the change and demands imposed by the desired sex role. (During this period the patient is both socially and vocationally a member of the desired sex.) Besides the bodily changes described above, the male transsexual has to adapt psychologically to the changes in his pattern of ejaculatory orgasm. Conversely the female transsexual, while retaining her basic orgasmic pattern, must adapt to a masculine pattern of sexual arousal. The next step is surgery. In the male this consists of castration, penile amputation, and the construction of a vagina from perineal skin. Following surgery considerable supportive psychotherapeutic counselling and guidance is needed.

Money and Gaskin (1970) reported several studies of sexually reassigned patients. Their findings agreed with earlier studies in that the majority of transsexuals who had a sex reassignment by surgery were subjectively happier following these procedures. Money and Gaskin state, in refutation of the argument that the eventual sexual or marital partner will be subject to a deception, that the partner is not deceived, and that the relationship is quite likely to be reciprocally supportive and beneficial. The evidence they cite in support of this statement has been referred to earlier (Chapter 6) when it was pointed out that because the post-operative male–female transsexuals met their partners in homosexual bars the criteria of partners' satisfaction could not be used to argue the case that the male–female transsexuals were now functionally heterosexual. What does not seem to be in doubt is that some individuals who have had the operation report being a good deal happier than they were beforehand.

Transsexualism: Prevention by Positive Learning in Infancy

Although the results of earlier attempts to help adult transsexuals to bring their attitudes into line with their physical features had been unsuccessful, this does not necessarily mean that attempts early in infancy would also be unsuccessful. Such an attempt was reported by Green et al. (1972b). They worked with 'feminine' young boys, and considered that, based on retrospective reports of childhood behaviour by adult males who want sex change surgery, 'there was reason to believe that these boys are pre-transsexuals'. Their data showed that the boys strongly preferred girls' clothes, girls' games, toys, activities and the companionship of girls, acted only the role of the female in games, stated their wish to be a girl, and steadfastly refused activities typical of boyhood, exactly as adult male to female transsexuals recall. Although long-term follow up data are not yet available, it does seem rather likely that these individuals would have matured into adult transsexuals.

Therapy was aimed at four objectives: the development of a relationship of trust and affection between the male therapist and the boy; heightening parental concern about the problem so that parents began to disapprove of feminine interests and no longer overtly or covertly encouraged them; promoting the involvement in the boy's life of the father, or a father substitute; sensitization of the parents to the inter-personal difficulties which are said to underlie the tendency of the mother to be overly close with the son and for the father emotionally to divorce himself from family activities. It can be seen that this is a mixture of behavioural and psychodynamic approaches.

Green *et al.* (1972b) describe five cases with whom they worked over a four year period. In all five there was a considerable shift towards masculine external behaviours and subjective self-image. (The fact that an environmental approach seems to have been successful with these individuals does not argue against a biological predisposition to develop the pre-treatment pattern of behaviour.) The oldest of the five boys was aged twelve at the time of report, at which time he had been treated for one year. The authors consider that this individual may represent the latest age period at which treatment of extensive cross-gender behaviour may be effective. Follow-up reports in adult years of external behaviour, subjective feelings, and sexual orientation will be of considerable interest, particularly if an untreated comparison group is available. This is a fascinating and important piece of work, and if satisfactorily extended and repeated by others would offer considerable hope to the parents of pre-transsexual individuals. Certainly, it seems a great deal less drastic to bring into line the beliefs and physical structure of an individual by changing these beliefs than inevitably seeking to alter physical structure.

Transsexualism: A Case of Apparent Reversal During Adolescence

An important single case study by Barlow *et al.* (1973) suggests that Green's view of 12 being the latest age for reversal may be pessimistic. A male transsexual aged 17 indicated his wish to try the masculine role in general behaviour and to change his sexual preference to heterosexual from being exclusively homosexual. Initial conventional aversion therapy was unsuccessful. Barlow and colleagues then concentrated on non-sexual but sex-related behaviours. They identified and systematically modified certain aspects of 'feminine' behaviour such as modes of sitting, walking, and standing. Next they turned to 'masculine' behaviour, shaping-up social behaviours, and vocal characteristics. A new social role was thus available. On the basis of this they tackled sexual behaviour, using positive conditioning procedures to establish heterosexual fantasy and arousal alongside their homosexual equivalent. Finally, they returned to aversion therapy. On this occasion homosexual responsiveness declined sharply in response to aversion. Very detailed measurements before, during, and after treatment indicated the specific effects of the procedures. One year after treatment, the boy, then 18, had no transsexual practices or thoughts, was almost exclusively heterosexual in preference and had a girlfriend, although sexual activity had not progressed beyond petting. Barlow *et al.* cautioned that their client may not have been typical of the general range of transsexuals, but their report does suggest that surgical reassignment may not be the only option therapists can offer transsexuals. Moreover, the initial re-shaping of sex-linked social behaviours has important implications for the treatment of the primary group of homosexuals.

Sex Offences: Rape

A number of approaches to the 'treatment' of rapists have been reviewed by Marshall *et al.* (1977). Stürup (1972) reported the results of *castration* of 900 Danish sexual offenders over a 30 year period (not all of them rapists). Only 1 per cent re-offered as against an expected rate of about 25 per cent for untreated offenders. However as Marshall *et al.* point out, 'Stürup estimated that 75 per cent would not re-offend . . . the rate fell to 7–10 per cent for a first offender. That is, at least 750 of Stürup's patients may have been needlessly castrated—a high price to pay for dubious benefits.' Another irreversible physical method (Roeder and Muller, 1969; cited by Marshall *et al.*, 1977) involves brain surgery, intended to eliminate sexual behaviour and intractable aggression. No empirical data as to the value of the procedure were presented. Marshall *et al.* (1977) argued that 'Society's aim of protecting its members from rapists would be best served by re-channelling the deviates sexual desires into acceptable outlets rather than eliminating them altogether.' They also point to such undesirable side effects as low self-esteem and a consequent increased risk of suicide which are associated with attempts to eliminate sexual desire.

As an example of a relatively acceptable physical procedure Marshall *et al.* cite hormonal intervention. Firstly the effects are reversible and secondly the temporary reduction of sexual arousability which results can be used to implement psychological training programmes, both to increase self-control of the deviant behaviour and to promote an alternative behaviour. Bancroft *et al.* (1974) carried out a well-designed trial which indicated that anti-androgens were, relative to oestrogen, both effective in temporarily reducing sexual arousability and free side effects. This temporary reduction may increase the effectiveness of a standard aversive procedure for reducing the attractiveness of stimuli associated with the deviant behaviour, which would form the next stage of a comprehensive approach.

The remaining steps all involve building behaviours. First, the establishment or re-establishment of arousal to non-deviant stimuli by shaping, fading, or directed masturbation. Next, improving knowledge of appropriate situational behaviours and of sexual anatomy, physiology, and skills. This requires first that existing gaps in knowledge are assessed and appropriately remedied using material adapted to each individual's general intellectual levels. Finally, making use of the improved knowledge in relevant situations, the objective is to produce social skills which are matched appropriately both to the situation and the response of the particular partner. Social skills, therefore, include not only knowing what to do and how to do it, but also the ability continually to monitor the partner's response. Social skills training is assisted by the use of live or videotaped models, by breaking up the skills into discrete components, the practice of those components, feedback to the individual concerned, and a gradual progress along an ascending hierarchy of skill difficulty. As with psychological problems in general it is vital to carry out a detailed analysis of the behavioural assets and deficits of the individual concerned in order to adapt the total range of techniques to that individual, bearing in mind targets which are both desirable and attainable.

Marshall et al. (1977) have been carrying out such a programme (omitting the use of chemical intervention) for several years within the Ontario Regional Penitentiary System, mainly with rapists. A comparison with a group psychotherapy programme has indicated significant advantages for the behavioural approach, both in measures of sexual response and social skills, and, most importantly, the rate of re-offending. The results to date are promising.

Sexual Offences: Exhibitionism

Rooth and Marks (1974) compared aversion therapy and 'self-regulation' (identifying the early eliciting stimuli for exhibiting, and developing and practising a repertoire of alternative behaviours) and relaxation. At the end of the treatment period aversion was the most effective. A complex cross-over design made follow-up difficult to evaluate.

There are a number of other reports of the successful behavioural treatment of exhibitionist behaviour, two of which (Evans, 1968; and MacCulloch et al., 1971) used anticipatory avoidance learning. The third (Reitz and Keil, 1971) described a method which required the exhibitionist to expose himself to a group of unresponsive nurses (the exhibitionist's positive reinforcement appears to be the expression of horror, fear, etc., on the face of the victim—see earlier in this chapter), the result being a reduction in the behaviour. In this method the aversive consequence is inattention by the 'victim'. In addition to training in avoidance, several reports have urged the importance of positive training in heterosexual social skills.

Sex Offences: Paedophilia

A number of reports have appeared of the behavioural treatment of paedophilia and are reviewed by Marks (1976). Essentially, the clients have had boys as their preferred sex partners, and the treatment methods employed have been those described in detail in the treatment of the homosexual preference in Chapter 6. A large-scale study is underway at Winson Green Prison, Birmingham, England (Perkins, 1977). This involves various categories of sex offenders, including a substantial number of paedophiles, and is similar to the Marshall et al. work in Canada in including detailed behavioural analysis and a wide range of procedures, with a particular emphasis on social skills training, likely to be very relevant to the apparent difficulty experienced by paedophiles in forming emotional relationships with other adults. Treatment does not begin until a release date is both near and is fixed so that consent is as free as possible, and may continue after discharge in the client's normal environment, so as to increase the possibility for generalization of any positive effects of treatment.

Sex Offenders: Concluding Comment

It might be thought that sex offenders, in contrast to people with psychological problems in general, do not seek help voluntarily, but instead would only enter treatment after arrest and conviction. A recently established walk-in centre in Memphis, Tennessee, USA, suggests that this belief might reflect both the sheer lack of services and the fear of self-incrimination. The Memphis service enables people to seek help voluntarily if they feel in danger of committing a sexual offence (Bancroft, personal communication, 1977). Such an approach is greatly preferable to the generally existing state of affairs from the point of view of both offenders and victims.

OVERVIEW

The acquisition of fetishist behaviours seems best explained by a combination of classical conditioning and very high sexual arousal, possibly related to abnormal brain functioning. Such behaviours seem largely confined to males as do all the sexual variations and sex offences reviewed in this chapter, with the exception of transsexualism. Once they are established the performance of fetishist behaviours is elicited by the now sexually toned fetish objects and their maintenance is assisted by the individual concerned being socially isolated with few or no alternative sexual outlets.

Essentially transsexual behaviour involves a strongly held belief that the person's physical sex is 'wrong' and often includes an active search to bring physical appearance into line with belief by means of surgery and hormones. Both social and biological explanations have been put forward. The most plausible seems related to one tentatively advanced for the primary homosexual: pre-natal feminization or masculinization due to hormonal influences in a direction contrary to that laid down by the individual's genetic inheritance. Once behaviour has begun along this sex-inappropriate track it may be socially reinforced.

The sadistic and masochistic types of sexual behaviour have attracted little research and the explanation we suggest is by analogy from laboratory studies, namely that of pairing and gradual shaping so that (in the case of masochism) the initially aversive event becomes positively reinforcing.

Under the heading of sexual offences we have confined ourselves to rape, exhibitionism, and paedophilia. Research reports are limited to the apprehended and convicted minority who may not be representative of the remainder. Rape is to some extent a sub-cultural phenomenon, carried out by young, relatively socially deprived males on females from the same setting. It is likely to be acquired, performed, and maintained according to general social learning principles, both by 'sub-cultural' rapists, many of whom may also be sexually active with consenting partners, and more socially isolated individuals for some of whom rape may be a partially aggressive rather than a solely sexual act.

Paedophilia excites particularly strong social condemnation despite unclear evidence as to long-term effects on victims. Social learning principles are likely to contribute to a comprehensive explanation; the apparent difficulty in forming emotional relationships with adults deserves careful investigation.

Exhibitionism seems very widespread, the majority of acts going unreported by victims. Once again social learning principles, both classical and instrumental, provide a helpful explanation, with social isolation an important setting event.

Methods of treatment are generally similar to those for other sexual behaviours and emphasize both the inhibition of the undesired behaviour and the training and enhancement of the desired alternatives. The results are promising for the most part. The great majority of transsexuals appear to seek sexual reassignment by medical means: the social consequences appear generally satisfactory to the clients concerned, providing careful social preparation is carried out beforehand. A few reports suggest the possibility of an alternative treatment option: training to live socially as a member of the genetic sex concerned rather than medical reassignment.

References

Achilles, Nancy. 'The development of the homosexual bar as an institution.' In J. H. Gagnon and W. Simon (Eds.), *Sexual Deviance*, New York: Harper & Row, pp. 228, 1967.

Amir, M. *Patterns in Forcible Rape*. Chicago: University of Chicago Press, 1972.

Ansari, J. M. A. 'A study of 65 impotent males.' *British Journal of Psychiatry*, **127**, 337, 1975.

Antoniou, L. D., Shalhour, R. J., Sudhakar, T. and Smith, J. C. 'Reversal of uraemic impotence by zinc.' *The Lancet*, Oct. 29, No. 8044, 895, 1977.

Apperson, Louise B. and McAdoo, W. G. 'Parental factors in the childhood of homosexuals.' *Journal of Abnormal and Social Psychology*, **73**, 201, 1968.

Aschner, B. 'Uber die Beziehungen zwischen. Hypophysis und Genitale.' *Archive fur Gynakologie*, **923**, 200, 1912.

Azrin, N. H., Naster, B. J. and Jones, R. 'Reciprocity counselling: a rapid learning based procedure for marital counselling.' *Behaviour Research and Therapy*, **11**, 365, 1973.

Bailey, S. *Common Sense About Sexual Ethics*. London, 1962.

Bancroft, J. H. J. 'A comparative study of aversion and desensitization in the treatment of homosexuality.' In L. E. Burns and J. L. Worsley (Eds.), *Behaviour Therapy in the 1970s: A Collection of Original Papers*. Bristol: Wright, 1970.

Bancroft, J. H. J. *Deviant Sexual Behaviour: Modification and Assessment*. Oxford: Clarendon Press, 1974.

Bancroft, J. H. J., Tennent, T. G., Loucas, K. and Cass, J. 'The control of deviant sexual behaviour by drugs. I. Behavioural changes following oestrogens and anti-androgens.' *British Journal of Psychiatry*, **125**, 310, 1974.

Bandura, A. *Principles of Behaviour Modification*. New York: Holt, Rinehart and Winston, 1969.

Bandura, A. *Aggression: A Social Learning Analysis*. New York: Prentice-Hall, 1973.

Bandura, A. and Jeffery, R. W. 'Role of symbolic coding and rehearsal processes in observational learning.' *Journal of Personality and Social Psychology*, **26**, 122, 1973.

Bandura, A. and Walters, R. H. *Social Learning and Personality Development*. New York: Holt, Rinehart and Winston, 1963.

Barclay, A. M. 'The effects of hostility on physiological and fantasy response.' *Journal of Personality*, **4**, 233, 1970.

Bardwick, J. M. and Behrman, S. J. 'Investigation into the effects of anxiety, sexual arousal and menstrual-cycle-phase on uterine contractions.' *Psychosomatic Medicine*, **29**, 468, 1967.

Barker, W. J. and Perlman, D. 'Volunteer bias and personality traits in sexual standards research.' *Archives of Sexual Behaviour*, **4**, 161, 1975.

Barlow, D. H. 'The treatment of sexual deviations: towards a comprehensive behavioural approach.' In K. S. Calhoun, H. E. Adams and K. M. Mitchell (Eds.), *Innovative Treatment Methods in Psychopathology*. New York: Wiley, p. 121, 1973.

Barlow, D. H. and Agras, W. S. 'Fading to increase heterosexual responsiveness in homosexuals.' *Journal of Applied Behaviour Analysis*, **6**, 355, 1973.

Barlow, D. H., Renolds, J. I. and Agras, W. S. 'Gender identity change in a trans-sexual.' *Archives of General Psychiatry*, **28**, 569, 1973.

Barr, R. F. 'Responses to erotic stimuli of trans-sexual and homosexual males.' *British Journal of Psychiatry*, **123**, 579, 1973.

Barraclough, C. A. and Gorski, R. A. 'Evidence that the hypothalamus is responsible for androgen-induced sterility in the female rat.' *Endocrinology*, **68**, 68, 1961.

Bauman, K. E. and Wilson, R. R. 'Premarital sexual attitudes of unmarried university students.' *Archives of Sexual Behaviour*, **5**, 29, 1976.

Beach, F. A. 'A review of physiological and psychological studies of sexual behaviour in mammals.' *Physiology Review*, **27**, 240, 1947.

Beach, F. A. *Sexual Behavior in Rats*. University of Wisconsin Press, pp. 263, 1958.

Beach, F. A. 'Experimental studies of mating behaviour in animals.' In J. Money (Ed.), *Sex Research: New Developments*. New York: Holt, Rinehart and Winston, 1965.

Beach, F. A., Noble, R. G. and Orndoff, R. K. 'Effects of perinatal androgen treatment on responses of male rats to gonadal hormones in adult-hood.' *Journal of Comparative and Physiological Psychology*, **68**, 490, 1969.

Beasley, R. 'Current status of sex research.' *Journal of Sex Research*, **11**, 335, 1975.

Bell, R. A. 'A reinterpretation of the direction of effect in studies of socialization.' *Psychological Review*, **75**, 81, 1968.

Bene, E. 'On the genesis of male homosexuality: an attempt at clarifying the role of the parents.' *British Journal of Psychiatry*, **111**, 803, 1965a.

Bene, E. 'On the genesis of female homosexuality.' *British Journal of Psychiatry*, **111**, 815, 1965b.

Bene, E. and Anthony, J. *Bene–Anthony Family Relations Test*. London: N.F.E.R., 1962.

Benjamin, N. 'Transvestism and transsexualism.' *International Journal of Sexology*, **7**, 12, 1953.

Bentler, P. M. 'Heterosexual behaviour assessment in males.' *Behaviour Research and Therapy*, **6**, 21, 1968.

Bentler, P. M. 'A typology of trans-sexualism: gender identity theory and data.' *Archives of Sexual Behaviour*, **5**, 567, 1976.

Bergeret, L. F. E. *The Preventive Obstacle or Conjugal Onanism*. New York: Turner and Mignard, 1898.

Bernard, J. 'The adjustment of married males.' In H. T. Christensen (Ed.), *Handbook of Marriage and the Family*. Chicago: Rand McNally, p. 675, 1964.

Berscheid, E. and Walster, E. 'A little bit about love.' In T. L. Huston (Ed.), *Foundations of Interpersonal Attraction*. New York: Academic Press, p. 356, 1974.

Berscheid, E., Dion, K., Walster, E. and Walster, G. W. 'Physical attractiveness and dating choice: a test of the matching hypothesis.' *Journal of Experimental Social Psychology*, **7**, 173, 1971.

Berscheid, E., Walster, E. and Bohrnstedt, G. 'The body image report.' *Psychology Today*, **7**, 119, 1973.

Berthold, A. A. 'Transplantation der Hoden.' *Archives of Anatomy and Physiology*, **42**, 1849.

Bieber, B., Bieber, I., Dain, J. J., Dince, P. R., Drellich, M. G., Grand, H. G., Grunolach, R. N., Kremer, M. W., Wilbur, C. B. and Bieber, T. B. *Homosexuality*, New York: Basic Books, 1962.

Binet, A. *Etudes de Psychologie Experimentale*. Paris, 1888.

Birk, L., Huddleston, W., Miller, E. and Cohler, B. 'Avoidance conditioning for homosexuality.' *Archives of General Psychiatry*, **25**, 314, 1971.

Blair, J. H. and Simpson, C. M. 'Effects of antipsychotic drugs on reproductive functions.' *Diseases of the Nervous System*, **27**, 645, 1966.

Boerhave, H. 'Institutiones medical.' In *Opera Medical Universa*, Geneva: Fratres de Tournes, 1728.

Box, S. *Deviance, Reality and Society*. London: Holt, Rinehart and Winston, 1971.

Brady, J. P. 'Brevital—relaxation treatment of frigidity.' *Behaviour Research and Therapy*, **4**, 71, 1966.

Brady, J. P. and Levitt, E. E. 'The scalability of sexual experience.' *Psychological Record*, **15**, 275, 1965.

Brehm, J. W., Gatza, M., Goethals, G., McCrommon, J. and Ward, L. 'Psychological arousal and interpersonal attraction.' Mimeo. Available from authors, 1970. (Cited by Berscheid and Walster, 1974.)

Bryan, J. H. 'Apprenticeships in prostitution.' *Social Problems*, **12**, 278, 1965.

Bullough, V. L. 'Homosexuality and the medical model.' *Journal of Homosexuality*, **1**, 99, 1974.

Byrne, D. and Griffitt, W. 'Interpersonal attraction.' In P. Mussen and M. Rosenzweig (Eds.), *Annual Review of Psychology*, Vol. 24, Palo Alto, California: Annual Reviews, 1973.

Byrne, D., Ervin, C. R. and Lamberth, J. 'Continuity between the experimental study of attraction and real-life computer dating.' *Journal of Personality and Social Psychology*, **24**, 1, 1972.

Callahan, E. J. and Leitenberg, H. 'Aversion therapy for sexual deviation: contingent shock and covert sensitization.' *Journal of Abnormal Psychology*, **81**, 60, 1973.

Calhoun, J. B. 'Population density and social pathology.' *Scientific American*, **206**, 139, 1962.

Carrier, J. M. 'Participants in urban American male homosexual encounters.' *Archives of Sexual Behaviour*, **1**, 279, 1971.

Cattell, R. B. and Scheier, I. H. *The Meaning and Measurement of Neuroticism and Anxiety*. New York: Ronald, 1961.

Cautela, J. R. 'Covert sensitization.' *Psychological Reports*, **20**, 459, 1967.

Chapman, J. D. 'Frigidity: rapid treatment by reciprocal inhibition.' *Journal of the American Osteopathic Association*, **67**, 871, 1968.

Clark, L. C. and Treichler, D. 'Psychic stimulation of prostatic secretion.' *Psychosomatic Medicine*, **12**, 261, 1950.

Cliffe, M. J. 'On an empirical calculus of stimulus magnitude.' *Archives of Sexual Behaviour*, **6**, 237, 1977.

Clinard, M. B. *Sociology of Deviant Behavior*. New York: Holt, Rinehart and Winston, 1968.

Coates, S. 'Homosexuality and the Rorschach Test.' *British Journal of Medical Psychology*, **35**, 177, 1962.

Colson, C. E. 'The evaluation of pornography: effects of attitude and perceived physiological reaction.' *Archives of Sexual Behaviour*, **3**, 307, 1974.

Coombs, C. H. 'Thurston's measurement of social values revisited forty years later.' *Journal of Personality and Social Psychology*, **6**, 85, 1967.

Cooper, A. J. 'A factual study of male potency disorders.' *British Journal of Psychiatry*, **114**, 719, 1968.

Cooper, A. J. 'An innovation in the behavioural treatment of a case of non-consummation due to vaginimus.' *British Journal of Psychiatry*, **115**, 721, 1969.

Cooper, A. J., Ismail, A. A. A., Smith, C. G. and Loraine, J. A. 'Androgen function in psychogenic and constitutional types of impotence.' *British Medical Journal*, **iii**, 17, 1970.

Court, J. H. 'Pornography and sex-crimes: a re-evaluation in the light of recent trends around the world.' *International Journal of Criminology and Penology*, **5**, 129, 1977.

Cox, B., Shirley, J. and Short, M. *The Fall of Scotland Yard.* Harmondsworth, Middlesex: Penguin, 1977.

Craighead, W. E., Kazdin, A. E. and Mahoney, M. J. (Eds.) *Behavior Modification, Issues and Applications.* Boston: Houghton Mifflin, 1976.

Curran, J. P. and Lippold, S. 'The effects of physical attraction and attitude similarity on attraction in dating dyads.' *Journal of Personality*, **43**, 515, 1975.

Curran, D. and Parr, D. 'Homosexuality: an analysis of 100 male cases seen in private practice.' *British Medical Journal*, **1**, 797, 1957.

Davies, B. M. and Morgenstern, F. S. 'A case of cysticercosis, temporal lobe epilepsy and transvestism.' *Journal of Neurology, Neurosurgery and Psychiatry*, **23**, 247, 1960.

Davison, G. C. 'Homosexuality, the ethical challenge.' *Journal of Homosexuality*, **2**, 195, 1977.

Davison, G. C. and Wilson, G. T. 'Attitudes of behaviour therapists towards homosexuality.' *Behaviour Therapy*, **4**, 686, 1973.

Dawkins, S. and Taylor, R. 'Non-consummation of marriage. A survey of 70 cases.' *Lancet*, **11**, 1029, 1961.

Dean, R. B. and Richardson, H. 'Analysis of MMPI profiles of forty college-educated overt male homosexuals.' *Journal of Consulting Psychology*, **28**, 483, 1964.

Demoor, P. and Denef, C. 'The puberty of the rat liver. Feminine pattern of cortisol metabolism in male rats castrated at birth.' *Endocrinology*, **82**, 480, 1968.

Dermer, M. and Thiel, D. L. 'When beauty may fail.' *Journal of Personality and Social Psychology*, **31**, 1168, 1975.

Deutsch, R. M. *The Key to Feminine Response in Marriage.* New York: Random House, 1968.

Devlin (Lord). *The Enforcement of Morals.* Proceedings of the British Academy, 1959.

Diess, P. 'Perinatal structural sex differentiation of the hypothalamus in rats.' *Neuroendocrinology*, **S**: 103, 1969.

Dion, K. K. and Dion, K. L. 'Self-esteem and romantic love.' *Journal of Personality*, **43**, 39, 1975.

Doerr, P., Kockott, G., Vogt, H. J., Pirke, K. M. and Dittmar, F. 'Plasma testosterone, estradiol and semen analysis in male homosexuals.' *Archives of General Psychiatry*, **29**, 829, 1973.

Doerr, P., Pirke, K. M., Kockott, G. and Dittmar, F. 'Further studies on sex hormones in male homosexuals.' *Archives of General Psychiatry*, **33**, 611, 1976.

Donnerstein, E., Donnerstein, M. and Evans, E. 'Erotic stimuli and aggression: facilitation or inhibition.' *Journal of Personality and Social Psychology*, **32**, 237, 1975.

Dorbar, R. R. 'Psychological testing of trans-sexuals: a brief report of results from the Wechsler Intelligence Scale, the Thematic Apperception Test, and the House-Tree Person Test.' *Transactions of the New York Academy of Sciences*, **2g**, 455, 1967.

Dörner, G. 'The influence of sex hormones during the hypothalamic differentiation and maturation phases on gonadal function and sexual behaviour during the hypothalamic functional phase.' *Endocrinology*, **56**, 280, 1970.

Dörner, G., Docke, F. and Moustafa, A. 'Differential localisation of a male and a female hypothalamic mating centre.' *Journal of Reproduction and Fertility*, **17**, 583, 1968.

Dörner, G., Rohde, W., Stahl, F., Krell, L. and Masius, W. G. 'A neuro-endocrine predisposition for homosexuality in men.' *Archives of Sexual Behaviour*, **4**, 1–8, 1975.

Doshay, L. G. *The Boy Sex Offender and his Later Career.* New York: Grune and Stratton, 1943.

Driscoll, R., Davis, K. E. and Lipetz, M. E. 'Parental interference and romantic love: the Romeo and Juliet effect.' *Journal of Personality and Social Psychology*, **24**, 1–10, 1972.

Edwards, A. L. *Edwards Personal Preference Schedule.* New York: Psychological Corporation, 1959.

Eibl-Eibesfeldt, I. *Love and Hate.* London: Methuen, 1971.

Ellis, A. 'The sexual psychology of human hermaphrodites.' *Psychosomatic Medicine*, **7**, 108, 1945.

Ellison, G. 'Vaginismus.' *Medical Aspects of Human Sexuality*, **6** (8), 34, 1972.

Epstein, A. W. 'Fetishism: a study of its psychopathology with particular reference to a proposed disorder in brain mechanisms as an aetiological factor.' *Journal of Nervous and Mental Diseases*, **130**, 107, 1960.

Evans, D. R. 'Masturbatory fantasy and sexual deviation.' *Behaviour Research and Therapy*, **6**, 17, 1968.

Evans, D. R. 'Exhibitionism.' In C. G. Costello (Ed.), *Symptoms of Psychopathology*, New York: Wiley, p. 560, 1970.

Evans, R. B. 'Childhood parental relationships of homosexual men.' *Journal of Consulting and Clinical Psychology*, **33**, 129, 1969.

Evans, R. B. 'Physical and biochemical characteristics of homosexual men.' *Journal of Consulting and Clinical Psychology*, **39**, 140, 1972.

Eysenck, H. J. *The Biological Bases of Personality*. Springfield, Ill.: C. C. Thomas, 1967.

Eysenck, H. J. 'Personality and attitudes to sex: a factorial study.' *Personality*, **1**, 335, 1970.

Eysenck, H. J. 'Personality and sexual adjustment.' *British Journal of Psychiatry*, **118**, 593, 1971.

Eysenck, H. J. 'The uses and abuses of pornography.' In H. J. Eysenck (Ed.), *Psychology is about People*. Harmondsworth: Penguin Books, p. 236, 1977.

Falk, M. '"Frigidity": A critical review.' *Archives of Sexual Behaviour*, **2**, 257, 1973.

Farkas, G. M. and Rosen, R. C. 'Effect of alcohol on elicited male sexual response.' *Journal of Studies on Alcohol*, **37**, 265, 1976.

Feder, H. H. and Whalen, R. E. 'Feminine behaviour in neonatally castrated and estrogen treated male rats.' *Science*, **147**, 306, 1965.

Feldman, M. P. 'The behaviour therapies and society.' In M. P. Feldman and A. H. Broadhurst (Eds.), *Theoretical and Experimental Bases of the Behaviour Therapies*. London: Wiley, p. 405, 1976.

Feldman, M. P. 'Helping homosexuals with problems.' *Journal of Homosexuality*, **2**, 241, 1977.

Feldman, M. P. and MacCulloch, M. J. *Homosexual Behaviour: Therapy and Assessment*. Oxford: Pergamon, 1971.

Feldman, M. P., MacCulloch, M. J., Mellor, V. and Pinschof, J. M. 'The application of anticipatory avoidance learning to the treatment of homosexuality—III. The Sexual Orientation Method.' *Behaviour Research and Therapy*, **4**, 289, 1966.

Feldman, M. P., MacCulloch, M. J. and MacCulloch, M. L. 'The aversion therapy treatment of a heterogeneous group of five cases of sexual deviations.' *Acta Psychiatrica Scandinavica*, **44**, 113, 1968.

Fenichel, O. *The Psychoanalytic Theory of Neurosis*. New York: Norton, 1945.

Festinger, L. *A Theory of Cognitive Dissonance*. Stanford: Stanford University Press, 1957.

Finck, H. T. *Romantic Love and Personal Beauty: Their Development, Causal Relations, History and National Peculiarities*. New York: MacMillan, 1891.

Finger, F. W. 'Changes in sex practices and beliefs of male college students during 30 years.' *Journal of Sex Research*, **11**, 304, 1975.

Fisher, G. and Howell, Leisla M. 'Psychological needs of homosexual paedophiliacs.' *Diseases of the Nervous System*, **31**, 623, 1970.

Ford, C. S. and Beach, F. A. *Patterns of Sexual Behaviour*. London: Methuen, 1952.

Freund, K. 'A laboratory method for diagnosing predominance of homo- or hetero-erotic interest in the male.' *Behaviour Research and Therapy*, **1**, 85, 1963.

Friedman, L. J. *Virgin Wives: A Study of Unconsummated Marriages*. London: Tavistock, 1962.

Furlow, W. L. 'Surgical management of impotence using the inflatable penile prosthesis.' *Mayo Clinic Proceedings*, **51**, 325, 1976.

Gagnon, J. H. and Simon, W. 'Introduction: Deviant behaviour and sexual deviance.' In J. H. Gagnon and W. Simon (Eds.), *Sexual Deviance*, New York: Harper & Row, 1, 1967.

Garfield, S. L. and Bergin, A. E. *Handbook of Psychotherapy and Behavior Change*. New York: Wiley, 1978 (Second edition).

Gebhard, P. H., Gagnon, W. H., Pomeroy, W. B. and Christenson, F. V. *Sex Offenders: An Analysis of Types*. New York: Harper and Row, 1965.

Gellhorn, E. and Loofburrow, G. N. *Emotions and Emotional Disorders*. New York: Harper and Row, 1963.

Giese, H. and Schmidt, R. *Studenten Sexualität*. Hamburg: Rowohlt, 1968.

Gillespie, W. H. 'Fetishism.' In I. Rosen (Ed.), *The Pathology and Treatment of Sexual Deviation*. London: Oxford University Press, 1964.

Goldstein, A., Hecutr, K. and Sechrest, L. *Psychotherapy and the Psychology of Behavior Change*. New York: Wiley, 1966.

Goldstein, M., Kant, H., Judd, L., Rice, C. and Green, R. 'Experience with pornography: rapists, paedophiles, homosexuals, transsexuals and controls.' *Archives of Sexual Behaviour*, **1**, 1, 1971.

Grady, K. L. and Phoenix, C. H. 'Hormonal determinants of mating behaviour; the display of feminine behaviour by adult male rats castrated neo-natally.' *American Zoologist*, **3**, 482, 1963.

Graham, S. *A Lecture to Young Men on Chastity Intended also for the Serious Consideration of Parents and Guardians*. Boston: C. H. Pierce, 1848 (Tenth edition).

Green, R., Fuller, M., Rutley, B. R. and Hendler, J. 'Playroom toy preferences of fifteen masculine and fifteen feminine boys.' *Behaviour Therapy*, **3**, 425, 1972(a).

Green, R., Newman, L. E. and Stoller, R. J. 'Treatment of boyhood "trans-sexualism".' *Archives of General Psychiatry*, **26**, 213, 1972(b).

Greenblatt, D. R. 'Semantic differential analysis of the "triangular system" hypothesis in "adjusted" overt male homosexuals.' Unpublished doctoral dissertation. University of California, 1966.

Griffitt, W. 'Sexual experience and sexual responsiveness: sex differences.' *Archives of Sexual Behaviour*, **4**, 529, 1975.

Guardian. Report of 29 September 1960. (Cited by Henriques, 314, 1958.)

Guardian. Report of 19 October 1966. (Cited by Henriques, 329, 1958.)

Guardian. Article of 12 September 1977, p. 9.

Gundlach, R. H. and Riess, B. F. 'Self and sexual identity in the female: A study of female homosexuals.' In A. J. Riess Jr. (Ed.), *New Directions in Mental Health*. New York: Grune and Stratton, 1968.

Guttman, L. 'The basis for scalogram analysis.' In S. A. Stouffer *et al.* (Eds.), *Measurement and Prediction*. Princeton: Princeton University Press, p. 60, 1950.

Hall, S. 'Vaginismus as a cause of dyspareunia: Report of cases and a method of treatment.' *Western Journal of Surgery, Obstetrics and Gynaecology*, **60**, 117, 1952.

Harlow, H. F. 'The nature of love.' *American Psychologist*, **13**, 673, 1958.

Harlow, H. F. 'Sexual behaviour in the rhesus monkey.' In F. A. Beach (Ed.), *Sex and Behavior*. New York: Wiley, p. 234, 1965.

Harlow, H. F. and Harlow, M. K. 'The effect of rearing conditions on behaviour.' In J. Money (Ed.) *Sex Research—New Developments*. New York: Holt, Rinehart and Winston, 1965.

Harris, G. W. 'Sex hormones, brain development and brain function.' *Endocrinology*, **4**, 627, 1964.

Hartman, W. and Fithian, M. *Treatment of Sexual Dysfunction: A Biopsychosocial Approach*. Long Beach, California: Center for Marital and Sexual Studies, 1972.

Haslam, M. T. 'Treatment of psychogenic dyspareunia by reciprocal inhibition.' *British Journal of Psychiatry*, **111**, 280, 1965.

Haslam, M. T. 'Psycho-sexual disorders and their treatment, Part I.' *Current Medical Research Opinions*, **2**, 240, 1974.

Hastings, D. 'Can specific training procedures overcome sexual inadequacy?' In R. Brecher and E. Brecher (Eds.), *An Analysis of Human Sexual Response*. Boston: Little, Brown. 1963.

Heller, C. G. and Maddock, W. O. 'The clinical uses of testosterone in the male.' *Vitamins and Hormones*, **5**, 393, 1947.

Henriques, F. *Modern Sexuality*. London: McGibbon and Kee, 1968.

Herman, S. H. 'An experimental analysis of two methods of increasing heterosexual arousal in homosexuals.' *Dissertation Abstracts International*, **33**, (1-B), 439, 1972.

Hess, H., Seltzer, L. and Shlien, M. 'Pupil response of hetero- and homosexual males to pictures of men and women: a pilot study.' *Journal of Abnormal Psychology*, **70**, 165, 1965.

Heston, L. L. and Shields, J. 'Homosexuality in twins.' *Archives of General Psychiatry*, **18**, 149, 1968.

Hill, M. and Lloyd-Jones, M. *Sex Education: The Erogenous Zone*. National Secular Society, 1970.

Himelhoch, J. and Fava, S. F. (Eds.), *Sexual Behaviour in American Society*. New York: Norton, 1953.

Hoenig, J. and Kenna, J. C. 'The nosological position of transsexualism.' *Archives of Sexual Behaviour*, **3**, 273, 1974.

Hohlweg, W. and Junkmann, K. 'Die hormonal-nervose reguluering der funktion des hypophysenvorderlappens.' *Klinische Wochenschrift*, **11**, 321, 1932.

Hohmann, G. W. 'Some effects of spinal cord lesions on experienced emotional feelings.' *Psychophysiology*, **67**, 211, 1966.

Hooker, E. 'The homosexual community.' In J. H. Gagnon and W. Simon (Eds.), *Sexual Deviance*. New York: Harper and Row, p. 167, 1967.

Howells, K. and Steadman-Allen, R. 'Emotional antecedents of rape.' Paper presented at Annual Conference of the British Psychological Society, Exeter, April 1977.

Huizinga, J. *The Waning of the Middle Ages*. London, 1955.

Jacobs, L., Berscheid, E. and Walster, E. 'Self-esteem and attraction.' *Journal of Personality and Social Psychology,* **17**, 84, 1971.

Jaffe, Y., Malamuth, N., Feingold, J. and Feshbach, S. 'Sexual arousal and behavioural aggression.' *Journal of Personality and Social Psychology*, **30**, 759, 1974.

Jenkins, M. 'The effect of segregation on the sex behaviour of the white rat.' *Genetic Psychology Monographs*, **3**, 461, 1928.

Jinks, L. and Fulker, D. W. 'Comparison of the biometrical genetical MAVA and classical approaches to the analysis of human behaviour.' *Psychological Bulletin*, **73**, 311, 1970.

Johnson, J. 'Disorders of Sexual Potency in the Male.' M. D. Thesis, University of Manchester, 1964.

Johnson, J. 'Androgyny and disorders of sexual potency.' *British Medical Journal*, **ii**, 572, 1965a.

Johnson, J. 'Prognosis of disorders of sexual potency in the male.' *Journal of Psychosomatic Research*, **9**, 195, 1965b.

Jones, W. Jr. and Park, P. 'Treatment of single partner sexual dysfunction by systematic desensitization.' *Obstetrics and Gynaecology*, **39**, 411, 1972.

Kallmann, F. J. 'Comparative twin study of the genetic aspects of male homosexuality.' *Journal of Nervous and Mental Diseases*, **115**, 283, 1952(a).

Kallman, F. J. 'Twin sibships and the study of male homosexuality.' *American Journal of Human Genetics*, **4**, 136, 1952(b).

210

Kallman, F. J. *Heredity in Health and Mental Disorder*. New York: Norton, 1953.
Kaye, H. E., Berl, S., Clare, J., Eleston, M. R., Gershwin, B. S., Gershwin, P., Kogan, L. S., Torda, C. and Wilbur, C. B. 'Homosexuality in women.' *Archives of General Psychiatry*, **17**, 626, 1967.
Kegel, A. 'Sexual functions of the pubococcygeus muscle.' *Journal of Obstetrics and Gynaecology*, **60**, 521, 1952.
Kellog, J. H. *Plain Facts for Old and Young*. Burlington, Iowa: I. F. Segner, 1882.
Kenyon, F. E. 'Studies in female homosexuality, IV. Social and psychiatric aspect.' *British Journal of Psychiatry*, **114**, 1337, 1968.
Kephart, W. M. 'Some correlates of romantic love.' *Journal of Marriage and the Family*, **29**, 470, 1967.
Kerckoff, A. C. 'The social context of interpersonal attraction.' In T. L. Huston (Ed.), *Foundations of Interpersonal Attraction*. New York: Academic Press, p. 3, 1974.
Kinsey, A. C., Pomeroy, W. B. and Martin, C. E. *Sexual Behaviour in the Human Male*. Philadelphia: Saunders, 1948.
Kinsey, A. C., Pomeroy, W. B., Martin, C.E. and Gebhard, P. H. *Sexual Behaviour in the Human Female*. Philadelphia: Saunders, 1953.
Klausner, S. Z. 'Sex life in Israel.' In A. Ellis and A. Abarbanel (Eds.), *Encyclopaedia of Sexual Behaviour*. New York: Hawthorn, 558, 1961(a).
Klausner, S. Z. 'Sex life in Islam.' In A. Ellis and A. Abarbanel (Eds.), *Encyclopaedia of Sexual Behaviour*. New York: Hawthorn, 545, 1961(b).
Klintworth, G. K. 'A pair of male monozygotic twins discordant for homosexuality.' *Journal of Nervous and Mental Diseases*, **135**, 113, 1962.
Kockott, G. 'Psychiatrische und lerntheoretische. Aspekte der Transsexualitat.' In *Sexualforschung: Kritik und Tendenzen*. Stuttgart: Enke-Verlag, 1970.
Kolarsky, A., Freund, K., Machek, J. and Polak, O. 'Male sexual deviation.' *Archives of General Psychiatry*, **17**, 735, 1967.
Kolaszynska-Carr, A. Unpublished Ph. D. Thesis, University of Birmingham, 1970.
Kolodny, R. C., Masters, W. H., Hendry, J. and Torro, G. 'Plasma testosterone and semen analysis in male homosexuals.' *New England Journal of Medicine*, **285**, 1170, 1971.
Kolodny, R. C., Jacobs, L. S., Masters, W. H., Torro, G. and Daughaday, W. H. 'Plasma gonadotrophins and prolactin in male homosexuals.' *Lancet*, **II** (7766) 18, 1972.
Kraft, T. and Al-Issa, I. 'The use of Methohexitone Sodium in the systematic desensitization of premature ejaculation.' *British Journal of Psychiatry*, **114**, 351, 1967.
Kraft-Ebbing, R. von. *Psychopathia Sexualis*. Philadelphia: F. A. Davis, 1894.
Langevin, R. and Martin, M. 'Can erotic responses be classically conditioned?' *Behaviour Therapy*, **6**, 350, 1975.
Lavrakas, P. 'Female preference for male physiques.' *Journal of Research in Personality*, **9**, 324, 1975.
Laws, D. R. and Rubin, N. B. 'Instructional control of a behavioural response.' *Journal of Applied Behaviour Analysis*, **2**, 93, 1969.
Lazarus, A. 'The treatment of chronic frigidity by systematic desensitization.' *Journal of Nervous and Mental Diseases*, **136**, 272, 1963.
Leckie, F. 'Hypnotherapy and gynaecological disorders.' *International Journal of Clinical and Experimental Hypnosis*, **12**, 121, 1964.
Lederer, W. J. and Jackson, D. D. *The Mirages of Marriage*. New York: W. W. Norton & Co., 1968.
Lemert, H. *Social Pathology*. New York: McGraw Hill, 1951.
Le Moal, P. 'The client of the prostitute.' In *The Participants in Prostitution*. Report of the International Abolitionist Federation Conference at Athens, 1963; Geneva, 1964.
Levi, L. 'Sympatho-adrenomedullary activity, diuresis and emotional reactions during visual sexual stimulation in human females and males.' *Psychosomatic Medicine*, **31**, 251, 1969.

Levitt, E. E. and Klassen, A. D. 'Public attitudes towards homosexuality: part of the 1970 national survey by the Institute for Sexual Research.' *Journal of Homosexuality*, **1**, 29, 1974.

Levy, N. B. 'Sexual adjustment to maintenance hemodialysis and renal transplantation: national survey by questionnaire: preliminary report.' *Transactions of the American Society of Artificial Internal Organs*, **19**, 138, 1973.

Lewis, C. S. *Surprised by Joy: The Shape of My Early Life*. London, 1955.

Lewis, D. J. 'Partial reinforcement: A selective review of the literature since 1950.' *Psychological Bulletin*, **57**, 1, 1960.

Leznoff, M. and Westley, W. A. 'The homosexual community.' *Social Problems*, **3**, 257, 1956.

Linton, R. *The Study of Man*. New York: Appleton-Century, 1936.

Lobitz, W. and Lopiccolo, J. 'New methods in the behavioural treatment of sexual dysfunction.' *Journal of Behaviour Therapy and Experimental Psychiatry*, **3**, 265, 1972.

Lockhart, W. B. *The Report of the Commission on Obscenity and Pornography*. New York: Bantam Books, 1970.

Loney, J. 'Background factors, sexual experiences and attitudes towards treatment in two "normal" homosexual samples.' *Journal of Consulting and Clinical Psychology*, **38**, 57, 1972.

Longford (Lord). *Pornography: The Longford Report*. London: Coronet Books, 1972.

Loraine, J. A., Ismail, A. A. A., Adamopoulos, D. A. and Dove, G. A. 'Endocrine function in male and female homosexuals.' *British Medical Journal*, **4**, 406, 1970.

Loraine, J. A., Adamopoulos, D. A., Kirkham, K. E., Ismail, A. A. A. and Dove, G. A. 'Patterns of hormone excretion in male and female homosexuals.' *Nature*, **234**, 552, 1971.

Loewenstein, J. *Treatment of Impotence*. London: Cassell, 1947.

MacLean, P. D. 'New findings relevant to the evaluation of psychosexual function of the brain.' In J. Money (Ed.), *Sex Research: New Developments*. New York: Holt, Rinehart and Winston 1965.

MacCulloch, M. J. and Feldman, M. P. 'On the aetiology of homosexuality.' *Revista Latino Americana de Psicologica*, **9**, 101, 1977.

MacCulloch, M. J. and Waddington, J. L. 'The biochemical basis of male and female homosexual behaviour in man.' *British Journal of Psychiatry*, (in press).

MacCulloch, M. J., Feldman, M. P. and Emery, A. E. 'The treatment by aversion therapy of an identical twin discordant for homosexuality.' Unpublished manuscript, Crumpsall Hospital, Manchester, 1967.

MacCulloch, M. J., Williams, C. M. and Birtles, C. J. 'The successful application of aversion therapy to an adolescent exhibitionist.' *Journal of Behaviour Therapy and Experimental Psychiatry*, **2**, 61, 1971.

Mahoney, M. J. *Cognition and Behavior Modification*. Cambridge, Mass.: Ballinger, 1974.

Mann, J., Berkowitz, L., Sidman, J., Starr, S. and West, S. 'Satiation of the transient stimulating effect of erotic films.' *Journal of Personality and Social Psychology*, **30**, 729, 1974.

Manosevitz, M. 'Early sexual behaviour in adult homosexual and heterosexual males.' *Journal of Abnormal Psychology*, **76**, 396, 1970.

Margolese, M. S. 'Homosexuality: a new endocrine correlate.' *Hormones and Behaviour*, **1**, 151, 1970.

Margolese, M. S. and Janiger, O. 'Androsterone/etiocholanolone ratios in male homosexuals.' *British Medical Journal*, **3**, 207, 1973.

Marks, I. M. 'Management of sexual disorders.' In H. Leitenberg (Ed.), *Handbook of Behavior Modification and Behaviour Therapy*. New York: Prentice-Hall, 255, 1976.

Marks, I. M. and Gelder, M. G. 'Transvestism and fetishism: clinical and psychological changes during faradic aversion.' *British Journal of Psychiatry*, **113**, 711, 1967.

Marshall, W. C., Williams, S. M. and Christie, M. M. 'The treatment of rapists.' In C. B. Qualls (Ed.), *Perspectives on Rape*. New York: Plenum Press, 1977.

Masters, W. H. and Johnson, V. E. 'The human female: anatomy of sexual response.' *Minnesota Journal of Medicine*, **43**, 31, 1960.

Masters, W. H. and Johnson, V. E. 'The sexual response cycles of the human male and female: comparative anatomy and physiology.' In F. Beach (Ed.), *Sex and Behaviour*. New York: J. Wiley & Sons, 1965 (a).

Masters, W. H. and Johnson, V. E. 'Counselling with sexually incompatible sexual partners.' In R. H. Klemer (Ed.), *Counselling in Marital and Sexual Problems (A Physicians Handbook)*. Baltimore: Williams and Wilkins, 1965 (b).

Masters, W. H. and Johnson, V. E. *Human Sexual Response*. London: Churchill, 1966.

Masters, W. H. and Johnson, V. E. *Human Sexual Inadequacy*. Boston: Little, Brown and Company, 1970.

Mathes, E. W. 'The effects of physical attractiveness and anxiety heterosexual attraction over a series of five encounters.' *Journal of Marriage and the Family*, **32**, 769, 1975.

Mathews, A. M. and Bancroft, J. H. J. 'The principal components of sexual preference.' Paper read to annual conference, British Psychological Society, April 1971. *Bulletin of the British Psychological Society*, **25**, 1971.

Mayer-Gross, W., Slater, E. and Roth, M. *Clinical Psychiatry*, London: Baillière, Tindall and Cassell, 2nd edition, 1968.

McConaghy, N. 'Subjective and penile plethysmograph responses following aversion relief and apomorphine aversion therapy for homosexual problems.' *British Journal of Psychiatry*, **115**, 723, 1969.

McConaghy, N. 'Subjective and penile plethysmograph responses to aversion therapy for homosexuality: a follow-up study.' *British Journal of Psychiatry*, **117**, 555, 1970.

McConaghy, N. 'Aversive and positive conditioning treatment of homosexuality.' *Behaviour Research and Therapy*, **13**, 309, 1975.

McConaghy, N. and Barr, R. F. 'Classical, avoidance and backward conditioning treatments of homosexuality.' *British Journal of Psychiatry*, **122**, 151, 1973.

McFall, R. M., Lillesand, D. and Bridges, D. 'Behaviour rehearsal with modelling and coaching in assertion training.' *Journal of Abnormal Psychology*, **77**, 313, 1971.

McGovern, K. B., Stewart, R. C. and Lopiccolo, J. 'Secondary orgasmic dysfunction. I: analysis and strategies for treatment.' *Archives of Sexual Behaviour*, **4**, No. 3, 265, 1975.

McGuire, W. J. 'The nature of attitudes and attitude change.' In G. Lindzey and E. Aronson (Eds.). *Handbook of Social Psychology*, Vol. 3. Reading, Mass.: Addison-Wesley, p. 136, 2nd edition, 1969.

Meichenbaum, D. H. and Goodman, J. 'Training impulsive children to talk to themselves: a means of developing self-control.' *Journal of Abnormal Psychology*, **77**, 115, 1971.

Melgren, A. 'Treatment of ejaculation praecox with thioridazine.' *Psychotherapy and Psychosomatics*, **15**, 454, 1967.

Merbaum, M. and Kazaoka, K. 'Reports of emotional experiences by sensitizers and repressors during an interview transaction.' *Journal of Abnormal Psychology*, **72**, 101, 1967.

Merritt, C. G., Gerstl, J. E. and Losciuto, L. A. 'Age and perceived effects of erotic pornography: a national sample study.' *Archives of Sexual Behaviour*, **4**, 605, 1975.

Meyer-Bahlburg, H. F. L. 'Sex hormones and male homosexuality in comparative perspective.' *Archives of Sexual Behaviour*, **6**: No. 4., 297, 1977.

Miller, N. E. 'Learning of visceral and glandular responses.' *Science*, **163**, 434, 1969.

Miller, R. E., Caul, W. F. and Mirsky, I. A. 'Communication of affects between feral and socially isolated monkeys.' *Journal of Personality and Social Psychology*, **7**, 231, 1967.

Mohr, J. W., Turner, R. E. and Jerry, M. B. *Paedophilia and Exhibitionism*. London: Oxford University Press, 1964.

Money, J. 'Components of eroticism in man: 1. The hormones in relation to sexual morphology and sexual desire.' *Journal of Nervous and Mental Diseases*, **132**, 239, 1961.

Money, J. and Brennan, J. G. 'Heterosexual vs. homosexual attitudes: Male partners'' perceptions of the feminine image of male trans-sexuals.' Paper delivered at the First International Symposium on Gender Identity, London, July 1969.

Money, J. and Ehrhardt, A. A. 'Fetal hormones and the brain: effect on sexual dimorphism of behaviour—a review.' *Archives of Sexual Behaviour*, 1, 241, 1971.

Money, J. and Ehrhardt, A. A. *Man and Woman, Boy and Girl*. Baltimore: John Hopkins Press, 1972.

Money, J. and Epstein, R. 'Verbal aptitude in eonism and prepubertal effeminacy.' *Transactions of the New York Academy of Sciences*, 29, 448, 1967.

Money, J. and Gaskin, R. J. 'Sex reassignment.' *International Journal of Psychiatry*, 9, 249, 1970.

Money, J. and Hampson, R. 'Imprinting and the establishment of gender role.' *Archives of Neurology and Psychiatry*, 77, 333, 1957.

Money, J. and Ogunro, C. 'Behavioural sexology: ten cases of genetic male intersexuality with impaired prenatal and pubertal androgenization.' *Archives of Sexual Behaviour*, 3, 181, 1974.

Morris, D. *The Naked Ape*. London: Jonathan Cape, 1967.

Morris, J. *Conundrum*. London: Faber and Faber, 1974.

Murstein, B. I., Goyette, M. and Cerren, M. 'A theory of the effect of exchange orientation on marriage and friendship.' Unpublished manuscript, 1974, cited by Walster *et al.*, 1976.

Neumann, F., Elger, W. and von Berswordt-Wallrabe, R. 'Intersexualität männlicher feten und hemmung androgenabhangiger funktionen bei erwachsenen tieren durch testosteronblocker.' *Deutsche Medische Wochenschrift*, 92, 360, 1967.

Nyrop, C. Storia dell' Epopea Francese nel Medio Evo. Turin, p. 353, 1888. (cited by Henriques, p. 325, 1958).

Obler, M. 'Systematic desensitization in sexual disorders.' *Journal of Behaviour Therapy and Experimental Psychiatry*, 4, 93, 1973.

Observer, 11 July 1965.

O'Connor, P. J. 'Aetiological factors in homosexuality as seen in R. A. F. psychiatric practice.' *British Journal of Psychiatry*, 110, 381, 1964.

Parker, N. 'Twins: a psychiatric study of a neurotic group.' *Medical Journal of Australia*, 2, 735, 1964.

Parks, G. A.,Korth-Schütz, S., Penny, R., Hilding, R. F., Dumars, K. W. Frasier, S. D. and New, M. I. 'Variation in pituitary-gonadal function in adolescent male homosexuals and heterosexuals.' *Journal of Clinical Endocrinology and Metabolism*, 39, 796, 1974.

Patterson, G. R., Hops, H. and Weiss, R. L. 'Interpersonal skills training for couples in the early stages of conflict.' *Journal of Marriage and the Family*, May, 291, 1975.

Patterson, G. R., Weiss, R. L. and Hops, N. 'Training of marital skills: some problems and concepts.' In H. Leitenberg (Ed.), *Handbook of Behaviour Modification and Behaviour Therapy*. New York: Prentice-Hall, 242, 1976.

Perkins, D. E. 'Development of a psychological treatment programme for sex offenders in a prison setting.' *Bulletin of the British Psychological Society*, 30, 179, 1977.

Pfeiffer, C. A. 'Sexual differences of hypophyses and their determination by the gonads.' *American Journal of Anatomy*, 58, 195, 1936.

Phoenix, C. H., Goy, R. W., Gerall, A. A. Young, W. C. 'Organizing action of prenatally administered testosterone propionate on the tissues mediating mating behaviour in the female guinea pig.' *Endocrinology*, 65, 369, 1959.

Pillard, R. C., Rose, R. M. and Sherwood, M. 'Plasma testosterone levels in homosexual men.' *Archives of Sexual Behaviour*, 3, 453, 1974.

Podell, L. and Perkins, J. C. 'A Guttman scale for sexual experience—a methodological note.' *Journal of Abnormal and Social Psychology*, 54, 420, 1957.

Pomeroy, W. B. 'Human sexual behavior.' In N. L. Farberow (Ed.), *Taboo Topics*, New York: Atherton, 1963.

Racey, P. A., Ansari, J. A., Rowe, P. E. and Glover, T. D. 'Proceedings: testosterone in impotent men.' *Journal of Endocrinology*, **59**, xxiii, 1973.

Rachman, S. J. (Ed.) *Critical Essays on Psychoanalysis*. Oxford: Pergamon Press, 1963.

Rachman, S. J. 'Sexual fetishism; an experimental analogue.' *Psychological Record*, **16**, 294, 1966.

Rachman, S. J. *The Effects of Psychotherapy*. Oxford: Pergamon Press, 1971.

Rachman, S. J. and Hodgson, R. J. 'Experimentally induced sexual fetishism: replications and development.' *Psychological Record*, **18**, 25, 1968.

Radzinowicz, L. *Sexual Offences*. London: MacMillan, 1957.

Rainer, J. D., Mesnikoff, A., Kolb, L. C. and Carr, A. 'Homosexuality and heterosexuality in identical twins.' *Psychosomatic Medicine*, **22**, 251, 1960.

Ramsay, R. W., van Velzen, V. 'Behaviour therapy for sexual perversions.' *Behaviour Research and Therapy*, **6**, 233, 1968.

Rasmussen, E. W. 'Experimental homosexual behaviour in male albino rats.' *Acta Psychologica*, **11**, 303, 1955.

Redbook Magazine. The Redbook Report: A Study of Female Sexuality. Issues of June, September and October, 1975.

Reiss, A. J. Jr. 'Sex offences: the marginal status of the adolescent.' *Law and Contemporary Problems*, 25, 1960.

Reitz, W. and Keil, W. 'Behavioural treatment of an exhibitionist.' *Journal of Behaviour Therapy and Experimental Psychiatry*, **2**, 67, 1971.

Rettig, S. and Pasamanick, B. 'Changes in moral values among college students: a factorial study.' *American Sociological Review*, **24**, 856, 1959.

Richardson, T. 'Hypnotherapy in frigidity.' *American Journal of Clinical Hypnosis*, **5**, 194, 1963.

Rickles, N. K. *Exhibitionism*. Philadelphia: Lippincott, 1950.

Roeder, F. and Muller, D. *German Medical Monthly*, **14**, 265, 1969.

Rooth, F. G. and Marks, I. M. 'Persistent exhibitionism: short-term response to self-regulation and relaxation treatment.' *Archives of Sexual Behaviour*, **3**, 227, 1974.

Rosen, I. 'Exhibitionism.' In I. Rosen (Ed.), *The Pathology and Treatment of Sexual Deviation*. London: Oxford University Press, 1964.

Rosenblatt, P. C. 'Cross-cultural perspectives on attraction.' In T. L. Huston (Ed.), *Foundations of Interpersonal Attractions*. New York: Academic Press, p. 79, 1974.

Rosenblatt, P. C. and Cozby, P. C. 'Courtship patterns associated with freedom of choice of spouse.' *Journal of Marriage and the Family*, **34**, 689, 1972.

Rubin, Z. *Liking and Loving: An Invitation to Social Psychology*. New York: Holt, 1973.

Rubin, Z. 'From liking to loving: patterns of attractions in dating relationships.' In T. L. Huston (Ed.), *Foundations of Interpersonal Attractions*. New York: Academic Press, 383, 1974.

Runciman, A. 'Sexual therapy of Masters and Johnson.' *The Counselling Psychologist*, **5**, 22, 1975.

Russell, A. and Winkler, R. 'Evaluation of assertive training and homosexual guidance service groups designed to improve homosexual functioning.' *Journal of Consulting and Clinical Psychology*, **45**, 1, 1977.

Sambrooks, J. E. and MacCulloch, M. J. 'A modification of the sexual orientation method and an automated technique for presentation and scoring.' *British Journal of Social and Clinical Psychology*, **12**, 163, 1973.

Sandler, J. 'Reinforcement combinations and masochistic behaviour: A preliminary report.' *Psychological Reports*, **11**, 110, 1962.

Sandler, J. 'Masochism: an empirical analysis.' *Psychological Bulletin*, **62**, 197, 1964.

Schachter, S. 'The interaction of cognitive and physiological determinants of emotional state.' In L. Berkowitz (Ed.), *Advances in Experimental Social Psychology*. New York: Academic Press, Vol. 1., p. 49, 1964.

215

Schachter, S. and Singer, J. E. 'Cognitive, social and physiological determinants of emotional state.' *Psychological Review*, **69**, 379, 1962.

Scheff, T. J. *Labelling Madness*. New York: Prentice-Hall, 1975.

Schein, M. W. and Hale, E. 'Stimuli eliciting sexual behaviour.' In F. Beach (Ed.), *Sex and Behavior*, New York: Wiley, 440, 1965.

Schmidt, G. and Sigusch, V. 'Changes in sexual behaviour among young males and females between 1960–1970.' *Archives of Sexual Behaviour*, **2**, 27, 1972.

Schmidt, G., Sigusch, V. and Schafer, S. 'Responses to reading erotic stories: male–female differences.' *Archives of Sexual Behaviour*, **2**, 181, 1973.

Schofield, M. *The Sexual Behaviour of Young People*. London: Longmans, 1965(a).

Schofield, M. *Sociological Aspects of Homosexuality*. London: Longmans, 1965(b).

Schofield, M. *The Sexual Behaviour of Young Adults*. London: Allen Lane, 1973.

Scott, J. F. *The Sexual Instinct*. New York: E. B. Trent & Co., 1889.

Scott, T. R., Wells, W. H., Wood, D. Z. and Morgan, D. I. 'Pupillary response and sexual interest re-examined.' *Journal of Clinical Psychology*, **31**, 433, 1967.

Semans, J. H. 'Premature ejaculation: a new approach.' *Journal of Urology*, **40**, 836, 1956.

Shapiro, B. 'Premature ejaculation: review of 1,130 cases.' *Journal of Urology*, **50**, 374, 1943.

Siegelman, M. 'Parental background of homosexual and heterosexual women.' *British Journal of Psychiatry*, **124**, 14, 1974.

Silverman, I. 'Physical attractiveness and courtship.' *Sexual Behaviour*, Sept., 22, 1971.

Silverstein, C. 'Homosexuality and the ethics of behavioural interventions.' *Journal of Homosexuality*, **2**, 205, 1977.

Simpson, G. M., Blair, J. H. and Amuso, D. A. 'Effects of antidepressants on genito-urinary function.' *Diseases of the Nervous System*, **26**, 787, 1965.

Skinner, R. B. *Science and Human Behavior*. New York: MacMillan, 1953.

Sluckin, W. *Early Learning in Man and Animal*. London: Allen and Unwin, 1970.

Small, M. P., Carrion, H. M. and Gordon, J. A. 'Small–Carrion penile prosthesis: New implant for management of impotence.' *Urology*, Vol. V. No. 4., 479, 1975.

Smith, P. E. and Engle, E. T. 'Experimental evidence regarding the role of the anterior pituitary in the development and regulation of the genital system.' *American Journal of Anatomy*, **40**, 159, 1927.

Snortum, J. R., Gillespie, N. F., Marshall, J. E., McLaughlin, J. P. and Mosberg, L. 'Family dynamics and homosexuality.' *Psychological Reports*, **24**, 763, 1969.

Sotile, W. M. and Kilman, P. R. 'Treatments of psychogenic female sexual dysfunction.' *Psychological Bulletin*, **84**, 619, 1977.

Spanier, G. B. and Cole, C. L. 'Mate swapping: perceptions, value orientations and participation in a Mid-Western community.' *Archives of Sexual Behaviour*, **4**, 143, 1975.

Spielberger, C. D. 'Theory and research on anxiety.' In C. D. Spielberger (Ed.), *Anxiety and Behavior*, New York: Academic Press, 1966.

Stevenson, I. and Wolpe, J. 'Recovery from sexual deviations through overcoming non-sexual neurotic response.' *American Journal of Psychiatry*, **116**, 737, 1960.

Stone, L. *The Family, Sex and Marriage in England, 1500–1800*. London: Weidenfeld, 1977.

Street Offences Act, 57, 1959.

Stürup, G. K. 'Castration: The total treatment.' In H. L. P. Resnick and M. F. Wolfgang (Eds.), *Sexual Behavior*. Boston: Little, Brown, 1972.

Swanson, H. H. and Gossley, D. A. 'Sexual behavior in the golden hamster and its modification by neonatal administration of testosterone propionate.' In M. Hamburgh and E. J. W. Barrington (Eds.), *Hormones in Development*. New York: Appleton-Century-Crofts, 1971.

Tanner, B. A. 'A comparison of automated aversive conditioning and a waiting list control in the modifications of homosexual behaviour in males.' *Behaviour Therapy*, **5**, 29–32, 1974.

Tanner, J. M. 'Current advances in the study of physique. Photogrammetric anthropometry and an androgyny scale.' *Lancet*, **1**, 574, 1951.

Tardieu, A. *Etude Medico-Legale sur les Attendants aux Molurs*. Paris: J. B. Baillère, 1857.

Tennov, D. 'Sex differences in romantic love and depression among college students.' *Proceedings of the 81st Annual Convention of the American Psychological Association*, 419, 1973.

Todd (Lord) *Royal Commission on Medical Education*. London: H.M.S.O., 1968.

Tolsma, F. J. *De Betekenis van der Verleiding in Homofile Ontivikekelingen*. Amsterdam: Psychiatrijuridicial Society, 1957.

Trower, P., Bryant, B. and Argyle, M. *Social Skills and Mental Health*. London: Methuen, 1978.

Udry, J. R., Bauman, K. E. and Morris, N. M. 'Changes in premarital coital experience of recent decade-of-birth cohorts of urban American women.' *Journal of Marriage and the Family*, **37**, 783, 1975.

Ulrichs, K. H. *Memnon: Die Geschlechtnatur des mannliebenden Urnings*. Schleiz: H. Heyn, 1868.

Walster, E., Aronson, V., Abrahams, D. and Rottmann, L. 'The importance of physical attractiveness in dating behaviour.' *Journal Personality and Social Psychology*, **4**, 508, 1966.

Walster, E., Berscheid, E. and Walster, G. W. 'New directions in equity research.' *Journal of Personality and Social Psychology*, **25**, 151, 1973b.

Walster, E., Walster, G., Piliavin, J. and Schmidt, L. ' "Playing hard to get": Understanding an elusive phenomenon.' *Journal of Personality and Social Psychology*, **26**, 113, 1973a.

Walster, E., Utne, M. K. and Traupman, J. 'Equity theory and intimate relationships.' Paper presented at the Conference on Human and Family Development: Social Exchange in Developing Relationships. Pennsylvania State University, 26–28 May 1976.

Ward, A. 'General practitioners and family planning in Sheffield.' *Journal of Biosocial Science*, **1**, 15, 1969.

Wengener, M. A., Averill, J. R. and Smith, D. D. B. 'Autonomic activity during sexual arousal.' *Psychophysiology*, **4**, 468, 1968.

West, D. J. 'Parental figures in the genesis of male homosexuality.' *International Journal of Social Psychiatry*, **5**, 85, 1959.

West, D. J. *Homosexuality* (3rd edition). London: Duckworth, 1967.

Whalen, R. E. 'Sexual motivation.' *Psychological Review*, **73**, 151, 1966.

Whalen, R. E. 'Differentiation of the neural mechanisms which control gonadotrophin secretion and sexual behavior.' In M. Diamond (Ed.), *Perspectives in Reproduction and Sexual Behavior*. Indiana: Indiana University Press, 1968.

Wheeler, S. 'Sex offences: A sociological critique.' In J. H. Gagnon and W. Simon (Eds.), *Sexual Deviance*. New York: Harper and Row, pp. 77, 1967.

Wiggins, J. S., Wiggins, N. and Conger, J. C. 'Correlates of heterosexual somatic preference.' *Journal of Personality and Social Psychology*, **10**, 82, 1968.

Wilson, J. G., Hamilton, J. B. and Young, W. C. 'Influence of age and presence of the ovaries on reproductive function in rats injected with androgens.' *Endocrinology*, **29**, 784, 1941.

Winch, R. F. *Mate Selection: A Study of Complementary Needs*. New York: Harper, 1958.

Wolfenden Committee. 'Our Approach to the Problem.' *Report of the Committee on Homosexual Offences and Prostitution*. London: H.M.S.O. Cmnd. 247, 1957.

Wölinder, J. 'Transvestism, definition and evidence in favour of occasional deviation from cerebral dysfunction.' *International Journal of Neuropsychiatry*, **1**, 567, 1965.

Wolpe, J. *Psychotherapy by Reciprocal Inhibition*. Stanford, California: Stanford University Press, 1958.

Woodward, M. 'The diagnosis and treatment of homosexual offenders.' *British Journal of Delinquency*, **9**, 44, 1958.

Wright, D. and Cox, E. 'Changes in moral belief among sixth-form boys and girls over a seven year period in relation to religious belief, age and sex difference.' *British Journal of Social and Clinical Psychology*, **10**, 332, 1971.

Yalom, I. D., Green, R. and Fisk, N. 'Prenatal exposure to female hormones.' *Archives of General Psychiatry*, **28**, 554, 1973.

Young, W. *Eros Denied*. New York: Grove Press, 1964.

Zimbardo, P. G. *Cognitive Control of Motivation*. Glenview, Illinois: Scott, Foresman, 1969.

Zondek, B. and Ascheim, S. 'Das hormon des hypophysenvorderlappen I. Testobjekt zum nachweis des hormons.' *Klinische Wochenschrift*, **6**, 248, 1927.

Zuckerman, M. 'Physiological measures of sexual arousal in the human.' *Psychological Bulletin*, **75**, 297, 1971.

Zuckerman, M., Persky, H. and Link, D. 'Relation of mood and hypnotizability: an illustration of the importance of the state, vs. trait distinction.' *Journal of Consulting Psychology*, **31**, 464, 1967.

Author Index

Abrahams, D., 79
Achilles, Nancy, 151
Adamopoulos, D.A., 155
Agras, W.S., 175, 198, 199
Al-Issa, I., 140
Amir, M., 187, 188
Amuso, D.A., 41
Ansari, J.M.A., 123, 124, 126
Anthony, J., 162, 163
Antoniou, L.D., 140
Apperson, Louise B., 162
Argyle, M., 175
Aronson, V., 79
Ascheim, S., 37
Aschner, B., 37
Averill, J.R., 41
Azrin, N.H., 86

Bailey, S., 3
Bancroft, J.H.J., 66, 153, 173, 199, 201
Bandura, A., 63, 64, 74, 133, 134, 194
Barclay, A.M., 42
Bardwick, J.M., 42
Barker, W.J., 90
Barlow, D.H., 175, 198, 199
Barr, R.F., 173, 181
Barraclough, C.A., 38
Bauman, K.E., 59, 104
Beach, F.A., 14, 20, 21, 36, 40, 41, 64, 192
Beasley, R., 5
Behrman, S.J., 42
Bell, R.A., 164
Bene, E., 162, 163, 165
Benjamin, N., 180
Bentler, P.M., 109, 110, 111, 117, 181, 183
Bergeret, L.F.E., 4
Bergin, A.E., 134
Berkowitz, L., 69, 70
Berl, S., 152, 163
Bernard, J., 77
Berscheid, E., 80, 81, 82, 83, 84, 85, 86

Berswordt-Wallrabe, R. von, 39
Berthold, A.A., 36
Bieber, B., 152, 161, 162, 163, 173, 174
Bieber, I., 152, 161, 162, 163, 173, 174
Bieber, T.B., 152, 161, 162, 163, 173, 174
Binet, A., 177
Birk, L., 174
Birtles, C.J., 200
Blair, J.H., 41
Boerhave, H., 3
Bohrnstedt, G., 86
Box, S., 22
Brady, J.P., 109, 110, 141, 143
Brehm, J.W., 82
Brennan, J.G., 181
Bridges, D., 74
Bryan, J.H., 17
Bryant, B., 175
Bullough, V.L., 3
Byrne, D., 76, 79

Calhoun, J.B., 36
Callahan, E.J., 174
Carr, A., 157
Carrier, J.M., 166
Carrion, H.M., 139
Cass, J., 199
Cattell, R.B., 40
Caul, W.F., 62
Cautela, J.R., 174
Cerren, M., 87
Chapman, J.D., 141
Christenson, F.V., 186, 187
Christie, M.M., 199, 200
Clare, J., 152, 163
Clark, L.C., 42
Cliffe, M.J., 153
Clinard, M.B., 16, 186
Coates, S., 173
Cohler, B., 174
Cole, C.L., 60, 105
Colson, C.E., 13

Conger, J.C., 66
Coombs, C.H., 7
Cooper, A.J., 123, 125, 126, 127, 138, 139, 142
Court, J.H., 12
Cox, B., 19
Cox, E., 7
Cozby, P.C., 78
Craighead, W.E., 134
Curran, D., 173
Curran, J.P., 80

Dain, J.J., 152, 161, 162, 163, 173, 174
Daughaday, W.H., 155, 156
Davies, B.M., 179
Davis, K.E., 82
Davison, G.C., 171, 172, 173
Dawkins, S., 142
Dean, R.B., 154
Demoor, P., 160
Denef, C., 160
Dermer, M., 80
Deutsch, R.M., 128
Devlin, Lord, 1
Diess, P., 39
Dince, P.R., 152, 161, 162, 163, 173, 174
Dion, K., 80, 84
Dittmar, F., 155, 156
Docke, F., 37
Doerr, P., 155, 156
Donnerstein, E., 67
Donnerstein, M., 67
Dorbar, R.R., 181, 182
Dörner, G., 37, 38, 39, 159
Doshay, L.G., 191
Dove, G.A., 155
Drellich, M.G., 152, 161, 162, 163, 173, 174
Driscoll, R., 82
Dumars, K.W., 156

Edwards, A.L., 190
Erhardt, A.A., 36, 40, 59
Eibl-Eibesfeldt, I., 78
Eleston, M.R., 152, 163
Elger, W., 39
Ellis, A., 182
Ellison, G., 143
Emery, A.E., 158
Engle, E.T., 37
Epstein, A.W., 178
Epstein, R., 181
Ervin, C.R., 79
Evans, D.R., 192, 193, 194, 200

Evans, E., 67
Evans, R.B., 154, 155, 160, 162, 166
Eysenck, H., 11, 110, 111, 115, 116, 117, 121

Falk, M., 140
Farkas, G.M., 68
Fava, S.F., 92
Feder, H.H., 39
Feingold, J., 67
Feldman, M.P., 134, 149, 152, 158, 171, 174, 190, 196
Fenichel, O., 184
Feshbach, S., 67
Festinger, L., 61
Finck, H.T., 76
Finger, F.W., 59
Fisher, G., 190
Fisk, N., 160
Fithian, M., 144
Ford, C.S., 14, 20, 21, 64, 192
Frasier, S.D., 156
Freund, K., 153, 179
Friedman, L.J., 143
Fulker, D.W., 158
Fuller, M., 166
Furlow, W.L., 140

Gagnon, J.H., 151
Gagnon, W.H., 186, 187
Garfield, S.L., 134
Gaskin, R.J., 182, 183, 196, 197
Gatza, M., 82
Gebhard, P.H., 59, 71, 89, 92, 99, 186, 187
Gelder, M.G., 196
Gellhorn, E., 41
Gerall, A.A., 38
Gershwin, B.S., 152, 163
Gershwin, P., 152, 163
Gerstl, J.E., 13
Giese, H., 116
Gillespie, N.F., 162
Gillespie, W.H., 179
Glover, T.D., 126
Goethals, G., 82
Goldstein, A., 133
Goldstein, M., 12, 13
Goodman, J., 74
Gordon, J.A., 139
Gorski, R.A., 38
Gossley, D.A., 36
Goy, R.W., 38
Goyette, M., 87

Grady K.L.,   39
Graham, S.,   3
Grand, H.G., 152, 161, 162, 163, 173, 174
Green, R.,   12, 13, 160, 166, 197, 198
Greenblatt, D.R.,   162
Griffitt, W.,   71, 76
Grundlach, R.N., 152, 161, 162, 163, 173, 174
Gundlach, R.H.,   168
Guttman, L.,   110

Hale, E.,   53
Hall, S.,   142
Hamilton, J.B.,   38
Hampson, R.,   182
Harlow, H.F.,   36, 62, 76, 167
Harlow, M.K.,   36
Harris, G.W.,   39
Hartman, W.,   144
Haslam, M.T.,   127, 142
Hastings, D.,   123, 137
Hecutr, K.,   133
Heller, C.G.,   155
Hendler, J.,   166
Hendry, J.,   155
Henriques, F.,   2, 3, 16, 17, 18, 184
Herman, S.H.,   175
Hess, H.,   153
Heston, L.L.,   157
Hilding, R.F.,   156
Hill, M.,   15
Himelhoch, J.,   92
Hodgson, R.J.,   177, 178
Hoenig, J.,   182
Hohlweg, W.,   37
Hohmann, G.W.,   41
Hooker, E.,   151
Hops, H.,   146, 148
Howell, Leisla M.,   190
Howells, K.,   188
Huddleston, W.,   174
Huizinga, J.,   2

Ishmail, A.A.,   126, 155

Jackson, D.D.,   85
Jacobs, L.,   82
Jacobs, L.S.,   155, 156
Jaffe, Y.,   67
Janiger, O.,   160
Jenkins, M.,   166
Jerry, M.B.,   189, 190, 191, 192, 193, 194
Jinks, L.,   158
Johnson, J.,   126, 139

Johnson, V.E.,   41, 43, 44, 45, 51, 52, 53,
    89, 121, 124, 125, 127, 128, 131, 136,
    138, 139, 140, 143, 144, 145, 146
Jones, R.,   86
Jones, W., Jr,   141, 142
Judd, L.,   12, 13
Junkmann, K.,   37

Kallman, F.J.,   157
Kant, H.,   12, 13
Kaye, H.E.,   152, 163
Kazaoka, K.,   74
Kazdin, A.E.,   134
Kegel, A.,   142
Keil, W.,   200
Kellog, J.H.,   3
Kenna, J.C.,   182
Kenyon, F.E.,   163, 164, 165, 168
Kephart, W.M.,   84
Kerckhoff, A.C.,   77
Kilman, P.R.,   141
Kinsey, A.C., 6, 7, 59, 65, 71, 89, 90, 92,
    93, 94, 95, 96, 97, 98, 99, 100, 101, 102,
    103, 104, 105, 113, 125, 128, 130, 137,
    150, 152, 155, 170
Kirkham, K.E.,   155
Klassen, A.D.,   9
Klausner, S.Z.,   103
Klintworth, G.K.,   157
Kockott, G.,   155, 156, 180
Kogan, L.S.,   152, 163
Kolarsky, A.,   179
Kolaszynska-Carr, A.,   67, 111, 112, 152,
    154, 163, 164, 167, 168, 169
Kolb, L.C.,   157
Kolodny, R.C.,   155, 156
Korth-Schütz, S.,   156
Kraft, T.,   140
Kraft-Ebbing, R. von,   4
Krell, L.,   159
Kremer, M.W.,   152, 161, 162, 163, 173, 174

Lamberth, J.,   79
Langevin, R.,   178
Lavrakas, P.,   66
Laws, D.R.,   153
Lazarus, A.,   141
Leckie, F.,   141
Lederer, W.J.,   85
Leitenberg, H.,   174
Lemert, H.,   16
Le Moal, P.,   65
Levi, L.,   42

Levitt, E.E., 9, 109, 110
Levy, N.B., 140
Lewis, C.S., 167
Lewis, D.J., 185
Leznoff, M., 151
Lillesand, D., 74
Link, D., 40, 41
Linton, R., 84
Lipetz, M.E., 82
Lippold, S., 80
Lloyd-Jones, M., 15
Lobitz, W., 145
Lockhart, W.B., 1, 10, 18
Loewenstein, J., 123
Loney, J., 151
Longford, Lord, 1
Loofburrow, G.N., 41
Lopiccolo, J., 145, 146
Loraine, J.A., 126, 155
Losciuto, L.A., 13
Loucas, K., 199

McAdoo, W.G., 162
McConaghy, N., 173, 175
McCrommon, J., 82
MacCulloch, M.J., 149, 152, 156, 158, 174, 190, 196, 200
MacCulloch, M.L., 196
McFall, R.M., 74
McGovern, K.B., 145, 146
McGuire, W.J., 59
Machek, J., 179
McLaughlin, J.P., 162
Maddock, W.O., 155
Mahoney, M.J., 134, 172
Malamuth, N., 67
Mann, J., 69, 70
Manosevitz, M., 162, 169, 170
Margolese, M.S., 155, 160
Marks, I.M., 196, 200
Marshall, J.E., 162
Marshall, W.C., 199, 200
Martin, C.E., 6, 7, 59, 65, 71, 89, 92, 137, 152, 170
Martin, M., 178
Masius, W.G., 159
Masters, W.H., 41, 43, 44, 45, 51, 52, 53, 89, 121, 124, 125, 127, 128, 131, 136, 138, 139, 140, 143, 144, 145, 146, 155, 156
Mathes, E.W., 79
Mathews, A.M., 66
Mayer-Gross, W., 184
Meichenbaum, D.H., 74

Melgren, A., 140
Mellor, V., 152
Merbaum, M., 74
Merritt, C.G., 13
Meyer-Bahlburg, H.F.L., 155, 156
Meznikoff, A., 157
Miller, E., 174
Miller, N.E., 61
Miller, R.E., 62
Mirsky, L.A., 62
Mohr, J.W., 189, 190, 191, 192, 193, 194
Money, J., 36, 40, 41, 159, 181, 182, 183, 196, 197
Morgan, D.I., 153
Morgenstern, F.S., 179
Morris, D., 56
Morris, J., 180
Morris, N.M., 104
Mosberg, L., 162
Moustafa, A., 37
Muller, D., 199
Murstein, B.I., 87

Naster, B.J., 86
Neulmann, F., 39
New, M.I., 156
Newman, L.E., 197, 198
Noble, R.G., 36
Nyrop, C., 2

Obler, M., 143
O'Connor, P.J., 161
Ogunro, C., 159
Orndoff, R.K., 36

Park, P., 141, 142
Parker, N., 157, 158
Parks, G.A., 156
Parr, D., 173
Pasamanick, B., 7
Patterson, G.R., 146, 148
Penny, R., 156
Perkins, D.E., 200
Perkins, J.C., 109, 110
Perlman, D., 90
Persky, H., 40, 41
Pfieffer, C.A., 38
Phoenix, C.H., 38, 39
Piliavin, J., 82, 83
Pillard, R.C., 155
Pinschof, J.M., 152
Pirke, K.M., 155
Podell, L., 109, 110
Polak, O., 179

Pomeroy, W.B., 6, 7, 59, 65, 71, 89, 91, 92, 99, 137, 152, 170, 186, 187

Racey, P.A., 126
Rachman, S.J., 133, 177, 178, 179
Radzinowicz, L., 186, 189, 192, 193
Rainer, J.D., 157
Ramsay, R.W., 152
Rasmussen, E.W., 166
Reiss, A.J., 17, 18
Reitz, W., 200
Rettig, S., 7
Reynolds, J.I., 198, 199
Rice, C., 12, 13
Richardson, H., 154
Richardson, T., 141
Rickles, N.K., 193
Riess, B.F., 168
Roeder, F., 199
Rohde, W., 159
Rooth, F.G., 200
Rose, R.M., 155
Rosen, I., 192, 193
Rosen, R.C., 68
Rosenblatt, P.C., 78, 85
Roth, M., 184
Rottman, L., 79
Rowe, P.E., 126
Rubin, N.B., 153
Rubin, Z., 81, 85
Runciman, A., 128
Russell, A., 175
Rutley, B.R., 166

Sambrooks, J.E., 152
Sandler, J., 184, 185
Schachter, S., 41, 81, 84
Schafer, S., 70
Scheff, T.J., 22
Scheier, I.H., 40
Schein, M.W., 53
Schmidt, G., 7, 8, 65, 70, 90, 103, 104, 105
Schmidt, L., 82, 83
Schmidt, R., 116
Schofield, M., 7, 14, 15, 65, 90, 91, 92, 93, 94, 100, 105, 106, 107, 108, 113, 114, 115, 116, 167, 168, 189, 190, 191, 192
Scott, J.F., 4
Scott, T.R., 153
Sechrest, L., 133
Seltzer, L., 153
Semans, J.H., 139
Shalour, R.J., 140

Shapiro, B., 124
Sherwood, M., 155
Shields, J., 157
Shirley, J., 19
Shlien, M., 153
Short, M., 19
Sidman, J., 69, 70
Siegelman, M., 164
Sigusch, V., 7, 8, 65, 70, 90, 103, 104, 105
Silverman, I., 79
Silverstein, C., 171, 172
Simon, W., 151
Simpson, C.M., 41
Singer, J.E., 41, 81
Skinner, R.B., 184
Slater, E., 184
Sluckin, W., 167
Small, M.P., 139
Smith, C.G., 126
Smith, D.D.B., 41
Smith, J.C., 140
Smith, P.E., 37
Snortum, J.R., 162
Sotile, W.M., 141
Spannier, G.B., 60, 105
Spierberger, C.D., 40
Stahl, F., 159
Starr, S., 69, 70
Steadman-Allen, R., 188
Stevenson, I., 174
Stewart, R.C., 145, 146
Stoller, R.J., 197, 198
Stone, L., 59
Stürup, G.K., 199
Sudhakar, T., 140
Swanson, H.H., 36

Tanner, B.A., 174
Tanner, J.M., 154
Tardieu, A., 4
Taylor, R., 142
Tennant, T.G., 199
Tennov, D., 80
Thiel, D.L., 80
Todd, Lord, 15
Tolsma, F.J., 191
Torda, C., 152, 163
Torro, G., 155, 156
Traupman, J., 85, 86, 87
Treichler, D., 42
Trower, P., 175
Turner, R.E., 189, 190, 191, 192, 193, 194
Udry, J.R., 104
Ulrichs, K.H., 4

Utne, M.K.,   85, 86, 87

Van Velzen, V.,   152
Vogt, H.J.,   155

Waddington, J.L.,   156
Walster, E.,   79, 80, 81, 82, 83, 84, 85,
    86, 87
Walster, G.W.,   80, 82, 83, 85
Ward, A.,   15
Ward, L.,   82
Weiss, R.L.,   146, 148
Wells, W.H.,   153
Wengener, M.A.,   41
West, D.J.,   161, 167
West, S.,   69, 70
Westley, W.A.,   151
Whalen, R.E.,   36, 39, 40
Wheeler, S.,   186
Wiggins, J.S.,   66
Wiggins, N.,   66

Wilbur, C.B., 152, 161, 162, 163, 173, 174
Williams, C.M.,   200
Williams, S.M.,   199, 200
Wilson, G.T.,   172, 173
Wilson, J.G.,   38
Wilson, R.R.,   59
Winch, R.F.,   77
Winkler, R.,   175
Wolinder, J.,   178
Wolpe, J.,   141, 143, 174
Wood, D.Z.,   153
Woodward, M.,   173
Wright, D.,   7

Yalom, I.D.,   160
Young, W.,   17
Young, W.C.,   38

Zimbardo, P.G.,   68, 69
Zondek, B.,   37
Zuckerman, M.,   40, 41, 42

Subject Index

Adolescent sexual behaviour, 96, 169
Adultery, 9
Affection, 78, 86, 126
Aggression, 67
Anatomy, of female genitalia, 33–35
  of male genitalia, 31–33
Androgen, 38, 40, 159, 160, 183
Androgen insensitivity, 159
Androsterone, 155
Anticipatory avoidance learning, 174, 200
Arousability, 40–42, 71, 127, 130
Arousal, 40–42, 68, 69, 71, 74, 81–83, 95, 122–125, 127–130, 145, 153
  and alcohol, 68
  copulation phase, 56
  excitement phase, 43–46
  failure in, 129
  matching rates of, 130–131
  mechanisms of, 41
  orgasmic phase, 43–46
  physiological measures of, 42
  plateau phase, 56
  post-coital phase, 56
  refractory period, 44
  resolution phase, 43–46
Attitudinal change, 61
Attraction, 76–80
Autonomic nervous system, 41
Aversion relief, 173
Aversion therapy, 173, 200

Behaviour therapy, 133
  in heterosexual dysfunction, 135–147
  in homosexuality, 173–175
Bentler Sexual Behaviour Inventory, 110, 111
Biosocial interaction, 112–113
Bisexuals, 36

Cerebral arousal centres, 40
Cerebral sexual centres, 36, 38, 159
Christian morality, 2, 8

Chromosomes, 25, 35
Classical conditioning, 62, 80
Clitoris, 33, 35, 51, 55, 128
Cognitive cues, 71
Cognitive dissonance, 61
Cognitive rehearsal, 74, 194
Consummation mechanism, 41
Contraception, 8, 15
Co-therapy principle, 136
Couple re-education, 141
Covert sensitization, 174
Cultural variations in sexual behaviour, 20–22

Dating, 115
Dimorphic behaviour, 35, 36, 159
Display of interest, 67
Double standards, 7, 8, 59
Drug therapy, 140, 142
Dyspareunia, 127, 129, 141

Early sexual experience, 94–96, 103–107
  in homosexuality, 168–170
Ejaculation, 44, 94–97, 196
  problems of, 124, 127, 139–140
Embryology of genitalia, 24–29
Equity theory, 85
Erotic stimulation, 69–71
Ethical principles of treatment, 170–173
Etiocholanolane, 155
Exhibitionism, 185, 192–195
  treatment of, 200
Extramarital coitus, 101–105

Fading, 175, 199
Fellatio, 55, 189
Female sexual dysfunction, 124–129
  treatment of, 140–143
Female sexual response cycle, 44–47, 51
Female transsexualism, 182, 197
Fetishism, 177–179
  treatment of, 195

224

First experience of coitus,   64–65, 126
Flagellation,   69, 184
Foetal hormones,
  see Pre-natal hormones
Follicle stimulating hormone,   37
Frigidity, *see* Orgasmic dysfunction
Frustration,   82

Gender identity differentiation,   183
Genitalia, *see* Anatomy
Genitalia stimulation,   43, 54, 55, 107
Gonadotrophins,   37, 156

Heart rate,   42, 46
Homogamy,   77
Homosexuality,   1, 4, 8, 9, 69, 95–99, 101, 102, 105, 149–152, 170
  anal-active,   166
  anal-passive,   166
  body build,   154
  child rearing influences,   160–166
  early sexual experience,   168–170
  ethical principles of treatment,   170–173
  genetic influences,   157
  hormones,   155, 159, 160
  incidence,   150
  personality,   153
  prostitution,   17, 18
  single sex environments,   166–168
  treatment,   173–175
Hormones, 37–41, 153, 155, 159, 160, 183
Hypophysical gonadotrophin,   38
Hypothalmus,   37, 39, 41, 183

Impotence,   123–126
  treatment of,   137–142
Incest,   185
Instrumental conditioning,   62
Instrumental responses,   63
Intersexuals,   182
Intimate relationships,   85

Kissing,   20, 55, 108, 115

Lesbians,   162, 163, 168
Love,   7, 76, 78, 80–86
Luteinizing hormone,   39, 155, 159

Male sexual dysfunction,   122–127
  treatment of,   137–140
Male sexual response cycle,   44, 48–50, 52–53
Marital satisfaction,   76

Masturbation,   3, 4, 12, 15, 69, 72, 74, 93, 95–100, 102, 104, 124, 172, 189
Masturbatory fantasy,   99
Mate selection,   77
Modelling,   64, 68
Multiple orgasm,   101

Nocturnal sex dreams,   96, 97, 100, 102
Non-genital stimulation,   55

Observational learning,   63
Oestrogen,   38, 39, 159, 160
Oestrogen feedback effect,   159
Optimal sexual environment,   138
Oral sex,   1, 4, 69
Orgasm,   40, 44, 52, 56, 59, 74, 94–102
Orgasmic dysfunction,   124–125, 128–131

Paedophilia,   12, 185, 188–192
  treatment of,   200
Pair formation,   56
Penile erection,   122–123, 137
Penis,   28, 29, 32, 52, 55, 139, 140
Permissiveness,   7, 8, 59, 65, 104
Personality, and sexual attitudes,   117–121
  and sexual behaviour,   115–117
Persuasive communication,   59
Petting,   96, 100, 103, 108
Physical attractiveness,   66, 79–80
Pituitary gland,   37
Plethysmograph,   42, 153, 178, 196
Pornography,   1, 9–13, 15, 18, 69–71
Premarital sex,   2, 7, 65, 78, 97, 100–107
Premature ejaculation,   124, 126–127
Pre-natal brain feminization,   183
Pre-natal hormones,   38, 159, 160
Primary homosexuals, 149, 156, 158, 159, 165, 168, 174, 176
Progestogen,   183
Prostitution,   16–18, 65
Psychotherapy,   132, 143, 173

Rape,   13, 168, 187–188
  treatment of rapists,   199
Relationship therapy,   146–147
Reinforcement,   63, 73–74, 170
Re-orientation of sexual preference,   173
Romantic love,   81–84

Sado-masochism,   184–185
Self-reinforcement,   63, 74
Sensate focus,   136, 138, 143

Sex education, 14−15
Sex surveys, 4, 5
  Eysenck, 11, 110, 111, 116−121
  Ford and Beach, 14, 20, 21
  Freud, 4
  Havelock Ellis, 4
  Kinsey, 5, 6, 7, 59, 65, 71, 90, 92, 94−103, 105, 150, 155
  Klausner, 103
  Kolaszynska-Carr, 112, 152, 154, 163, 167
  Masters and Johnson, 5, 43
  Redbook, 104, 105
  Schmidt and Sigusch, 90, 103, 104
  Schofield, 92−94, 106−108, 113, 115
Sexual activity scale, 110
Sexual arousal, *see* Arousal
Sexual attitudes, 104, 117−121, 129
Sexual deprivation, 72
Sexual dimorphism, 35, 36, 159
Sexual drive, 97, 125, 137
Sexual imagery, 99
Sexual offences, 3, 9, 12, 13, 185−201
Sexual orientation, 101, 152
Sexual orientation method, 152
Sexual reassignment, 196
Sexual retraining, 143−146
Shaping, 199
Single sex environments, 166−168

Social attitudes, 5, 7, 9, 11
Social learning, 58−65
'Squeeze' technique, 139
Systematic desensitization, 141, 174

Temporal lobe epilepsy, 178
Testosterone, 155, 159
Transsexualism, 166, 177−184
  treatment of, 196−199
Transvestism, 177
Treatment of, couples, 143−148
  ejaculatory problems, 139−140
  exhibitionism, 200
  female sexual dysfunction, 140−143
  fetishism, 195
  homosexuality, 173−175
  male sexual dysfunction, 137−140
  paedophilia, 200
  rapists, 199
  transsexualism, 196−199
Trial marriage, 78

Vagina, 27, 33, 51, 122, 124, 127
Vaginal dilators, 142
Vaginal exercises, 142
Vaginismus, 124, 127, 141
Virginity, 6, 7, 61

Women's Liberation, 8, 152